Director's Cut

Director's Cut

Book 3

ALTON GANSKY

ZONDERVAN™

GRAND RAPIDS, MICHIGAN 49530 USA

ZONDERVAN™

Director's Cut
Copyright © 2005 by Alton L. Gansky

Requests for information should be addressed to:
Zondervan, *Grand Rapids, Michigan 49530*

Library of Congress Cataloging-in-Publication Data

Gansky, Alton
      Director's cut / Alton Gansky.
            p. cm.—(The Madison Glenn series; bk. 3)
      ISBN-10: 0-310-25936-3 (softcover)
      ISBN-13: 978-0-310-25936-7 (softcover)
      1. Women mayors—Fiction.   2. Chauffeurs—Crimes against—Fiction.
      3. Motion picture industry—Fiction.   4. Political campaigns—Fiction.
      5. California—Fiction.   I. Title.
      PS3557.A5195D565 2005
      813'.54—dc22

                                                                              2005013985

Interior design by Michelle Espinoza

Printed in the United States of America

05 06 07 08 09 10 11 12 /❖ DCI/ 10 9 8 7 6 5 4 3 2 1

Director's Cut

chapter 1

From my place in the shadows, I could see her radiate a glow that would cower Helen of Troy, Cleopatra, and every other historical beauty. She was trim, with hair so black it threatened to absorb every photon of light from the room; a face the color of cream hosted large, innocent eyes.

Only the crimson flow of blood oozing through her fingers detracted from her beauty.

My lungs paused as I watched her draw her hand from her chest, look at the thick cherry red fluid that covered her palm and dripped from between her fingers, then raise her eyes to the man who had pulled the trigger.

She worked her mouth but no words came.

A second later she collapsed.

"Excellent," a voice shouted. A man seated several feet in front of me rose and applauded. "Did that work for you, Catherine?"

The beautiful young woman rose from the stage, holding out her red-tinted hand. A middle-aged woman scurried from behind the side curtains. She held a white towel in her hand and began cleaning the mess from the actress's hand.

"It worked fine, Mr. Young." She glanced down at the red spot on her gown. "Did I get enough on me?"

"You did it just right—and I've told you to call me Harold. We're not student-teacher anymore. If anything, you're teaching me."

I rose from my seat, uncertain if this was a good time to make my presence known, and walked down the aisle formed by long tables set in rows. Behind me were horseshoe-shaped booths and above them a balcony for other patrons of the Curtain Call, Santa Rita's only dinner theater.

"It's hard to change old habits," Catherine said. "You're the one who got me into this crazy business." Her eyes shifted to me. "Maddy! You're back."

I smiled as Catherine made eye contact. I hadn't seen her since she graduated high school and moved off to a college in New York. She had grown another inch and filled out where women fill out. As a teenager, she had been slow to develop physically but nature had made up for lost time.

Catherine pulled away from the woman with the towel and trotted down the stage steps to the main floor. She held out her arms to me, then stopped midstep. She looked at her gown again, which still oozed with stage blood.

I closed the gap between us, placed my hands on her shoulders, and gave her a kiss on the forehead. "It's been a long time."

"Much too long." Her smile dazzled even in the dim light of the theater.

"Can I have the houselights, please?" Young bellowed.

Overhead lights swept away the shadows that filled the small theater. "Okay, everyone, that's it for today. Good work. One more dress rehearsal tomorrow. Dinner will be on me. Strike the set and set up for act one."

The handful of actors moved from the platform and stagehands took their places.

"Mr. Young—I mean Harold—this is my cousin Maddy. She's the mayor. Her name is Madison Glenn. Isn't that a great name? Maddy, this is Harold Young. He teaches drama at the high school, and he's directing this play."

The director returned his attention to us. He was stocky with a bald dome, thick black eyelashes, and a round head. His eyes traced my face and form, then smiled through thin lips. I judged him to be well north of fifty. Extending his hand, he said, "I'm pleased to meet you, Mayor. I voted for you and plan to vote for you for congress."

"Thank you. May your tribe increase." I shook his hand.

"I see beauty runs in the family." His smile broadened and he gave my hand a squeeze. I didn't like it.

"Thank you." I extricated my hand. "Catherine got most of the beauty genes."

I felt conspicuous next to her. I try not to compare myself to others, especially other women. Women who worry to extremes about their appearance annoy me, probably because I battle the same disease. Standing next to Catherine made me feel old and just a few years removed from qualifying for senior citizen discounts at restaurants. I'm thirty-nine, Catherine is twenty-five; my dark brown hair hangs to my shoulders and goes limp if it catches sight of a cloud, my cousin's black hair shines like obsidian and falls in graceful curls several inches beyond her shoulders. Our skin displayed the same cream color all the women in our family own, but mine had seen a decade and a half more of life. I stood five foot six; Catherine was two inches taller.

"You're being modest, Mayor," Young said. "Have you ever thought of acting as a career?"

That made me laugh. "I'm a politician. Some would say that I am already in the business."

"Touché."

"When did you get back?" Catherine asked. She looked at Young and explained, "Maddy was out of town when I arrived."

"About half an hour ago," I said. "I was in Sacramento for the governor's annual report to California mayors."

"Sounds exciting," Young said.

"If you like talking about taxes, crime, population shifts, and faltering budgets, then it's a hoot. Otherwise, it would put a lifetime insomniac into a coma. Government business is an acquired taste."

"You're coming by to see the house, aren't you?" Catherine said. "Or do you have to go to the office?"

"If I go to the office now, I'll be gang tackled by a week's worth of postponed work. I think I'll save that joy for tomorrow."

"Great, let me change and then we can go." She turned, then stopped. "Did you drive?"

"Yes. I left my car at the airport and drove straight here after I landed."

She frowned. "Maybe I should call Ed."

"Ed?"

"The studio provided a limo. Ed Lowe is the chauffeur." My face must have betrayed my amusement. "It's not my limo. The studio is in the final script revisions for my next movie. I have to go into Hollywood this week for a reading. They don't want me driving on the LA freeways. This way they know I'll be safe *and* on time."

"I can follow," I said.

"If you don't mind driving, I'll call Ed and tell him not to come. I want to spend as much time with you as I can. Taking two cars doesn't make sense."

"That's fine with me."

"Great. I'll make the call and change. Harold will entertain you while I'm gone."

"It'll be my pleasure," he said.

Catherine trotted up the steps to the stage, then disappeared behind the stage right curtains.

"She's a bundle of energy, isn't she?" Young said.

"I haven't seen her for years, but I remember her having enough energy to power the neighborhood."

"Let's have a seat while we wait." He walked to the nearest table and pulled a chair out for me, then did the same for himself. He waited until I sat before lowering himself into the armless chair. He leaned an elbow on the table.

"I don't know how you do it," I admitted. "Pulling a play like this together with so little practice."

"Little practice? We've been working on this for more than a month."

That confused me. "I understood Catherine didn't arrive until the day before yesterday."

"That's right. Her first practice was Monday . . . Ah, I see." He smiled and gave a knowing nod. "It's not uncommon for the stars of a show to arrive just in time for the last few rehearsals. Usually, they've played the part before or they study their lines on their own. Then they show up to run through their paces, fine-tune their performance to the director's specifications, and learn their blocking."

"Isn't it hard to practice without the star of the show?"

"No, not really." He shifted in his seat. "We use stand-ins during the early rehearsals. The stand-ins become the understudies. These days, the quality actors belong to unions or guilds and small-time operations like this one can't afford to pay what it costs to tie up a name actor for several weeks."

"So, this is Catherine's second day on the job?"

"We're lucky to get her at all. Her last movie has made her a star. Everyone who's anyone in showbiz wants her for something. Our show is going to run for six weeks but we only get her for three, then she has to fly off to location for her next movie."

"That's where the understudy comes in."

"Right. The dinner theater will run the show for six weeks, then a new show comes in."

"Are you directing that one too?"

He looked embarrassed. "No. Neena lets me do one show a year. The rest of my time is spent teaching high school drama."

"Neena . . . ?"

"Neena Lasko. She owns the Curtain Call dinner theater. I take it you've never met."

"No. Actually," I said, "this is my first time here."

"They do good work and serve up a great meal. You owe it to yourself to come by now and again. I see every one of their shows and I haven't been disappointed yet." He paused, then said, "Where are my manners? Can I get you some coffee or a soda?"

I declined.

He studied me for a moment. "You must be very proud to have Catherine as a cousin. There aren't many actresses who skyrocket to fame like she did."

"I am proud, but as I said, I haven't seen her in years. Catherine is the youngest daughter of my father's sister. They used to live in Santa Rita, but after Catherine moved off to college, they took an early retirement and relocated to Boise, Idaho."

"Okay, I'm ready."

Catherine had started speaking before she reached our table. She was wearing a dark blue T-shirt with the words "Way Off Broadway" stenciled on the front, blue jeans, and orange canvas shoes. She had pulled her hair into a ponytail. The stage makeup was gone and hadn't been replaced. She looked several years younger, if that was possible.

"That was quick," I said and stood.

"Actors learn to change quickly," she said, then paused. "I'm not sure what to do. I tried to get hold of Ed, but he's not answering his cell phone."

"Do you know where he went after he dropped you off?" I asked.

"He said he was going to get the limo washed, then go back to my house to wait for my call. This is so unlike him. He was my driver during the filming of my first movie and he was always on time and available."

"Maybe his cell phone died," Young said. "It happens to me all the time."

"I suppose," Catherine said, "but he's not answering the house phone either."

"Well," I said, "we can wait for him to show up or go on to your house. It's your call."

Catherine thought for a moment as if weighing a momentous decision. "Let's go. I'll try his cell phone again once we're on the road."

"If he shows up here," Young said, "I'll tell him you two flew the coop."

We thanked him and I led the way to the door.

With me was the nation's newest star.

chapter 2

Catherine's home was in the north part of the city, just this side of Santa Barbara. It would be a lovely drive with the cobalt blue ocean to our left, green hills to our right, and an azure sky above lit by a golden sun. There would also be the many colors of cars and trucks packed on a freeway designed to hold half the contents it bore each day during rush hour. My silver Lincoln Aviator would add to the mix. There was nothing I could do about that.

As mayor, I receive calls, letters, and email almost daily, complaining about the growing traffic problem. People want me to fix it, and I can't blame them. I have a form letter I send to each one, thanking them for their interest in our city and reminding them I am the mayor, not the governor. I can complain, make requests for freeway improvement, but as long as Santa Rita has the Los Angeles basin to the south and Santa Barbara to the north there is going to be traffic and it is going to get worse each year.

"I had forgotten how pretty it is here." Catherine sat in the passenger seat and gazed out the window. Under the direct rays of the sun and without the mask of makeup we women usually wear, I could see the sparkle in her eye and the beginnings of crow's-feet. She was just twenty-five but the pressures of living on her own and doing whatever overnight successes do had begun to place the patina of age on her youthful face. "I missed the ocean."

"They have an ocean on the East Coast." I shifted lanes to pull around an eighteen-wheeler that was blocking my view of the traffic ahead. At the blistering thirty miles an hour we were traveling, it would take me awhile to pull past the truck.

"It's not the same. Besides, I didn't get out of the city much. I worked a couple of plays before signing on to the movie. I was pretty busy."

"Busy isn't bad," I said. "It beats the alternative."

"True." She sighed and laid her head back on the seat. She seemed drained.

"You okay?" I asked.

She kept her eyes closed but smiled. "Couldn't be better. The last few months have been a whirlwind. My agent told me not to take this play. He said it was too much strain to move into a new house, rehearse for a play, and study a script for my next movie." She raised her head again and blinked a couple of times. "He's right, of course, but I wanted to do the play anyway."

"Why?" I pressed the brake pedal as the traffic continued to coagulate in front of us. "Not that I'm not happy to see you. It's not every day I get to hang out with the rich and famous."

She laughed lightly. "I was just thinking how proud I felt about being related to the mayor."

That made *me* laugh. "I've been in city government for over a decade and mayor for three years, and most people who live in the city couldn't pick me out in a police lineup. Local politics is not the way to become famous. Of course, that was never my goal."

Out of the corner of my eye I caught her staring at me. "I'll bet that will all change when you become Congresswoman Maddy Glenn. How's that going?"

"The campaign?" I glanced at her. "Wait a second, you didn't answer my question. Are you trying to turn the conversation around to me?"

She shifted in her seat and repositioned the seat belt. "Sorry, I've developed the habit of diverting attention from myself."

"Why would you do that? I thought attention was one of the benefits of being a star."

"Yeah, so did I."

She looked uncomfortable, and I wondered if I had just crossed the line. I chastised myself. I tend to form opinions quickly and swerve past small talk. Over the years I had annoyed more people than I could count.

"When I first became interested in acting, I thought how wonderful it would be to be recognized on the street, to sign autographs, do talk shows and everything else that goes with it, but that got old quick." She paused as if remembering something painful. "I learned it wasn't popularity I crave, but art. I love acting. I want to be the best actor I can be."

I nodded. "I once met a novelist who told me the same thing. He said he couldn't wait to do a book signing, but after a few episodes of that he decided that he was much happier putting words on a page than signing his name."

"Don't get me wrong," Catherine said. "I enjoy being well known, but it isn't what drives me. I'm doing the play because I feel like I owe my friends in Santa Rita something and because stage acting is more challenging than movies. When you make a film there is no audience except the crew, and they're paid to be there. Onstage you can hear the audience and get immediate feedback. There's nothing like it. Does that make sense?"

I told her it did, then added, "It's similar in my world. I hate campaigning. I prefer to be busy with governing rather than running for office. Still, it's the price I pay for my passion."

"We all pay a price," she said. "Some days are more expensive than others."

That sounded heavy with history. I cut my eyes her way, then returned them to the road. I kept silent to allow her time to elaborate but nothing came. There are awkward times when I don't know whether to push for more information or back away. To do the former could be construed as prying, the latter as being insensitive. I had been with Catherine less than thirty minutes, and even though she was family we had never been close, certainly never confidantes. It wasn't time to press.

She broke the silence. "I'm sorry. That sounded heavier than I meant it to. So tell me about the campaign. How's it going?"

I changed lanes again. "Not great," I said. "The general election is less than a month away, and I'm behind in the polls. Not much, but enough to make sleeping difficult."

"My mother told me that you won the primary by a big margin."

"She heard that all the way up in Boise, did she?"

"Your mother is proud of you," Catherine said. "She calls my mom and talks about you, and then my mother talks about me."

"Where would we be without mothers?"

"Someone has to start the fan clubs."

I smiled at that. "Well, your mother was right. When they counted the votes, I was the Republican nominee for the vacant house seat, and Robert Till has gone back to being a county supervisor."

"So now you're running against the Democratic contender?"

"Garret Kinsley. He's a powerhouse. Well funded, heartthrob handsome, educated, and a dynamite speaker. He served as ambassador to Argentina. He's a well-tanned Adonis with brains and has a political organization some consider the best in Southern California. He demolished Assemblywoman Wilma Easton in the primaries. Her political life is in a coma. I may be next."

"How big is the gap in the polls?"

I was impressed with the question. Catherine was more politically savvy than most people. "The Santa Rita *Register* did a poll last week. Kinsley leads me by 6 percent."

"That doesn't sound like much," Catherine said.

"It's huge this late in the game. My campaign manager thinks the poll is flawed and badly constructed, but I think she's just trying to keep my spirits up."

"You're not giving in, are you?"

"No way. I'm committed to the goal. It's not over until the votes are cast."

"Can I do anything?"

I hadn't expected that. "I appreciate the offer."

"I'll do anything I can to help. Does your campaign need funds? I want to contribute. Money's not a problem."

"There are limits on how much an individual can contribute to a candidate, but every little bit helps. We're having one last fundraiser to raise money for television time and one more direct mail."

"Maybe I could come to that. Would that help?"

I paused. "Yes, it might, but I don't want you to think that—"

"Of course not. I asked you; you didn't ask me. When is it?"

"A week from Monday night."

"The next exit is mine," Catherine added calmly.

"Nuts, I wasn't paying attention." I checked my mirrors. Getting over to the exit lane would require the help of several kind drivers or some pushy driving on my part. I planned on the latter, signaled, and began a steady merge to the right. To my surprise no one honked. Such is driving in Southern California.

After I successfully elbowed my way to the exit, Catherine said, "You'd do great in New York. It takes attitude to drive there."

"It takes body amour to drive here," I said. "Would a week from Monday work for you? What about the play?"

"The theater is dark Monday and Tuesday. I'm free that night. I might have to show up a little late if they call me to Hollywood for a script meeting, but I should be back by late afternoon."

"We're holding it at the Spaghetti Warehouse. It begins at six o'clock."

"Shouldn't be a problem then. Take the exit and stay right. It's not far."

I did as instructed. I also made a note to call Nat as soon as I could. Natalie Sanders is my campaign manager and the last-minute addition of movie star Catherine Anderson would thrill her and send her scrambling to get word out. I just made her life much more difficult.

I felt good.

chapter 3

"That's odd," Catherine said as I turned into the long drive that led from Virgil Street to her house.

I had successfully negotiated the freeway off-ramp and pressed the large SUV up the hill to the rarified air of Oak Crest Knolls, one of the most prestigious neighborhoods in Southern California. I live in a three-thousand-square-foot house built by my late husband. It sits right on the beach. Most consider it a luxury house—I know I do—but in the "The Knolls" it would be considered a starter home.

We had just driven through the land of Mercedes, Humvees, and homes one could buy beginning in the low seven figures. It was the area of the city that if you had to ask how much it cost, you didn't belong. It was also a land of political hostility toward me. I was persona non grata here. Last year, the residents felt their five- and ten-thousand-square-foot mansions deserved the prestige of a Santa Barbara address. They petitioned to be annexed by Santa Barbara city and found open arms and smiles, and why not? Homes that large on five-acre lots could bring in a lot of revenue.

I wasn't keen on letting my city lose the revenue and surrendering a few square miles of prime property to boot. I led the fight against the homeowners' association and the city to the north. The entire council backed me on it. It was one of the few times we'd agreed on anything. Since then, the residents have harbored a well-oiled hatred toward me. I had learned to live with it. I couldn't help noticing that many of Garret Kinsley's contributors had addresses from this little section of paradise.

"What's odd?" I asked as I pulled along the drive.

"The limo." She pointed. A black, stretch Lincoln Town Car sat on the sweeping drive in front of the house.

I hadn't noticed it. My eyes were glued to the monster before me. A massive, two-story, French country chateau sat—no, *loomed* before me. I wasn't certain what I expected. A large home, sure, but this stunned me. It stood like a castle on a bare lot. Landscaping was in place but had yet to fill out the grounds. Thin trees seemed intimidated by the gentle breeze: ground cover lay in clumps as if gathering strength for the job that lay before them. A year from now, the property would be verdant beyond anything I'm capable of imagining.

"What about the limo?"

"Ed didn't answer his cell phone when I called, so I tried the house. When he didn't answer there, I assumed something was wrong with his cell service and that he might be on his way to pick me up."

"Makes sense," I said.

"How did he get back before us?" She shook her head and frowned. "I don't think he left at all. I wonder if . . ."

I started to press for the rest of the sentence but decided I was again being too nosy. Pulling behind the limo, I parked, set the brake, and slipped from my seat. Catherine was already out.

I took a step back and looked at the house. It was two stories tall with an elegant hip roof dressed with dark, flat tile. Stark white trim accented the windows and a large arch that led to the front porch and entry door. The walls bore stone of various shades of gray and charcoal painted siding. The windows were an assortment of shapes: oval, square, and arched.

"Come in and I'll show you around," Catherine said. "I need to warn you that we got final inspection just last Friday and there's still a lot of cleanup to do."

"I understand," I said, following her to the front door. I expected her to produce a key, but instead she pressed the buttons on a small numeric keypad. I heard a click and a thunk as the door unlocked. "Cute."

"The house has a top-of-the-line security system. I enter a code here and it not only unlocks the door but it turns off the alarm. It also records when the code is used and stores the information on a device that can be read by my home computer. If someone tries to defeat the system, it records the number of attempts, the time of day, and activates the security camera."

"I don't see a camera."

"That's the point." She smiled. "There are security cameras in several key spots around the lot. They're not working yet, but should be by the end of the week."

"There's always something left undone when building a new house."

I followed her into the entry. I'm used to entering a large home, but this house took my breath away. Black marble covered the floor; the Venetian plaster wall to my right boasted several arched niches tall and wide enough to hold a child. They were empty. Before me was an open, sweeping staircase that led to the floor above. The stringers were a curved, dark wood that I didn't recognize. I guessed mahogany.

It took ten steps to cross the foyer and plunge into the living room. The space was enormous and a thick mottled blue carpet

covered the floor and ran up the center of the stairs. Empty bookshelves lined one wall and two white half-hemisphere chandeliers
hung from the vaulted ceiling.

To the side of the staircase was a raised planter and fountain
that curved in harmony with the stairway. Aside from that, the room
was empty.

"Furniture is due to arrive over the weekend," Catherine said.
"It looks pretty empty now."

"You're staying here without furniture?"

"The bedroom has most of its furnishings," she said. "It's all I
need right now. The interior designer is pulling everything together.
I have no head for those things. I grew up in a small home, so this
is all new to me."

I remembered her house, a sixteen-hundred-square-foot Craftsman-
style bungalow in one of the city's early subdivisions.

"How many rooms?" I asked as I moved to the center of the living space.

"Six bedrooms, an office, a rec room, a media room, and a den, plus
the usual kitchen, breakfast nook, dining room, and five bathrooms."

"And you plan on living here alone?" I tried to imagine the place
filled with furniture. Over my head hovered an open beam ceiling.
Across the long wall were thick, ivory-colored drapes that reached
from the floor to a rod ten feet above. Above the cornice were a
series of narrow rectangular windows. Wood blinds that matched
the stairway blocked the light. The wall faced west, which meant the
afternoon sun would pour in.

"I hope not," she said.

I turned to her. "Oh?" I smiled. "You have a husband-to-be waiting in the wings?"

She chortled. "No, Maddy, I don't. Not that I haven't been asked.
In fact, I get about twenty proposals a week from love-struck fans."

She stepped to the stairs, bent, and picked up a small plastic device that looked like a television remote. She pressed a button and the dark wood blinds opened. The late afternoon sunlight streamed in. I could see a few shreds of clouds ornamenting the sky.

"If not a husband . . ."

"I'm hoping to convince Mom and Dad to move back to Santa Rita. It's one reason I built my home here. They're not getting any younger, and I would love to have them around."

"You're a good daughter," I said. "Not many people your age would want to have their parents around. It would cramp their style."

"I don't have a style; I'm just a very fortunate performer. No one knows how long fame will last. This time next year, I may be a used-to-be."

"Somehow I doubt that."

She frowned and glanced around. "I wonder where Ed is. We've made enough noise to wake the dead."

"Bathroom?" I suggested. "Or the media room?"

"There's nothing in the media room yet," Catherine said. She returned the remote to the third tread. "I'm going to take a quick look around. I'll be right back and we can continue the tour."

"Okay." I watched Catherine move up the stairs with an easy grace. What a young woman she had become. The best I could tell her fame and newly earned wealth had not gone to her head. Her comment about wanting her parents around warmed my soul.

I surveyed the empty room and rocked on my heels. I felt like an empty bottle floating on the wide ocean. There was no place to sit, no magazines to read, no . . . nothing. I thought of the landscape I had seen out front and wondered what lay behind the house. Surely there was a pool, and I was willing to bet next week's salary the lot had one of the best views in Santa Rita.

Catherine had opened the blinds over the transom windows with a remote. I directed my gaze back to the stairs and saw the plastic device right where she had placed it a moment ago.

I could have just walked to the draped wall and pulled on the curtains until I found where they met, then peeked at the backyard, but then I wouldn't have had the opportunity to play with the remote. What fun was that?

I studied the gizmo and it looked straightforward enough. It had two sets of long buttons. Each end of each button had an arrow: open and close. *Simple.*

Pressing the right side of the top button, I watched the wall, ready for the curtains to part. Instead, the wood blinds closed again. A fifty-fifty chance and I blew it. For me, luck is a word you find in the dictionary and little more. I depressed the lower button and drapes parted like curtains on the stage. *Apropos.*

The wall of curtain pulled back to reveal tall and wide windows overlooking the ocean and a broad and deep backyard. The diminishing light had changed the cobalt blue of the ocean to a churning green-gray. A few miles off the coast, heavy clouds gathered, preparing themselves for the near daily entrance to shore. Marine layer, meteorologists call it. In Santa Rita we wake up to it almost every morning and watch it slip in most evenings. It was part of life on the coast.

I let my eyes trace the rear yard. Dark brown pavers covered a rear patio that was circumscribed by a short curving wall of flagstone. To one side a portion rose higher than the rest of the wall. Water poured from it and into what I assumed was a pool. I couldn't actually see the pool since it was sequestered behind the landscape wall. Several young trees populated the edge of the landscaping near the house. Any farther out and they would block the view of the ocean and no one committed such a crime in Santa Rita.

In the middle of the window wall was a pair of tall French doors. I approached and opened them. The fountain played music with its water. There's something about the sound of running water that puts me in a good mood.

I started across the threshold, then froze midstep by a knife-sharp scream.

For half a second I thought I set off the security alarm, but then I recognized the unique human timbre. I snapped around, my heart knocking like the beat of a hummingbird's wings.

Catherine stood on the stairs a half-dozen steps down from the second floor balcony that ran the length of the living room.

"What?" I shouted.

Her hands were at her mouth, her eyes wide. The color drained from her face like water from a sink. I sprinted toward her, stepping up the treads as fast as I could. I took her by the shoulders. "What? What is it?"

She shook her head. Her shoulders began to shake. I looked up the stairs and along the balcony. I saw nothing. Then it occurred to me that I was facing the wrong direction.

My stomach fluttered and my mind told me not to turn around. I turned anyway.

From the elevated perch of the stairway I could gaze through the window, over the landscape wall, past a terrace I hadn't seen from ground level, and into the large, oval pool.

In the middle of the pool, facedown, floated a man. He wore dark pants, dark coat, and dark shoes. And something else was dark in the clear, crisp water—blood.

My fluttering heart seized. My quivering stomach turned to lead. I could feel blood draining from my head.

"Ed?" I asked softly.

Catherine whimpered, "Yes."

My gaze was glued to the still figure. Less than a second passed when I thought I saw his arm move.

"Call 9–1–1." I scampered down the stairs and started for the open door. I took a moment and stole a glance over my shoulder. Catherine hadn't budged. I turned and pointed at her. "Call 9–1–1. Do it now."

She looked at me, then blinked. Her mind reengaged. She started down the steps.

I resumed my course, shooting through the open door. Had I seen him move? Was there still a chance that he was alive? I bolted over the patio and down a short run of stone steps. Stopping at the edge of the pool I hoped to see him move again. Nothing. I scanned the area, looking for a long pole to pull the unconscious man to the side. Didn't pools have rescue poles or was that just public pools?

Seconds mattered. Seconds meant life or death. Every atom in me said not to do it. It was too much to expect of anyone. No one would blame me if I waited for the professionals.

I kicked off my pumps and stepped over the edge.

The water engulfed me in cold fingers, and I felt the surface crash over my head. The water blurred my vision. I pushed off the bottom and toward the floating chauffeur, coming up on his left side. Reaching across his torso, I took hold of his arm and pulled, rolling him onto his back.

He stared at the sky with open, unblinking eyes.

There was a small hole in the side of his head.

I stifled my own scream and pushed away from the dead man.

I was too late.

Much, much too late.

chapter 4

The wind was picking up, blowing in from the ocean and torment- ing me through my wet clothing. One of the firemen, who had been first on the scene, had given me a wool blanket. I clung to it like it was a life preserver. I was shaking, more from shock than from the chilling breeze—swimming with a dead man unsettled me.

Catherine stood at my side, her fair skin pale, and her eyes afloat in tears. I heard her sniff several times and knew her dam had just developed a new crack. She hovered so close our shoulders touched. I wanted to put my arm around her, but my wet arm would only chill her more. Together we stood next to one of the stone terrace walls. The wall was four feet tall and marked off a stretch of planter. Like the rest of the lot, the landscaping here was incomplete. Sev- eral plants waited for workers to remove them from the plastic pots and nestle them into the ground. Leaning against the wall were sev- eral tools: two shovels, trowels, and a short pickax.

Her backyard was abuzz with activity. Several firemen, draped in heavy yellow Nomex coats and equally yellow helmets, stood to one side. Their job was done. Once released by the police or the county coroner's office, they would climb back on their pumper and return to the fire station. With nothing to do, paramedics packed their kits. The hole in Ed Lowe's head had convinced them heroic efforts were useless.

Two uniformed police officers stood to the side of the pool and watched as a dark-haired man in a snappy blue suit and white latex gloves hunched near the body. His hair was black and his eyes dark. When he stood erect, that anthracite hair hovered six feet two inches above the ground. His eyes were keen and kind, and when he smiled he showed teeth that shamed pearls. Detective Judson West is the darling of the Santa Rita police and the only detective that works homicide. I counted him a friend.

He arrived ten minutes after the fire department and five minutes after the paramedics declared the chauffeur dead. When he stepped through the rear door, he saw me and shook his head.

West rose and addressed the two uniformed officers. "Tape it off. In fact, tape off the whole lot."

"Front yard too?" one of the policemen asked.

"The killer didn't parachute in. For now, we assume the bad guy came up the drive, so I want it all cordoned off."

The men began to move. West approached the fire captain and said something to him. The captain nodded and motioned for his men to leave.

West turned to me. I shivered. He made me feel uncomfortable in the most wonderful way, and I was compelled to fight it.

He looked me over, then smiled. "Swimming fully clothed can be . . . awkward."

"You should try it in pantyhose," I said.

"No thanks." He paused. "Are you all right?"

"Shaken," I admitted. I looked at the body of Ed Lowe lying on the stone rim of the pool, right where the firemen had left him. The scene was too bizarre to believe, but no amount of denial would change the situation or erase the image branded on my brain. To avoid thinking, I resorted to courtesy. "Catherine, this is Detective Judson West. Detective West, this is Catherine Anderson. This is her home, her pool, and . . . her chauffeur."

West smiled. "I saw your movie. Let's go inside."

I had dealt with West often enough over the last year and a half and knew he was thinking of more than just my comfort. He didn't want us contaminating his crime scene more than we already had. We followed his lead and entered the house. As we crossed the back threshold the front door opened. A man and a woman, both in their early thirties, stepped in. They wore olive green Windbreakers with patches over their left pockets that read Santa Rita County Sheriff's Department.

The two looked at West then Catherine then me. Their eyes lingered longer on my wet form. They identified themselves as field investigators from the county crime lab. West had called them. Santa Rita, like many cities, was too small to fund its own crime lab. We have a contract with the county for scientific investigations.

"GSW to the head. He was found in the pool. The fire department removed the body from the water about fifteen minutes ago. I need a full workup including prints in the house."

"Got it," the woman said. "ME?"

"Medical Examiner is on the way and should be here in the next ten minutes."

"Does the deceased have a name?" the woman asked.

"Ed Lowe," Catherine whispered.

"Ed . . . Hey, aren't you—"

"Yes, she is," West interrupted. "The body is in back."

They got the hint and moved through the house.

"Thank you, Detective."

"Don't mention it." He gave her one of his patented smiles. "I'm afraid I'm going to have to ask some questions."

"I understand," Catherine said. She looked like a china doll that had been rolled down a rocky slope.

"Perhaps you should start from the beginning."

I spoke up. "I drove Catherine home from—"

West raised a hand. "Excuse me, Mayor, but as you said, this is Ms. Anderson's home, Ms. Anderson's pool, and Ms. Anderson's chauffeur. I would like to hear from her first."

"I was just trying—"

"Just trying to help. I know." He turned back to Catherine and raised an eyebrow.

She cleared her throat and told West how I had met her at her rehearsal, how she had tried to reach Mr. Lowe, and how I had driven her home. That part flowed easily enough, but when she got to the part about seeing the body in the pool, a tear slipped down her smooth cheek. She told it anyway.

"I can't see the pool from here," West said. "How could you see the body?"

"I was on the stairs. Maddy had just opened the drapes. With the drapes open you can see the whole backyard, even the lower areas."

"Then what?"

"Maddy told me to call 9–1–1 and I did. I gave the operator all the information, then ran after Maddy. When I got there she had pulled Ed . . . the body, to the side of the pool. I helped her crawl out."

West looked at me. "You jumped in?"

I nodded. "I thought I saw the man move. I thought maybe he had fallen in and hit his head. When I got to him, I saw how wrong I was."

"But you still had the presence of mind to pull him to the side of the pool."

"I guess. I wasn't doing a lot of thinking at the time. I was just acting on instinct."

Turning back to Catherine, West asked, "How long have you known Mr. Lowe?"

"About a year. He drove for me during the filming of my first movie. We did a lot of shooting in Southern California."

"So he's your regular chauffeur?"

"He's not my chauffeur. I mean, I don't pay him. The studio does. After we finish shooting this movie, I'll be on my own again. Thankfully. I hate being driven around."

I watched West bite his lower lip. Any other place than a murder scene, I might have thought it cute and endearing. He studied Catherine for a moment, then asked, "What was your relationship to Mr. Lowe?"

"My relationship?" Catherine tilted her head to the side.

"Was he ever more than a chauffeur?"

"Judson West!" I snapped.

"Excuse me?" Catherine replied.

"Let me clear something up here," West said. "There has been a murder and I am a homicide detective. That means I have to ask questions and some of those are going to be unpleasant. That's my job." He looked at me. "You of all people should know that, Mayor. We've been through enough together for you to know how this works."

He was right, of course, and I almost hated him for it.

"He was my chauffeur and nothing else, Detective. Ed was kind, polite, and always the gentleman." She stared him hard in the eyes. "Is that clear enough? He was old enough to be my father."

"What did you do after you helped Mayor Glenn out of the pool?"

"I came back in the house and made another call," Catherine said.

"To whom?"

"It doesn't matter," she said.

"I'll decide that, Ms. Anderson. Whom did you call?"

"Frank Zambonelli—Franco, actually. He's my publicist."

"Your publicist?"

She rubbed her forehead. "I know it sounds petty and shallow, but it's not what it seems. I haven't been in the business very long and I've only made one movie, but I've learned enough to know that the movie biz is cutthroat. For some, the only way to the top is to climb over their competition. I wanted the producers to know what happened so they wouldn't be caught off guard by the media."

"Why not call them directly?" West pressed.

"Who? The producer?" Catherine looked puzzled. "I don't know. Franco came to mind first."

West peered out the window wall. I followed his gaze. The two field investigators were taking photos of everything. They moved quickly, perhaps goaded on by the setting sun, which was now amber and painting the clouds salmon pink.

"Ms. Anderson, did Mr. Lowe act differently today? Tense? Worried? Anything like that?"

"No. He picked me up at ten o'clock and drove me to the Curtain Call, then left. He was going to get the car cleaned and run a few errands for his boss. Then he was supposed to pick me up after rehearsal."

"She's starring in a play at the dinner theater," I added.

"Where does Mr. Lowe spend his evenings? Does he drive back to Hollywood for the evening? Does he stay here?"

Catherine frowned. It was an unnatural expression for a face used to smiling. "He doesn't stay here, Detective. Look around. There's no furniture except what is in my bedroom, and no one stays there but me." Her words were getting warmer as the shock gave way to the indignity of being questioned in her own home.

"So if he didn't stay here, where did he stay?"

"I don't know. I recall him saying he had a condo in Glendale. That's north of Hollywood."

"I know where—"

"I just remembered something." She furrowed her brow. "Ed said something about being put up in a room, a hotel. He said it was someplace near the shore."

"You don't recall the name of the hotel?" West pressed.

"No. I had just gotten off the plane in Burbank. He picked me up at the airport. It's a bit of a drive from Burbank to Santa Rita. I used the time to go over my lines for the play."

"You flew into Southern California."

"I still have an apartment in New York," Catherine said. "I attended a party the night before, stayed up too late, then caught an early flight out the next morning."

West seemed thoughtful, like a man trying to place a piece of a jigsaw puzzle in the right place. "Why would Mr. Lowe wait for you here, a place with almost no furniture, I assume no television, when he had a hotel room to go to?"

"There's a television in my bedroom, but I doubt he would have watched it," Catherine said. "But that doesn't matter. As you can tell, the house is brand new. Have you ever had a house built for you, Detective?"

"No, I'm a buy-what's-there guy."

"It's a pain," Catherine said. "The carpet layers can't lay carpet until the painters are done, but they can't paint until the finish carpenters are done, which they can't do until the drywall people tidy up, which they can't do until inspectors pass on the electrical and so on. You get the idea. And when the work is done, it's often done incorrectly. I was having a problem with the electrical in this room. Ed offered to stay at the house until the electrician came and made things right."

"Did the electrician come?"

"I assume so. When I left this morning the automated drapes and blinds didn't work. Now they do."

"Automated . . . Never mind. I'm going to need the name of the person responsible for hiring Mr. Lowe."

"That would be Stewart Rockwood. He's the executive producer." She recited his phone number from memory. She also gave him the address.

"You have all that memorized?" West said. "I'm impressed."

Catherine shrugged. "It's what actors do, memorize."

"Do you know if Mr. Lowe had family?"

Her face clouded. "No, I'm sorry, I don't."

It took me a second to realize that she wasn't apologizing for not having an answer but for not bothering to have asked Ed Lowe. Catherine was always a sensitive spirit.

"Just so that you know, Ms. Anderson, people are going to be in and out of here for quite a few hours. Do you have a place you can stay tonight?"

"She's staying with me, Detective," I said before Catherine could answer. "You know where I live and you have my private number."

He let slip a little knowing chuckle. "That I do, Maddy . . . Mayor."

Catherine gave me a confused look, then asked West, "May I pack a few things?"

"I'll have to go with you," he said.

"You shouldn't treat her like a suspect," I snapped. "She's a victim."

"I'm not a treating her like a suspect, but I'm not going to change my procedure to preserve your feelings. If we're lucky, we'll catch the killer, and when he or she goes to trial I don't want some public defender raking me over the coals for not preserving the evidentiary quality of the crime scene. I'm trying to protect the evidence, the scene, and you two."

I struggled for a sharp retort but came up empty.

"This way, please," Catherine said. She started up the stairs.

West paused partway up the treads and looked out the windows as if checking our story. I could see him looking down toward the pool. A second later, he was up the stairs and following Catherine to her bedroom.

I walked to the open doors and pretended to watch the field investigators do their work. Within a minute, the medical examiner arrived, and I pointed him to the backyard. No matter how difficult my job became, it would never be as taxing as what these guys did day in and day out.

At least I hoped it never would.

chapter 5

Catherine's cell phone rang four times from the time we left her house and drove to my home. The trip took only half an hour, the traffic being thinner southbound than the reverse. Still, it was a taxing drive.

The first call had been her publicist. I couldn't hear what he said, but her side of the conversation gave me enough to know that he was asking about her health and mental state. She ended that conversation with, "Okay, Franco, I'll see you then." That call was followed with one from Stewart Rockwood, the producer; one from a Patty Holt, Rockwood's aide; and another call from Franco the publicist—again.

"Kind of makes you want to turn that thing off, doesn't it?"

"They're worried about me. They didn't say so, but I think they're also worried about fallout."

"Fallout?" I pulled down my street and up the driveway, then paused while I waited for the garage door to rise.

"Publicity is a two-edged sword. Bad press can make or break a movie."

"Bad press can make a movie?"

"Sometimes."

"It's a shame that's not true in politics."

I guided the car into the garage and exited. Catherine did the same, dragging a designer duffel bag with her. She held it to her chest like it was a teddy bear and she was a frightened eight-year-old. We walked through the door that joined the garage with the house. I had been gone for a week, and it felt good to be home.

My house is more than a home; it is my cocoon, the place I return each night and lock out the world. My husband, who grew up buried to his neck in comic books, called the place his Fortress of Solitude. If Superman could have a Fortress of Solitude, why couldn't Peter? But Peter wasn't Superman, a fact made clear the night I received a phone call from the Los Angeles police telling me my husband had been killed during a carjacking. The thugs got the BMW, and my husband got a bullet.

That was almost ten years ago—plenty of time to get over the violent tragedy. I wasn't over it. Not a day goes by when I don't see his face when my eyes close; not a week passes when I don't catch a whiff of his aftershave.

I live alone in three thousand square feet of house. The exterior walls wore diagonal cedar siding proudly. The floor plan is open on the first floor with one room flowing into the next. The kitchen and dining room run the length of the back, and a large living room dominates the rest of the floor. I have a guest room on the lower floor and several bedrooms on the second. Also on the second floor is my office. I converted it from the rec room that had been one of my husband's favorite places. On both floors, large windows face the ocean, small windows face the street.

I grew up in a much smaller home, a saltbox design. My parents still live there and I have dinner with them once a week. Our house was small but I never experienced poverty. My father still teaches history at the University of Santa Barbara, and Mother is a retired music teacher. They earned good money but never enough to buy a house on the beach.

My husband's family is different. Peter's father owns a commercial flooring company: Glenn Structural Materials. Anyone who's walked into a bank, high-rise, or large commercial building in any of the western states has probably walked on Peter's flooring. He was on a sales trip in Los Angeles when he was murdered.

Peter's life insurance policy allowed me to pay off the house. I don't make enough money as mayor to pay for the home I live in. Peter's father continues to pay his salary as if his son were still alive. For months I told him he didn't need to do that, but he convinced me he did. "Twice a month, when I sign his paycheck, I feel as if he's still here." I never argued the point again.

Over the last year and a half, two great tragedies have happened in my home—horrors I refuse to talk about. If this house hadn't been Peter's dream, I might have left it long ago. I can't leave.

"Wow," Catherine said. "This is a blast to the past. I haven't been in here since I was a kid."

I looked at the twenty-five-year-old. She still looked like a kid to me. "It's been a long time."

"I used to think this was the biggest house ever built." She set her duffel on the first tread of the stairs and walked into the living room.

"It's more than big enough for me." I walked through the entry. An antique mirror given to me by my parents last Christmas hangs on the wall. The image staring back was frightening. My hair hung like spaghetti, my eyeliner was now more smear than line, and my clothing, which had dried in the warm car, looked as if I had pulled them from beneath a rock. Halloween had come early.

"How have you been able to look at me and keep a straight face?" I asked.

"I'm an actor. Besides, I keep seeing poor Ed floating in the pool."

"I'm amazed the medical examiner didn't take me away instead." I meant it to be funny, but it flopped. Neither one of us was in a joking mood.

Pulling away from the mirror, I said, "Let's go upstairs. I'll show you your room, then I'm going to take a shower and change clothes. I've had all of me I can stand."

Catherine followed up the stairs, and I showed her the guest room, the bathroom, and the closet where I keep linens.

"You should call your parents," I said. "It's better they hear the news from you than through the media."

"Do you think they'll hear about it all the way up in Boise?"

"You're a national name now, sweetheart. I'm afraid if word gets out, the whole country will know. It's been my experience that media goes wherever you don't want them to."

I left her on her own and made my way to the master bath. A few moments later I was disrobed and standing with my head beneath the pounding stream of the shower. The water was hot enough to make my skin sting. Steam rose in embracing billows, but it couldn't drive the chill of terror that lingered from my up-close-and-personal experience with the corpse of Ed Lowe.

This morning I had coffee with mayors from around California as we discussed recent legislation about how the state controlled local taxes. Since then I had flown back from Sacramento, gone swimming in a pool laced with the pink of blood, been interviewed by my friend and homicide detective Judson West, and now I stood in the flow of a shower while my cousin, one of Hollywood's hottest properties, sat in my house.

I was unsettled. At first, I attributed the feeling to being on scene at a murder, but there was a nagging something pulling the strings at the back of my mind.

I thought of Catherine and how well she was handling the event. Aside from the scream on the staircase, she had been rock solid. It was easy to see the strain on her face and in her body language, but ... *but what?*

The inkling slipped away like the shower water cycled down the drain. Adrenaline was driving my brain, I decided. I allowed myself another five minutes in the warm womb of the shower before setting to work with soap and washcloth. Fifteen minutes later, I walked down the stairs, wrapped in a cozy terrycloth robe and my hair wrapped in a towel turban.

Catherine sat at the dining room table eating an apple she had cut into thin segments. A few slices of cheddar cheese were on a small plate. The portions were lined up like yellow-orange soldiers. Next to the plate was her cell phone. I was barefoot so I made little noise as I crossed from the stairs, through the living room, and to the edge of the dining area. She was staring out the rear sliding glass doors, watching the surf roll to the shore and the white gulls soar over the sea.

I started to say something, then stopped when Catherine took one cheese slice from its column and rank on the plate and placed it on one of the apple segments. She did so with agonizing precision. Once she positioned the cheese just right, she raised the morsel to her mouth and took a small bite.

"I see you found something to eat," I said.

Catherine let out a yelp and sprang to her feet, spinning to face me. Her eyes widened and her mouth hung open, barely holding its cargo of snack.

She swore.

"Whoa, easy there." I felt horrible. "I didn't mean to frighten you. Maybe I should wear a cowbell."

She raised a hand to her chest as if doing so could slow her heart. She took a few deep breaths, and I was afraid she was going to aspirate the apple and cheese.

"You scared me."

"I noticed. I'm sorry." I watched her for a moment, then went into the kitchen. "How about some tea?"

Her jaw began to work again: chewing had resumed. A good sign.

"Got anything herbal?"

"I got it all. Herbal, black tea—"

"Cranberry? I like tea with cranberry."

"One of my favorites. Cranberry it is." I put the pot on the burner and began heating water. From the pantry I pulled a box of Celestial Seasons Cranberry Cove and set it on the counter. "So, is that comfort food?" I nodded at the cheese and apple slices.

"Comfort food?"

"Food we eat because it makes us feel good. I'm prone to chocolate, grilled cheese sandwiches, tomato soup, chocolate, Mexican cuisine, and occasionally I eat chocolate."

Catherine laughed. "I guess apples and cheese qualify. It's my father's favorite snack."

"Did you call them?"

"Yes. They're worried like everyone else, but I told them I was with you. That made them feel better."

"I'm glad." I walked to the table and sat down. Catherine took her seat again. I looked out the glass doors and watched a brown tern dive-bomb headfirst into the ocean only to reappear a moment later. Politics was tough, but at least I didn't have to get wet with every meal.

"What do you think will happen next?"

"West is a good detective. Very thorough. He'll look into every detail. You can expect to be interviewed again. Probably a couple more times."

"Sounds like you speak from experience."

"I do. I've seen him in action twice before. He's smart, polite, and dogged."

"He started to call you 'Maddy.'" Catherine studied the cheese as if her startled leap from the table might have jarred things out of place.

"We're friends, which is sometimes awkward."

"How is it awkward?"

I waited for her to start nibbling again, but she made no move for the food. "He's a detective on the police force, and I'm the mayor. In a way, I'm his boss, even though I don't and can't interfere with police investigations."

"He's sweet on you," she said with a thin smile. "I could see it in his eyes."

I shrugged. "We had one date, but it was uncomfortable."

"He didn't try anything."

A laugh slipped out. "No, not at all. We just had pie and coffee. You know how these things go. That was months ago."

"So you're still footloose and fancy-free, as my mom used to say."

This conversation was going down a path I didn't want to walk. I was doing my best to find a way to change the subject when the phone rang. I was thankful for a convenient out. Rising, I walked to the kitchen counter where rested one of my cordless phones. I answered.

"Why is Doug Turner calling me about a murder and mentioning your name?"

It was a very familiar voice. "Hi, Nat. I'm fine. Thank you for asking."

"Don't be coy with me, kiddo. I know where you live, work, and have access to your campaign funds. What happened? Doug Turner called me through the campaign office. He's trying to reach you. I'll bet he's been calling city hall as well. Have you checked your messages?"

"I've been a little busy."

"He used the word *murder*, Maddy. Please, oh please, tell me you didn't trip over another body."

"I have never tripped over a body."

"You know what I mean."

I did know. In January of this year, I went to work and found someone had parked an ugly green AMC Gremlin in my parking place. The someone was still in the car. He was also dead.

There was a long, dark pause on the other end of the line. Natalie Sanders is my campaign manager. A former news anchor, she is beautiful, brilliant, tech savvy to a fault, a research genius, opinionated, and driven. She is all that and more. Those who meet her for the first time may notice the wheelchair, but not for long.

I filled her in. "You say Doug Turner knows about it?"

"Oh yeah. He knows, and I'm betting other reporters will know soon enough, and most of them aren't weighed down by scruples like Doug." There was a pause, and for a moment I thought I could hear the motor of her mind humming. "You dove in the pool?"

"I thought I saw him move and thought he might still be alive."

"That might be the angle."

"What angle?"

The doorbell rang. Catherine was up and moving to the front door. I followed, the cordless phone still pressed to my ear.

"I'm thinking of how to spin this so it doesn't look like you attract dead bodies like sugar attracts ants. Who have you spoken to?"

"Who is it?" Catherine asked at the door.

I heard a muffled, "Um ... Floyd ... Floyd Grecian."

I put my hand over the phone and whispered to Catherine. "Let him in."

She did.

"We need to be ahead of the curve on this, Maddy. What are you doing tonight?"

"I have company." I told her about Catherine.

"Why does that name ring a bell?"

"She's the actress."

"She's at your house?"

"Yes. She's my cousin."

"Whoa!" Floyd Grecian said. He looked at Catherine, then at me, then back at Catherine.

"Come in, Floyd." I motioned him in with my free hand. He gave me a strange look. It hit me: my aide had never seen his boss barefoot, in a robe, with a towel perched on her head.

"I'm ... um ..." He looked at Catherine. "You're ... um ... I mean ..."

Floyd is a wonderful assistant. Newly graduated from college, he was attentive, loyal, hardworking, a whiz on the computer, and sharp—sometimes. He was also one of the few innocents left in the world. At times he was clumsy, easily frustrated, and like now, a little tongue-tied.

"Hi, I'm Catherine Anderson." She held her hand out to Floyd.

Floyd stammered. "I know ... I mean, it's good to meet you ... no, *great* to meet you. I saw your movie three times."

"May I come over? I have other news."

I wanted to ask what news, but I was in a three-way conversation and had only two ears and one brain. "Sure. I'll find something for dinner."

"Don't bother, I'll pick up something."

"Nothing too spicy."

Nat promised to be prudent in her food selection and rang off. I turned my attention to the two young people standing in my foyer. "Someone want to close the door?"

"Oh," Floyd said. "I'm ... I'm sorry. It's just ... just ..."

"Floyd," I said, "close the door."

He did, then turned and looked at me, then at Catherine. His brain was overloaded. Movie star to his right, robe-clad mayor to his left.

I fought down my rising embarrassment at being seen fresh from the shower by an employee I worked with daily.

"As you can tell, Floyd, you caught me off guard. I wasn't expecting you."

He nodded but said nothing.

"Floyd, what are you doing here?"

He blinked several times as if he had to think about the answer. "Oh, I was worried. Doug Turner has been calling you at the office, and I tried to call to let you know. You didn't answer your cell phone, and when I called the house all I got was your answering service. I called the airport, and they said your plane landed. Mr. Turner said he wanted to talk to you and that it was very important."

"My cell phone is working. You shouldn't have had any problem—" I frowned at myself as I realized the problem. "I turned it off on the airplane and forgot to turn it back on." And I accuse Floyd of being flaky. "Doug didn't say what he wanted?"

"No," Floyd answered. "You know how he is. Reporters want answers but never want to give them."

"Doug Turner?" Catherine asked.

"He's—"

"He's—"

Floyd and I spoke in unison and stopped on the same syllable.

"Go ahead, Floyd." It was his chance to impress Catherine.

"Doug Turner is the lead reporter for the Santa Rita *Register*. He covers politics and major crime. Actually, he covers whatever he wants."

Catherine looked at me. I watched her face pale. "He's a reporter?"

"Yes," I said. "That was my campaign manager on the phone. He's been calling her too. She's coming over and bringing dinner."

"How did he find out so soon?" Catherine asked.

"I imagine the newspaper uses scanners to monitor police calls. Most news media do."

"I was afraid of this."

"What?" Floyd asked. "Police? Scanners? Reporters? What's going on?"

"I'll explain," I said, "but not while standing in the foyer. Let's at least go to the dining room and sit at the table . . . Better yet, I'm going to go get dressed. Catherine can explain things. You feel up to that?" I looked at her.

"Yeah, I can do that."

I headed up the stairs.

chpter

I slipped into jeans a size too large and therefore reasonably comfortable, a pair of canvas deck shoes, and a sweatshirt with Temple University emblazoned on the front. I didn't go to Temple. I
graduated from San Diego State University. I had the Temple sweatshirt for the same reason I had one from Yale, Princeton, Brown,
Baylor, and a dozen more. I collect them. I've been asked why I collect them, but I have no answer. Some people collect snow globes,
others souvenir spoons, and still others dolls. I collect college shirts
because I want to.

Catherine and Floyd were seated at the dining room table when
I reemerged. Both had a cup of tea in front of them. I had forgotten
about the teapot. It was a good thing Catherine hadn't.

The scene was amusing. Floyd was leaning over the table as if he
needed to be a couple inches closer to Catherine to convince himself that she wasn't an illusion, a fantasy conjured up by his twenty-
something mind. The funny thing was the teacup. Floyd doesn't
drink tea. I guess he couldn't tell Catherine no.

Catherine exuded poise and confident self-awareness. She was
comfortable before a camera, a theater filled with people, or an audience of one. I felt pride rising like the tide.

"Do you have dinner plans, Floyd?" I entered the kitchen and prepared my own cup of tea.

"Um . . . no."

"Join us tonight. I'm sure Nat will bring enough for you too." He beamed. Christmas had come in October.

Over the next thirty minutes, I pumped Floyd for information about the office. While I was in Sacramento, I had called him daily, but now I wanted to know all the dull details. Besides, it was far more pleasant than talking about a murder victim in Catherine's pool.

Catherine sat in silence, a slight smile on her perfect face, as she feigned interest in city government. Ever the actor.

I heard the honk of a car horn from the front of the house.

"I bet that's Nat," I said and rose from the table. "Come on, Floyd, you can show us that chivalry isn't dead by carrying the food in." He was up in a second. Catherine followed.

We stepped onto the front stoop just in time to see the side door of the van open and a metal lift emerge. A blond woman in an electric wheelchair moved onto the flat metal bed and the unique elevator lowered her to the grass strip that separated the street from the sidewalk.

"She's crippled," Catherine whispered as Floyd moved to greet Nat.

"After you get to know her," I said, "you'll never use the word to describe her again."

Nat said something to Floyd and he disappeared into the van, emerging moments later with his hands filled with white paper sacks. Once he was out of the vehicle, Nat pulled a small remote from a cloth bag that hung from the right armrest and pressed a button. The remote activated the lift, which rose and disappeared into the van. The door closed as if by magic.

Nat approached and stopped at the four-inch-high stoop. I stepped down to the walkway and moved to the back of Nat's wheelchair. I put a foot on a small bar that protruded from the back of the chair and pushed down on the handles by her shoulders. The chair rocked back, and I pushed it forward until its front wheels were on the concrete porch. I lifted as Nat powered the chair, and a second later we were inside the house.

The evening was warm for October, and the breeze that had chilled me at Catherine's had settled to a whisper. We moved out to the deck at the back of the house and set up to eat. The sun painted an amber racing stripe on the surging, darkening ocean.

I made introductions while I unpacked the sacks of food Nat had brought.

"Grinders!" I grinned as I pulled one long sandwich out. "I love these. Did you get them with olive oil?"

"Jimmy won't let you leave the restaurant without it," Nat said. "I ordered them over the phone, and they brought them out to me."

"We always called these hoagies," Floyd said.

"Hoagies, grinders, submarine sandwiches, call them what you will, but they're great. Especially if Jimmy made them." I passed the sandwiches out, then took my place at the redwood table that took up a third of my deck.

Catherine took hers and slowly opened the wrapper. She moved with such deliberateness she made me think of someone trying to diffuse a bomb.

I took a bite. Green bell pepper, ham, provolone, tomato, oregano, and other treasures seduced my taste buds. The thought of calories percolated to the top of my mind but another bite drove the nagger away.

"What made you choose Jimmy's Mafia Pizzeria?" I asked.

"It was on the way, and he also sent a campaign contribution of two hundred and fifty bucks."

"So it was a politically motivated decision?"

Nat laughed and peeled back the sandwich wrapper with her one good hand. She bent forward, resting one end of the grinder on the table, and bit into the other end. Natalie Sanders once graced the airwaves of a major Los Angeles news station. She was the darling of the industry and was often called upon to fill in on national programs. No one doubted that one day she would be the Tom Brokaw of national news. That was before the news van she was riding in tumbled down an embankment. Months and hundreds of hours of therapy later, Nat returned to her life. But it wasn't the life she left.

Commercial news stations sell beauty more than information. Men and women who look like they've been peeled off some catalog anchor prime-time news shows. If they hadn't earned degrees in journalism, most could have made a good living as underwear models.

Insurance had set her up for the rest of her life, but she was not one to do nothing. Her mind operates like a fine Swiss watch and the thought of becoming addicted to soap operas and Court TV was repugnant, so she started her own business. Nat is a researcher. People, companies, local governments hired her to search for facts. With her computer skills and her connections in the news business, she became the most sought-after researcher on the West Coast. Working from her home, she scours the databases and the Internet looking for the one bit of information that can take a news story from the mundane to the spectacular or give a Fortune 500 company an edge on its competition.

When I entered the race for congress, she was my first choice for campaign manager. Our friendship has grown every day since.

I caught Nat watching Catherine. Floyd was watching too but with a different look in his eye. Catherine studied the messy grinder, then lifted it, taking care to touch it with just her fingertips. She took the tiniest bite and then returned the sandwich to the center of the wrapping paper she had so carefully spread before her. The bite she took wasn't enough to fill her mouth, but she chewed it like she had chowed down half the contents.

I felt like a pig and drew a napkin across my face to wipe away some errant olive oil.

We chatted about my trip to Sacramento, about Catherine's play, her new home, and a few other odds and ends. I also told her about Catherine's offer to be a part of our last fund-raiser. Nat remained polite through all of it, but I could see that she was growing impatient. I told her everything about the body in the pool.

I waited for Hurricane Nat to blow in. She narrowed her eyes, worked her jaw, pursed her lips, but said nothing.

"Word's going to get out," I said. "Turner will be polite, but he'll no more give up this story than a bulldog will surrender a bone."

"You actually jumped in the pool," Nat said. It wasn't a question; it was a well-chewed statement. "That may work for us."

"That's what you said on the phone. How?" All eyes shifted to Nat.

"Look, I know you weren't thinking campaign issues when you took that leap into the bloody water. You were just being Maddy and doing what Maddy does, looking out for others. It was a heroic effort even if it was futile."

"Wait a minute, Nat," I said. "I don't want to make political mileage out of a murder. It doesn't seem right."

"I'm not saying we weave it into speeches or put out a press release, just that we make sure the press knows about it."

"What good will that do?" Floyd wanted to know.

"We've faced an uphill march in this campaign, Floyd," Nat explained. "First, Maddy isn't that well known outside of Santa Rita. The congressional district includes areas beyond our city limits, areas where the name Madison Glenn doesn't mean anything.

"Second," she continued, "we're up against an opponent who exudes confidence, strength, and courage. Garret Kinsley was an ambassador, and the public doesn't view ambassadors as politicians. The title carries an untarnished dignity with it. He faced a woman opponent in the primaries, and he demolished her but he did it so smoothly that even she felt honored. Women love him; men want to be him.

"The third problem has to do with the appearance of strength and personal resolve. We live in frightening times. People want a strong hand at the helm. A member of congress can only legislate. He or she can't do much about bringing a sense of safety to the district, but voters don't seem to care about that. Polls show most voters see Garret as better able to deal with such matters."

"That's crazy," Floyd said.

"Sometimes, Floyd, unfounded assumption is more powerful than fact."

"I don't understand," Catherine said. "How does Maddy's jumping in the pool help?"

"It took courage to do that and a willingness to act. Most people wouldn't think of doing what she did."

"I didn't think about it," I said. "I just reacted."

"All the better." Nat paused, then added, "Talk to Doug Turner. In fact, talk to him first. Let him have a lead on this. We might need a favor later." She looked at Floyd. "Can you retrieve Maddy's office messages from here?"

"Sure, the city uses the telephone company's service. I can call from anywhere."

"Do it. If we're lucky there will be calls from some of the local television stations."

Floyd left the table and walked to the cordless phone I had left on the kitchen counter.

"Lucky?" I said, but I knew where she was going. "I'm not real comfortable with this."

"Of course you're not. I'd think less of you if you were." Nat gave me one of her straight-in-the-eye looks. "I'm not asking you to ham it up. Just tell the truth. You were visiting a family member, discovered the body, and tried to help. You were too late. Oh, and you have every confidence in the work and skill of the Santa Rita police. Got it?"

I said I did.

Floyd returned and he looked stunned. "There is another call from Mr. Turner, two calls from television stations, and one from a radio station."

"News or music station?"

"It's the local easy listening station," Floyd said.

Nat shook her head. "Forget them. Radio news fades faster than a flower in an oven." She fell silent again for a moment. "Maddy, how do you feel about Doug coming to your home?"

"I try to keep where I live secret."

"Doug is trustworthy on this. I can threaten to run him over if he releases your address."

It was my turn to think. Doug Turner had always been professional. In some ways, I owed my campaign to him. After I had been particularly testy with him while trying to conceal my plans for higher office, he said, "Why is it that every time a politician is thinking of running for higher office, they deny it when asked? It's like they're ashamed of wanting to do more for the community." Those words burrowed into my thinking like a worm in an apple. When the time came to commit to the campaign, his words echoed in my brain.

"Okay," I agreed. "He's the only media man I trust that much."

"Good, it will go a long way with him," Nat said. "Why don't you call him? I'll call the television stations back. They're going to want some tape so we need to set up a place to meet. It's too late for the early evening news, but the eleven o'clock people will eat it up."

"Are you sure this is a good idea?" Floyd said.

"To do nothing is to invite disaster," Nat replied. "Our best defense is a quick offense. If we're careful, this will run a day or two, then drop from the news."

Running for office is like being on a bus. Some days you get to drive; other days you sit on the backseat. Knowing when to do what is the trick. I trusted Nat and told her so.

"One last thing." Nat made eye contact with Catherine. "You have some decisions to make."

"I do?" Catherine had been picking at her sandwich, pinching off small bites and placing them in her mouth. She covered her mouth as she spoke as if she had a wad of food ready to fall out. I doubted she had eaten enough to dirty her teeth.

"I assume you have a publicist," Nat said.

"Yes. Franco Zambonelli. I called him right after I called the police. He said he was coming up to see me."

"That doesn't surprise me," Nat offered. "I think we should hide you away while Doug Turner is here. You're news and he'll want to talk to you about your chauffeur and his murder at your new home. There's good journalistic mileage in that. I don't think your publicist would like us meddling in his work."

"You may be right," Catherine said.

"I'm pretty sure I am. Can you reach him?"

"I can call his cell phone."

"It sounds like we all have calls to make," Nat said, and pulled her cell phone from the cloth caddy. Catherine reached for her cell phone, and I took the cordless from Floyd.

Poor Floyd looked lost.

chapter 7

Nat had been right about the television stations. She had also been wrong. None wanted "tape" so we didn't need to set up a place for a press conference. I was relieved. The early evening news was already over by the time I called. That left only the ten and eleven o'clock broadcasts. Only one station was local; the others operated out of LA. Murder stories are so common in the greater Los Angeles area they barely make the news, unless they are unusually gruesome. All three stations were content with a phone interview. We emailed a publicity photo to each station, which they appreciated. Television thrives on visuals.

Each interview was a clone of the previous. The reporter thanked me, asked a few general questions, pretended to be moved by the horror of swimming with a corpse, and then thanked me again. I referred them to the police for any specifics. They seemed satisfied—for now.

Doug Turner was a bit of a mystery. He was noble and professional and I could trust him—even if he was a reporter. But I couldn't find him. I called his office and left a message with his editor who promised to page him. There was nothing to do but wait for his call.

The breeze had picked up again, so we moved from the rear deck into the living room. I built a fire in the fireplace and we gathered around. Catherine entertained us with tales of her New York experiences, made us laugh as she recounted a few gaffes she had made from the stage, and told how different making movies was than straight theater. She even told us about the early product commercials she made. We listened, asked questions, and laughed at the appropriate times.

Floyd sat enraptured by each tale. I started to ask him how Celeste was doing but bit my tongue. Celeste and Floyd were evolving into an item. While some people fell in and out of love as quickly as the weather changed, Floyd and Celeste moved forward at glacial speeds. To ask about Celeste now would embarrass the young man. I let it go.

Anyone looking at the scene might have mistaken the gathering in my living room as a small party, but we knew better. We were avoiding the horror of the day. Catherine told her humorous stories because entertaining was her coping mechanism. Her eyes, however, no longer flickered as they did when I picked her up at the theater, and her shoulders were slightly rounder than before. She was being brave, but as every person who has been forced to be courageous knows, bravery isn't the absence of fear. Anxiety, shock, confusion, and uncertainty not only remain, they're fanned to searing flames. The courageous are merely people who keep doing what needs to be done despite what they feel. Catherine had just joined those ranks.

The soft melody of tinny music filled the room—a Mozart aria. Catherine's cell phone was sounding. We fell silent as she exchanged a few words. She looked at me. "It's Franco. He needs directions."

"Do you want me to give them?"

She handed me the phone. The voice on the other end was nasal and tinted with a New Jersey accent. With a name like Franco, I was expecting Italian. I asked where he was and then gave him step-by-step directions to the house. I handed the phone back to Catherine and she made her good-byes.

"He said he'd be here soon." Catherine looked at me. "I know about the need to keep our lives private. I appreciate your opening your home to me and letting Franco come by."

"That's what family is for," I said. "Franco sounds like an East Coaster."

"He grew up in New Jersey, then moved to New York. Later he moved his publicity firm to LA to work with the film people. There's more business in movies than in theater."

"How long has he been your publicist?" I asked.

"Almost a year now. He did the publicity for the production house, and then I hired him a few months later. He's one of the best."

"Did he get you the part in the next movie?" Floyd wondered.

Catherine gave him a smile, and I was pretty sure Floyd was going to melt into my sofa. "Publicists don't represent actors to producers and directors, agents do. Franco represents me to the media. In a sense, by getting my name well known, he's responsible for the continued interest in my work, but deals are made by agents."

"So you have an agent?" Nat said.

"Two. I have one agent in Hollywood. She deals with the film industry. I also have an agent in New York who represents me to the Broadway and off-Broadway producers. I also have a business manager."

"Wow, Catherine," I said. "It sounds like you're a small business."

"As an actor, I am, but there's nothing small about the movie business. Millions of dollars flow like water. Every day deals are made and broken by the dozen. It's important to have people you trust around you."

"And you trust all these people?" I wondered.

"Mostly, but never completely." She pursed her lips, and her eyes shifted to the fire.

"What do you mean?" I said.

"The first thing you learn in the business is that the waters are filled with sharks. When you're an actor, people act like you're the most important thing in their lives, but what they really want is access to your money or influence. There have been many actors who have had their bank accounts emptied by people they trust."

Sadness oozed through me. There was something heartbreaking in seeing innocent youth tarnished with the realities of life. Sitting on my sofa was an overnight success, a sudden millionaire, a beauty who could be recognized on any street in America, and she was only twenty-five. At an age when most are trying to form a career, she had already achieved wild success. Her face and manner radiated her youth, but her eyes were revealing hard-earned wisdom of someone twice her age. I was proud of her.

"It sounds like you've taken precautions," Nat said.

Catherine turned her gaze to Nat. "I have to. My business manager handles all my bills, but he doesn't have access to my bank accounts. He submits a detailed list of bills to pay, and I transfer money. He advises me on investments but knows I'll always get a second opinion."

Nat raised her well-arched eyebrows. "You got him to agree to that?"

"He had no choice. It was the price of doing business with me."

Nat laughed. "Maddy, I think you should drop out of the race and let Catherine run. Congress needs people with common sense."

"Watch it," I said. "Are you saying I have no common sense?"

"I would never say that." She winked.

Floyd leaned forward, eyes wide. "How does someone become an agent? I mean, can anyone become an agent? Do you have to go to school?"

Dear, dear Floyd. Floyd is a professional wannabe. He doesn't know what he wants to be, so he wants to be everything. Since he's come to work for me, he's expressed interest in becoming a businessman, politician, and even a police officer. He is like a moth who can't decide which source of light to circle. His father is Lenny Grecian—Reverend Lenny Grecian—my pastor. Pastor Lenny spent his youth surfing, then driving a truck. Someplace along the line he discovered faith, or faith discovered him. Some of Pastor Lenny's initial lack of focus must have been genetically transferred to Floyd.

"It's a hard business, Floyd," Catherine said. "More fail at it than succeed."

The doorbell rang. I rose, approached the door, and put my eye to the business end of the security peephole. Bathed in the yellow light of the front porch stood a man with a head as hairless as an egg; dark, thick eyebrows nestled on a round face.

"Who is it?" I was being overcautious but past events have made me leery about opening the door to nighttime visitors.

"Franco Zambonelli." The door muffled his words.

I unlatched the locks and opened the door. "I'm Maddy Glenn. Please come in."

"Thank you."

He was shorter than me by three inches and was round above the belt. He wore a beige sport coat over a white dress shirt, no tie, black slacks, and New Balance running shoes. I was pretty sure he had never run in them.

I closed the door and led Mr. Zambonelli to the others. Catherine stood and smiled. "Hi, Franco." Her words were soft.

"Hi, nuthin'," he said. He stepped forward and gave her a brief hug. His accent was thick. "You okay, kid?"

"I'm fine." She motioned to me. "This is my cousin, Mayor Madison Glenn—"

"Just Maddy," I said.

Catherine introduced the others. Franco did a double take when Catherine introduced Nat. It was a common reaction. I had done the same thing when I first met her. Beauty in a wheelchair was jarring. It shouldn't be, but it was.

Franco then looked at me. "Mayor? Really. You're mayor of this little berg?"

Little berg? "Yes, Mr. Zambonelli, I'm the mayor of Santa Rita." I bit my tongue and tried to change the subject. "May I offer you a drink?"

"Scotch, if you have it."

"I'm afraid I don't. I don't have anything with alcohol—"

"Oh, one of those, eh? Doesn't matter. I knocked back a coupla' double lattes on the drive over. I'm a little wired."

That was an understatement. "Have a seat, Mr. Zambonelli—"

"Call me Franco. Back in Jersey they call me Frankie Z., but for some reason that makes youse California types think of the Mafia."

Catherine returned to her place on the sofa, leaving the middle space open between her and Floyd. Franco looked at Floyd.

"You mind if I sit there, kid? I need to talk to my client."

Floyd stood and searched for another place to sit. He looked emotionally injured. I patted the empty portion of the love seat. As Floyd joined me, I gazed at Franco and wondered how badly my campaign would be hurt if I pummeled him with the fireplace poker.

"Okay," Franco said to Catherine. "Tell me what's new. About the murder, I mean."

"Not much," Catherine said. "The police showed up and took over. They asked me a lot of questions, and Maddy too. They said they'd be processing the scene until late tonight, so Maddy said I could stay with her."

"Did the cops mistreat you, kid? Did they push you around any?"

Catherine blinked several times. "No, why would they do that?"

"I'm just looking out for your well-being, baby. That's all. Just your well-being." He turned to me. "What kinda cops you got here?"

"What do you mean?" I stuffed down a little more irritation.

"You know. Are they straight or on the take?"

He gave no indication he knew how offensive the question was. "The Santa Rita police department is one of the best law enforcement agencies in the country."

"No offense meant, Mayor, it's just that I know how these small-town police departments are. This is the perfect situation for someone to make a name for himself: beautiful movie star, rich, big home and all that."

"The detective is Judson West, and he learned his craft in San Diego, one of the nation's largest cities. He is skilled and fair."

"Like I said, no offense meant." He returned his attention to Catherine. "Would you prefer a hotel? I can set you up with a suite in Santa Barbara or Thousand Oaks."

I caught Nat looking at me. I couldn't decide if she was silently pleading with me not to hurt the man or begging me to.

"I want to stay with Maddy. Besides, this is where I told the police I would be if they needed to contact me."

"I understand, baby. I understand. But will you be comfortable enough here?"

I snapped my jaw shut to stem the tsunami of snide remarks. Wisecracks and threats flowed from my brain to my mouth like a flash flood. I have always had trouble controlling my mouth. It's a family trait. Some months ago I became a person of faith. I see things differently now, but the old nature was still there and I still lost more internal battles of discipline than I won. I learned that a Christian's words were to be "seasoned with salt." I was sensing more pepper than salt. I took a deep breath and let it out slowly.

"I'm fine here, Franco," Catherine said. "Really. I should be able to go home tomorrow or the next day."

"Okay, okay. I'm just trying to do what's best for you." He scooted closer and took her hand in his. "Who else have you spoken to?"

"Nothing's changed since I spoke to you last on the phone."

"This little play you're doing; have you spoken to the director to tell him that he'll have to replace you?"

"Why would I do that?" Catherine asked.

"Listen, kid . . ." He looked at me, then the others. "Could we have a moment here?"

That was it. "You're asking me to leave my living room in my home in my city—"

"It's okay," Catherine said to Franco quickly. "I want them here. They're my friends, and they've given me good advice."

I caught a glance at Floyd who looked ready to pop buttons.

Catherine continued. "It was Nat who told me to wait until you got here before talking to anyone else. I trust her and Maddy. And Floyd."

"Okay, sweetheart. If they're good with you, then they're good with me. Now back to this play thing. I spoke to Stewart Rockwood and Chuck Buchanan and they're afraid that adverse publicity could damage the project. They want you to drop off the radar scope for a month or so, come back to Hollywood and focus on the movie."

"I am focused on the movie," Catherine retorted. "We're just going over script reviews now. Principle shooting doesn't begin for several weeks."

"I know, I know, but it would ease their minds. You've done Broadway and the big screen, kid, you shouldn't be doing dinner theaters and local stock."

Catherine fell silent. I couldn't advise her. As much as it galled me, I could see Franco's point.

Catherine lowered her head, and I readied myself to hear her acquiesce. When she looked up she said, "I made a promise, and I'm going to keep it. There's nothing in my contract that says I can't do local theater. I'm going to do my part."

"Be reasonable, Catherine," Franco whined. "You're a star now, not a beginner."

"I've made up my mind," Catherine said. I had a new reason to be proud of her.

"I can't talk you out of it?" Franco tilted his head to one side and put on his best hangdog look. It was pathetic.

"No."

Franco looked at me as if I was using some kind of mind control on his client. I raised my hands. "Don't look at me; I'm just the lowly mayor of a little berg."

He frowned. Nat bit her lip and tried to force down the corners of her mouth. Floyd shifted nervously.

"Have you spoken to the media?" Franco said.

"Maddy did, but she didn't tell them about me or that I was staying here."

"Good. That's real good."

My life was complete. I could now die happy.

He continued. "If the media starts bugging you—say, at rehearsals or something—refer them to me. You have my cell number. Better yet, maybe I'll sit through the rehearsals. That way I can run interference for you."

"Okay," Catherine conceded.

Franco rose and I joined him. "Is there a decent hotel around?"

The image of Sleep Right motel popped to the front of my mind. Most people referred to it as the Flea Bite motel. It was run-down, dirty, and the place where the city's few prostitutes and drug dealers hang out. I fought the urge to give him the address. I also had to squelch the nagging desire to tell him to try Thousand Oaks or Santa Barbara. Instead, I referred him to one of the business hotels near the center of town.

I walked him to the door and wished him a good night. It took work, but I did it. He thanked me and shook my hand.

Earlier that day, I had plunged into blood-tinted water in a useless effort to save a man's life. I ended up dragging a corpse to the side of the pool, yet I felt dirtier after shaking Franco Zambonelli's hand.

chapter

The hardest part about travel is coming home. No matter how short the trip, say to Sacramento, and no matter how mundane the task, say a mayors' meeting with the governor, it was always difficult to come back to a desk backed up with work. I strolled into my office at ten minutes to eight. I had been gone over a week, but it felt longer.

I hesitated at the door between Floyd's office and my own. On most days, I love my job. Coming to the office was a joy. Like today, I would enter, sit behind a large cherry desk—a gift from my husband—read the Santa Rita *Register* and the *Los Angeles Times* to get my brain in gear, then dive into the work.

This morning I needed an extra moment. From the threshold I could see the number of files demanding my attention was twice what I expected it to be and three times what I *wanted* it to be. A stack of pink While You Were Out slips rested near the phone.

Time to get to work.

I set my purse inside one of the desk drawers and then glanced through the files. The city manager had sent up a file on a possible expansion of a park in the center of the city; the city attorney had forwarded the notification of a lawsuit against the city that had been dropped; Tess Lawrence had typed up and delivered her version of the city council meeting she chaired while I was gone; and the local redevelopment agency filed a report on cost estimates to refurbish the downtown library. There was a memo from our Local Agency Formation Commission; a letter from a citizens group against special city taxes; and a request to speak to the local chamber of commerce.

The telephone messages were many but none urgent and for that I was thankful.

I was tired.

After "Frankie Z." had left—I still had to laugh at the moniker—Catherine, Nat, Floyd, and I visited a little longer. I broke out some pound cake and anointed the servings with Cool Whip. Catherine declined with a comment about her need to fit into costumes. Several of my "costumes" had stretch waists, so I ate my portion without guilt. I figure swimming while fully dressed allowed me some reward.

Floyd left soon after, and Catherine went to bed. Nat and I talked for another fifteen minutes before I walked her to the van. At last alone and in bed, I settled in for sleep that wouldn't come for another hour and a half. My body was ready, but my brain still had hashing to do. I hate nights like that.

Now I was back in familiar territory ready to take on the day's challenges.

"Coffee?"

I looked up and saw Fritzy standing in my door. She held a large cup.

"Did you make it?" I asked.

"Of course." Her smile threatened to touch her ears.

"In that case, I'll take a great big, steaming mug."

"Lucky for you, I just happen to have one here." She stepped into my office and placed the cup on my desk. "Welcome home, Madam Mayor."

I thanked her. Fritzy is an institution at city hall. A gray-haired woman with ever youthful eyes, she had become a dear friend. I had always admired the way she handled the reception desk and the way she made others feel welcome and valued. This past January she endured a horrible tragedy. I was thrown into the mix. I watched her weather the storm with the kind of strength poets wrote about. The dark time forged a new bond between us, one that neither my role as her boss or our age difference could dilute.

I took the cup and sniffed the rich aroma. The woman knew how to make coffee. "You're the best, Fritzy. I'm thinking of adopting you."

"I'm more trouble than I'm worth. Is there anything I can do for you?"

"I don't think so. I'm just getting my head back in the game. Did Floyd cause you any problems?"

She laughed. "Oh no. He's a wonderful boy. He did wander around a little lost while you were gone."

"That's our Floyd, but he's not a boy, Fritzy. He's a college grad."

"From where I stand, anyone his age is a boy." She hesitated. I had a feeling I knew what was coming next. "I heard about what happened yesterday. It's horrible. And what you did. You amaze me."

"Well, when you don't bother to think, you can do those things."

"A murder at your cousin's house. Horrible. Just horrible."

"It's in the hands of the police now," I said and opened the *Register*.

"What's she like?"

"Who?" I looked up again.

"You know who. Catherine Anderson."

I got it. "She's . . . Catherine. A little older, just as pretty, smart, and talented. I left her sleeping in the guest room."

"I loved her movie."

"It was a big hit," I admitted.

"I saw it twice."

"I take it you want to meet her," I said.

"That'd be wonderful." Fritzy's smile broadened. Something I didn't think was possible.

"I can't promise anything, but I'll see what I can do. Maybe I can get you a ticket to opening night or something. No promises though. Remember, I'm only the mayor."

"That would be great," Fritzy said. "I mean, if it's not too much trouble."

"I'll ask her later this morning. I plan to pick her up a little before ten and drive her to rehearsal. We'll see what she has . . . to . . . say."

A small article just below the fold on the front page of the *Register* kidnapped my attention: "Man Slain at Star's Home." I had expected the article. The murder was news after all. What surprised me was the byline: Vincent Branch. Branch was the *Register*'s editor. Why wasn't Doug Turner's name there? He had made the initial calls and when I spoke to Branch the previous evening, he acted like the story was Doug's.

Thinking he might have been pulled off for another story, I rifled through the newspaper. No articles by Doug. That wasn't conclusive of anything. When I spoke to Branch it was early evening. He would have to put the paper to bed soon so it would be on doorsteps this morning. If Doug had been reassigned, his new article might not be out until tomorrow or even later. It was odd but not bizarre. The news business was volatile and could change in minutes; breaking news often upstages political news conferences, at least at the city level.

I shook off the distraction and read the article. It was brief, succinct, and offered few facts. I could see Branch typing like crazy to get something about the murder in the paper. Unlike its large cousins, the *Register* operates with a small staff, small enough that Branch had to occasionally pick up the slack. I decided I'd have to ask Doug what happened the next time I spoke to him.

"I'm here." Floyd walked into the room. "Can I get you a cup of—? Oh." He looked at the mug on my desk.

"Fritzy beat you to it."

Floyd just stood there. I stared at him. He stared at me. I love Floyd dearly, but at times he seems to orbit a different planet than the rest of us. Fritzy excused herself.

"Yes?" I prompted.

"Oh. I was just wondering if there was anything special today."

"Special? No, nothing special. I plan to review files and get caught up on messages until ten, then I need to pick up Catherine and take her to the Curtain Call for rehearsal. After that I have a luncheon with the chamber of commerce. At two I meet with the Community Development Department and at three, I brief the council about my meeting in Sacramento."

"It sounds like a full day," Floyd said. "Do you want me to pick up Catherine for you? I could take her to rehearsal."

So that was it. "What would Celeste say about that?"

He shrugged. "We kinda broke up. It was her idea."

That surprised me. Floyd was no ladies' man, but his refreshing honesty and his ability to take himself lightly was attractive. "When did this happen?" I motioned him to take a seat.

"Last week." He sat, his round shoulders drooped another inch.

I waited for more but nothing came. This was going to be a question-and-answer situation. "Did you have a fight?"

He shook his head and gazed at the edge of my desk and rubbed the arm of the chair with his right thumb. "I think she's seeing someone else. Someone at the college."

Celeste had just started her junior year at USB. Floyd was two or three years older and already out of college. They had hit it off, and I thought they made a great couple. Floyd isn't every girl's cup of tea, but he has a good heart and a fine mind even though the latter occasionally gets lost in youthful fog.

"I'm sorry, Floyd. These things are always tough." Now I understood his barely concealed interest in Catherine. Of course, Catherine had the kind of beauty that broke men's hearts when she walked down the street.

"It's okay."

"Nonsense. A broken relationship hurts and shouldn't be minimized. What makes you think she's seeing someone else?"

He shrugged again. "I dunno."

"Floyd, do you have any reason to believe that she is seeing someone else? Has she told you that? Have you seen her with another man?"

"No."

I waited again. Nothing. I pressed on. "When was the last time you spoke to her?"

"Last week. I called her, and she said she was too busy to talk."

"Was she?"

"Was she what?"

"Floyd, maybe she *was* too busy to talk. You know how overwhelmed we get sometimes. Maybe she was telling you the truth."

"Maybe."

"It's up to you, but here's what I think you should do. Call her up and offer to meet her for lunch. She probably has classes today. Drive up there and meet her at the White Gull. Have some chowder or order burgers. See what she says. If she turns you down, then at least you know your hunch was right. If she has lunch with you, you may discover that you're worrying over nothing. How's that sound?"

"Good, I guess."

"I'll call ahead and make sure they have a table for you. In fact, I'll arrange to make the whole thing my treat." The White Gull was one of my favorite Santa Barbara restaurants. It sat on the ocean's edge. Even during a business lunch it was romantic.

"Okay. Maybe you're right."

"What do you mean, 'maybe'? Have you ever known me to be wrong? Don't answer that. Just go pull those stats on new business licenses I asked you to compile. I'll need it for my luncheon."

Floyd walked from the office.

I read through the papers and digested what I needed from the files on my desk and returned a few phone calls. That took a little over an hour. At a quarter past nine, I started perusing the business license information Floyd had gathered for me. Cities have several forms of income. The primary sources of revenue come from three taxes: property tax, the uniform local sales tax, and the vehicle license fee. We also receive money through state and federal aid, special assessments, and fees. That's why most cities work so hard to get businesses to move into city limits. More businesses mean more jobs, more tax revenues, and additional fees. A healthy city has a growing business base. Ours has fluctuated over the last three years and I had dedicated myself to improving Santa Rita's tax record without damaging our unique Edenesque setting.

That's what I planned to tell the chamber of commerce at their monthly luncheon. I also planned to talk about my run for congress.

I was immersed in the numbers of new businesses and examining the charts Floyd had prepared when he called through the open door between our offices. "A Ms. Catherine Anderson is on the phone for you."

Ms. Catherine Anderson? That was awful formal. I looked at the phone. Line one was lit but not blinking. Floyd had not put her on hold. The ceremonial announcement was for her benefit.

I picked up. "Hey, you. How'd you sleep?"

"Pretty good. Thanks for leaving the coffee on for me."

"It was nothing. Did you eat yet?" I asked.

"I never eat breakfast," she said. "I need a favor."

"Need me to pick you up sooner?" I guessed.

"I forgot my movie script. I left it at the house. I usually study it in the mornings before going to rehearsal. Can we swing by and pick it up before going to the theater?"

"I don't know if you can get in. Have you heard from Detective West?"

"No, but I need that script. I have a meeting with the director and cast tomorrow morning, then I have to rush back for the play."

"You are one busy girl," I said. "You go ahead and get ready. I'll call West and check on the status of the house." I hung up. "Floyd, see if you can ring up Detective West. He may be at headquarters."

"Did I hear my name?"

The unexpected voice made me jump. West walked through the outer door into Floyd's office and stepped to my threshold.

"I was just going to call you." I stood. "Long night?" He looked drawn. The ace-up-his-sleeve smile usually perched above his chin was missing and the skin beneath his eyes looked dark. The only clue I had that he had gone home yesterday was his change of clothes.

"You don't know the half of it." A formal man, he stood at the doorway until I invited him in. He closed the door behind him and took the seat I offered.

"Want some coffee?" I offered.

"No thanks."

"Fritzy made it."

"Okay. Black, please."

I buzzed Floyd over the intercom and placed an order for coffee, then I lowered my fanny back into the desk chair. "That was Catherine. She left something in her house and wants to know if she can pick it up. Poor thing, she's putting up a good front, but I can tell this is weighing on her like a wet bag of cement."

"I suppose so," West said. "Scientific investigation finished up last night. I finished an hour later. I've declared the house clear. She can go back now if she wants."

"Find anything?"

He paused at that.

"You did, didn't you? You found something at the house."

"No, not at the house." He leaned forward.

There was a knock on the door, and West stopped midsyllable. The doorknob made some noises but the door didn't open. I pinched off a smile. "Do you mind?"

West rose and opened the door. Floyd stood on the other side. He had been trying to juggle two cups of coffee and open the door at the same time.

"Sorry," he said and entered. He placed the coffee mugs on my desk and took away the now empty cup Fritzy had left. As he exited, he closed the door behind him.

West sat down, took the coffee, and said, "Doug Turner is in the hospital. As of an hour ago, he was in a coma."

"Wha—What?" I felt sick. Acid boiled in my belly. The words came too quickly and slapped me hard across the mind.

"He came by the scene last night. Took a few photos, interviewed me, then took off. At this point, we're not exactly sure what happened. He was found in his car. He had driven off Aberdeen Canyon

Road. The car rolled several times, and the accident investigators think he may have done an end over."

"An end over?"

"The car flipped end over end."

The image fanned the nausea boiling in my stomach. I opened my mouth to say something but my mind refused to cooperate. West filled in for me.

"A passerby saw lights shining up the slope. Fortunately for Turner, the other driver has a curious streak. He saw the headlights of the car and then called for the police."

As much as I fought it, the image of Doug Turner careening over the edge of the road, rolling and flipping his way to the bottom, flashed like a strobe in my brain. The area West described was just a couple of miles from Catherine's house.

Santa Rita has three basic areas of geography. A portion of the city ran along the sugary sands of the coast. The "flatlands," as the locals called it, was a wide expanse on the other side of the 101 freeway. Businesses, parks, government buildings, schools, and the like were built there. Immediately east of that rose the gently rolling hills where the expensive homes were built. Those hills meet in valleys, some with steep sides. Aberdeen Canyon was one such gorge.

"I know that road," I said. "The canyon side has barricades along the side. Are you saying that Doug went through or over the railing?"

"No." West folded his hands and pressed his lips into a line. "The railing was gone. All that was left were the short posts that held it."

That made no sense. "The city and county share in the maintenance of the residential roads. This year's budget reflected our efforts to improve safety on the hillside roadways."

"I know," West said. "The accident investigators believe that the rails were removed by high school or college kids. Lately, there's been a rash of thefts. They're taking everything they can get their hands on. For the moment, the best guess is that it's a right of passage for some group of teenagers. Tagging was and remains a problem, but this is something new."

"Why would they do that?" The thought was repulsive. "That kind of game could get someone killed . . ." I prayed I wasn't being prophetic.

"We have officers on it," West said and sipped his coffee.

"Will you be working that investigation too?"

"No. Believe it or not, it's considered petty theft, unless—"

"Unless Doug dies, then it's homicide, right?"

"Yeah, that's pretty much it." He studied me. I knew West well enough to know that he was concerned about how the news would affect me. West was a friend, and he wanted to be more. For a time, although I fought it tooth and nail, I thought I wanted the same thing, but the more time I spent with him, the more I realized that romance was not in the works. We had been through several grueling, soul-shredding events, but all that did was prove that friendship could be strengthened but love could not be forged. I had accepted that fact. He hadn't.

"You okay?" He fingered the rim of his coffee cup.

"Stunned. That word doesn't say it. I'm . . . I'm . . . speechless."

He smiled. "I never thought I'd see that." It was a kind gesture meant to lighten a dark moment.

"I'm a little surprised myself."

We fell into an awkward silence. My mind juggled a dozen thoughts, and my emotions quarreled with each other. Courage wanted to take control, but sadness demanded equal time. I prayed in silence. *Oh God. Dear God. Sweet Jesus.* It wasn't eloquent but it was the best I could muster.

"Well," West said, standing. "I need to be going. The ME is doing the autopsy on Catherine's chauffeur in about half an hour. I need to go observe."

"One of the great benefits of your job."

"When I left San Diego, I thought I'd see a lot fewer people on the metal table, but lately it seems like I should have an office down there. I'm afraid the world is catching up with your city, Mayor. It's a shame, really. Eden is falling."

It was my turn to study West. He wore a cloak of weariness; a weariness that didn't come from the loss of some sleep—his heart was fatigued, his soul aging faster than it should.

I rose and looked into his eyes. West's determination and strength was almost legendary among the police force, but I saw the eggshell spirit of the man. He could be powerful, determined, and had a will of iron. Nothing cowed him. Yet, behind the badge, beneath the veneer of masculinity, was a man who frayed at the edges as quickly as the rest of us. He would never admit it, and I would never ask him to.

"You'll keep me posted?" I asked.

"I always do."

He set the coffee cup down, gave me a quick but penetrating stare in the eyes, sucked out some of my strength, then left.

As a child, I visited my grandparents and saw an old washing machine, the kind with rollers on the top for squeezing water out of just-washed clothing. I felt like I had just passed through a pair of those rollers.

I stepped into Floyd's office. "Floyd, please ask the city manager and city attorney to meet me in my office."

"Sure. What time?"

"I want them here in ten minutes. Call Tess, too. The deputy mayor should be in on this."

Floyd looked at me. "You look pale. Are you all right?"

"No, Floyd. I'm not."

I went back into my office, closed the door, sat in my chair, and closed my eyes. For a moment, I wished I had stayed in Sacramento.

chapter

ometimes being mayor and being human seems like mixing oil and water; today was becoming one of those days. Ten minutes after West left I had three people in my office: Tess Lawrence, deputy mayor and frequent thorn in my flesh; Fred Markham, city attorney and all-around nice guy; and Russell Elliot, the city manager. My leisurely morning had dissolved in the heat of change. I was to pick up Catherine earlier than planned, and the news West brought me required immediate action. I got straight to the point and laid out what West had revealed about Doug Turner's accident.

"That's horrible," Russ said. "Is he going to be all right?" Russ is a quiet, reflective man who has helped make Santa Rita one of the best cities in California. I valued his leadership, his opinion, and his honesty.

"I don't know," I said. "I pray so." My stomach still quivered.

"Doug may have been a reporter but he was always an honest reporter," Fred Markham said. Fred is one of my favorite people at city hall. He had joyful eyes, an insatiable mind, and spoke plainly. We were lucky to have him, especially in light of the number of offers he received from larger, better-paying cities. I once threatened to nail his feet to the floor. I wanted to keep him as long as possible.

"I see the problem," Tess Lawrence said. She stood by the door, allowing Fred and Russ to sit in the only two guest chairs in my office. To an outsider, it might look as if she was being polite, but I know her too well. Tess wanted the advantage of being the only one standing.

Tess and I have a rocky history. Until this year we could barely stand to breathe the same air. She is often argumentative, obstinate, manipulative, aggressive, rude, ambitious, and as cuddly as a snowman. In the past, I have described her as an iceberg in pantyhose. Now, I restrain myself.

Some months back, during a difficult time for the city and for me, we had knocked heads like bighorn sheep, but when the air cleared I had come to see a different side to the woman with short white hair and a permanently etched frown. I learned of her artistic side. I also learned that she had a heart, bled when cut, and had feelings as genuine as mine. We had come a long way, but we weren't taking our lunches together. The thawing of our professional relationship had been good for everyone, especially me, since she was my deputy mayor.

"I thought you might," I said. She was insightful. "Share your thinking."

Tess crossed her arms and stepped to the side of my desk, addressing Fred and Russ. "I'm preaching to the choir here, but we need to consider the legal ramifications of the accident. A citizen driving on a city street steers off the road and is nearly killed. He may die yet. If he lives, he may sue. If he dies, his famil—" She looked at me. "Does he have family?"

I didn't know. "His mother passed away in January, but that's all the family I know of. I'm afraid I never asked." *Great, now I felt guilty.*

"We'll have to assume he does. Even a brother or sister could launch a wrongful death suit. His medical bills are going to be enormous. I assume the *Register* has some sort of health insurance for its employees, but that means that they might try and recover some of their costs. We can add to that Mr. Turner's auto insurance. They're certain to see us as having some pretty deep pockets."

"I'll get started on an assessment," Fred said. He seemed to have aged five years in the last five minutes. "I'll also refresh my memory on the city's liability insurance."

I looked at Russ. The city manager scratched his head. "I've never heard of anything like this," he said. "Oh, I've heard of kids stealing traffic signs but not often. Those things are attached in a way that makes them difficult to remove. Removing a segment of traffic rail would take a good piece of work. I'll get hold of the Public Works Department and see how far these pranks have gone."

"I want that rail fixed as soon as possible," I said, snapping more than I meant.

"The key is to show we weren't negligent," Tess said. "If it appears we were aware of the problem and did little or nothing to prevent it, the court will hand us our heads on a platter. Damage control will be the order of the day."

"What if we are negligent?" I asked. It was an uncomfortable thought.

"We're not," Tess said. "It's important, no, it is imperative that we give the idea that the city is limited in this matter. Do you want me to handle the media on this?"

She was in rare form.

"It's vital that we put the right spin on this," Tess added. "The city could lose a lot of money—"

"We don't have all the facts yet, Tess. There's nothing to spin. I want to know the truth." I stood so I could be eye-to-eye with Tess. Her lips were drawn tight and her expression could be read by everyone in the room. She was a severe woman in attitude and appearance.

It was an image she cultivated around city hall. On the campaign field, she could appear warm, caring, and open. Those elements were in her—somewhere—and percolated to the surface from time to time. Most days, she was just plain difficult. This was one of those days. We had had a few warm moments, but this wasn't going to be one of them.

"First, we don't know that the city is liable. Second, we don't know Doug Turner's intent. I agree we need to be ready, but our first goal is to ascertain the truth and not become defensive. I want to know as much as I can before we decide on a course of action. Let's keep our options and our eyes open. Russ, I need your report from the public works people as soon as possible. I plan to follow up with the police. Fred, see what you can do about getting the police report on the accident."

"I have a question," Fred said, rising. "I read the paper this morning, and there was nothing in it about Turner's accident."

"I don't know for sure," I said, "but my guess is that the paper had already been put to bed. By the time Doug was found and the paper learned of it, the presses would have been rolling."

"That makes sense," Fred said.

"All right, folks," I said. "Let's learn what we can as fast as we can." I shifted to see Tess better. "Tess, I need you to work with Fred on this. I'm going to accept your offer to handle the media. Don't spin anything. At the moment we don't know enough to spin anything."

She softened and nodded. Tess was as smart as they come, and despite her sometimes prickly personality and hair-trigger temper, she could assess a situation faster than anyone I knew. From the look she gave me, I could tell she understood what else I was doing. I was giving her more "face time" with the media. There was no secret that she wanted to sit in the mayor's seat. It was one reason she took the appointment as deputy mayor. "Deputy mayor" looks better on a ballot than "council member." If I won the congressional seat, then she would become acting mayor and make a run for the job. If I lost the campaign, then she remained deputy mayor and would take me on in the next citywide election.

My office emptied, and I felt the sudden cold of being alone. Yesterday I shared a pool with a murder victim; today, a respected acquaintance lay in a coma after visiting the site of the murder. I had a feeling I would be facing my own media problems.

I glanced at the clock. It was time to pick Catherine up. I grabbed my purse and left the office behind.

Catherine met me at the curb in front of my home. I had called her to tell her I was on my way. The unplanned meeting with Tess, Fred, and Russ, as well as some slower-than-usual traffic, had put me a few minutes behind. I pressed the car forward trying to make up for the lost minutes. I have a thing about arriving ahead of schedule. I hate being late even if it's just to drop someone off.

Before we could head to the Curtain Call, we had to swing by Catherine's home. The side trip would double the time, but it needed to be done. I worked my way to the freeway and proceeded north. The sun dropped diamonds on the undulating ocean. The Pacific is aptly named. Looking at it always gave me a sense of peace. No matter what happened around me, the ocean never changed. That was how I had come to think of God. My faith was still new, and I was still growing, having more to learn than I thought possible. Through the difficult and even life-threatening events in my life, God had been there, unaltered by the chaos that surrounded me. Like the ocean, he could change everything around him, and not be changed in the process. There was comfort in that.

We arrived at Catherine's home, and I pulled up the long drive. Hanging from one of the newly planted trees was a piece of yellow police ribbon, flapping in the gentle ocean breeze. Once it had cordoned off the area and marked it as the scene of a vicious crime, now it was just the detritus left behind by police investigators.

I parked on the driveway near the limo, still parked in the same spot as yesterday, and exited with Catherine. The dirt bore the countless footprints of policemen who had searched the grounds.

"The landscapers are scheduled to put down sod next week," Catherine said. She seemed sad. The bruised ground, along with the tape remnant, was a reminder of what she had experienced the day before.

"It will be beautiful when it's done." I hoped the kind words would be salubrious words.

She tested the door and found it locked. At least West and his team locked up after leaving. Catherine punched in her code on the keypad and the same "thunk" I heard yesterday sounded again. We walked into the foyer. She stopped suddenly and looked around. Black smears were on the walls. Fingerprint powder. We walked into the living room and saw the same thing. They had gone over the house from top to bottom.

The curtains were still open and my eyes were drawn to the patio, terrace, and the pool I knew to be just out of sight. An arctic wind blew through me, and I tensed. It was all coming back in nauseating detail. I tried to force the memories from my mind.

"There's still police tape around the pool," Catherine said. She had already started up the stairs and apparently was no more successful at not looking than I had been. I could see she had blanched as she gazed through the windows.

I walked up to meet her. From her position on the stairs we could see down to the pool. She was right. Several pieces of outdoor furniture had been moved close to the pool's edge and used as support for the tape.

"Why would they do that?" she asked.

I knew and felt worse for knowing. "Your chauffeur . . . bled in the pool. The pool will need to be cleaned. There are businesses that specialize in . . . residue cleanup. That's what the police call it. State law requires that the cleanup crew be certified."

"I guess you have to know almost everything to be mayor," Catherine said. "I would never have thought of it."

I didn't tell her that I once had such a crew in my own home. "Let's get your script and get going." She went upstairs as I descended, found the remote control that operated the drapes, and closed them. There was no need for Catherine to come home to that sight again.

I waited. I heard a door slam, then another. Catherine appeared at the top of the stairway. "I can't find it. I know I left it in my bedroom, but it's not there."

"Did you check the other rooms?"

"Yes, but it's not there. Since they're empty, I had no reason to put it there. I've even checked the bathroom. It's gone."

She scampered down the stairs and searched the lower floor. A few minutes later she came back empty-handed.

"Nothing?" I asked.

"I don't understand. I have a place in my bedroom where I keep it. I know it was on the nightstand when I left for rehearsal yesterday morning."

"Did you take it with you? Could you have left it in the limo?" I sounded like my mother. When I was young and lost something, Mother always started a litany of possible places I could have misplaced it. It annoyed me then. Now I was annoying myself.

Catherine thought for a moment, then said, "No. I didn't take it with me."

"Would Ed have moved it? Maybe he planned to bring it to you when he picked you up yesterday."

She moved outside. I followed her to the parked limo and watched as she tried to open the rear passenger door. It was locked. She tried another door but with the same result. I approached as she rounded the vehicle. The tinted windows made it difficult to see in. Placing my hands to the window, I peered in and was able to make out the seats and a few other familiar items, but no script.

"The car is locked."

I started to ask about the keys but thought better of it. Most likely, Ed Lowe had them on his person when he was shot and killed.

"I need that script." She was coming unglued. I walked around the long, black car and placed my hands on her shoulders.

"Can you get another one?"

She nodded. "Yes. I can call and the studio will send out another, but they won't be happy."

"Things get lost. They'll understand."

"No, you don't get it. Scripts are secret. Producers and directors don't like the public getting their hands on early scripts. It can lead to all kinds of problems."

"Okay, here's what we're going to do. You need to be at the Curtain Call pretty soon, so I'm taking you there. You focus on the play. I'll call Detective West and see if he or any of his people took the script. Perhaps they took it for some kind of evidence or something." I was making it up as I went. "While I drive you to the theater, you can call your producer or director or whomever and ask them to send you a new one. They can email it to me if they want."

"They won't email it, especially to a stranger. I'm telling you, Maddy, movie people are paranoid about these things. You should see the contract I had to sign, preventing me from revealing anything about the movie, shooting schedule, actors, or anything else until they give me the go-ahead."

"I'm sorry," I said. "It's all I can think of to do right now."

A sigh escaped her lips. "You're probably right. The police must have it. I can't think of what else could have happened to it."

We locked up the house and started down the drive. As we did, a thought rose within me. *Would someone kill for that script?*

When I reached the end of the driveway, I turned to my right.

"That's not the way we came," Catherine said. She was searching her purse for her cell phone. I hoped that hadn't gone missing as well.

"I know. I'm taking a different way out. We'll end up on the freeway at about the same time. I should have you at the theater a few minutes early."

"Okay." She found her phone and began entering numbers. A few moments later, I heard her give her name and ask for Charles Buchanan. She sat in silence. I assumed she was on hold. Moments later, Catherine launched into the story about the missing script. I could only hear one side of the conversation, but I was able to glean that Buchanan was conciliatory and perhaps worried about Catherine's well-being. "I'm fine. Really, I'm fine." She said that ten times if she said it once.

My mind began to wander. We had been driving for only five minutes when I pulled to the shoulder. Catherine gave me a funny look. I mouthed, "I'll be right back." She continued her phone conversation as I slipped from the driver's seat.

I felt chilled despite the fact that it was a warm October day. Along the coast of Southern California, October isn't that much different from May. Days are shorter. Nighttime temperatures are a little lower. But that's it. My chill came not from a breeze but from what was before me. I walked toward a gray metal railing. Posts rose every six feet. The railing was shaped like a rounded W, attached to the posts by thick carriage bolts. The rail was separated from the uprights by a block of wood. The bolt traveled through the metal rail, wood block, and metal uprights. I peered at the back of the post. The bolt was attached with a large washer and a pair of metal nuts. With the right tools, it would be easy to remove the rail.

I walked a few feet farther along the road and stopped in front of three twisted and bent posts. Their rail was nowhere to be seen. Just beyond the posts, a steep, heavily planted slope shot downward. Some of the plants had been uprooted, and I could see gouges in the bare ground where something hard had impacted the earth.

This was where Doug Turner's car had plummeted off the road. The bent metal uprights had been unable to stop it. I shivered. It was a long way down Aberdeen Canyon. It was amazing that Doug was only in a coma and not dead.

I pulled myself away from the sight and walked back to the car. Catherine was off the phone.

"Why did you stop here?"

"A rail is missing," I said. "I wanted to look at it."

"Doesn't the city hire people to do that?"

"Yes, we do." I started the car. "How did the call go? Are they sending a script up?"

"Yes, and a new driver. Since I have to be in Hollywood in the morning and back in time for opening night, they're sending a new chauffeur. The script and chauffeur will arrive by dinner tonight. They're going to meet me at the theater."

"So I don't need to pick you up."

"No. I'll be fine."

"You're welcome to stay with me again."

"Thank you, but I'll be okay . . ." She paused. "Okay, maybe one more night, but I have to leave early in the morning."

"I rise pretty early. It won't be a problem. Dinner?"

She shook her head and her long raven hair shimmered in waves. "Remember? Harold is buying the cast dinner tonight. Do you want me to see if I can get you invited?"

"Sounds fun, but I still have some catching up to do. I'll wait up for you, and we can have hot chocolate or something."

"Okay. I shouldn't be late. I need my sleep."

Fifteen minutes later, I dropped Catherine at the front door of the Curtain Call theater.

chapter 10

I made it back to the office in time to gather and review my notes, making changes based on the business license information Floyd had compiled. The speech would be short, and then I'd entertain questions. I was to speak after lunch, which meant that I'd eat very little. Most public speakers forgo eating right before they speak. It cuts down on throat clearing and sleepiness. It was bad enough when the audience dozed off after lunch; it was unforgivable when the speaker did so.

On my drive from the office to the Ocean Green Country Club—a golf course with a meeting room large enough for the active members of the chamber—I kept noticing guardrails. Some were different than what I had seen a couple of hours before. The rails were wider, some fixed to wood posts instead of metal, and some higher. All my life, I had passed these low-lying barricades that line streets and freeways and had never taken notice of them. Now I couldn't stop thinking of them and when I did, I was immediately immersed in thoughts about the murder that took place at Catherine's and her missing script.

I forced my brain to change gears. I was about to speak to the business leaders of Santa Rita, and I needed to be at my best. Some of the people had contributed to my campaign for congress, others opposed my election. Some were CEOs of billion-dollar businesses, others were struggling mom-and-pop shops. All deserved a mayor who was prepared and had something to say.

As I pulled into the parking lot of the country club, I could see I should have left sooner. The lot was full. Either there was a major golf tournament I didn't know about, or I would be speaking to a packed house. I hoped for the latter. I found a spot at the far end of the lot, guided my Aviator into the stall, and marched across the pavement to the country club meeting hall.

The place was abuzz. One reason people join the chamber is to network. When I walked in I saw hands being shaken, cards being exchanged, and pats being delivered to backs.

It was showtime.

I left the country club feeling good about the speech. No one dozed off, no one made snide remarks masked as questions, and no one asked a question I didn't have an answer for—always a danger. My relief was short-lived as thoughts of what remained in the afternoon loomed before me. I had a two o'clock with the Community Development Department and a briefing meeting with the council. I should head straight back to the office.

I didn't.

Instead, I called Floyd and asked him to push the CDD meeting back fifteen minutes, then I directed my vehicle toward Pacific Horizon Hospital.

PHH is a four-story structure that sits on the east side of the freeway, hunkered down in the gentle hills. It is a glass and concrete structure that refuses to blend in with its surroundings. It had all the style and form of a refrigerator. It wasn't pretty to look at, but those who worked within its walls made the place memorable and the architecture forgivable. PHH boasted some of the best-trained and brightest minds in medicine. Only high-end research hospitals could brag about a better staff, and even then, they would get an argument from the patients.

I parked and walked into the lobby. My head was down, and I realized that leaving the world of the well for the cosmos of the afflicted had unsettled me. It wasn't that sick people made me uncomfortable; it was that I spent time here this past winter, and it held a negative association. I had anchored my past uncomfortable experience with PHH.

The lobby was expansive. To one side was a group of worn and faded chairs and sofas. The room could seat fifty or sixty people, but only a handful of people populated the area, sitting in clumps like mushrooms on a spring lawn, each group as far from the others as the furnishings allowed.

I set a course for the information desk manned by two silver-haired ladies dressed in pink. They had kind eyes afloat on dour expressions, as if waiting for this morning's prune juice to do its work. One was short and thin as if crafted from drinking straws. The other was broad from shoulder to hips and her cheeks bore several layers of rouge. Hospital volunteers. Women who chose public service to pass hours otherwise spent alone in front of a television. As I stepped to the oak desk, they looked up at me but said nothing.

I smiled. "My name is Madison Glenn. I'm here to see Doug Turner."

"Is he a patient?" the thin one said.

I blinked. "Yes, he's a patient."

The thin woman asked, "What is his name?"

I smiled again. "Doug Turner. Maybe Douglas Turner. He was admitted last night."

"Is that Turner with a T?" Before both women were clipboards with several sheets of paper. I could see patient names and room numbers.

"Yes, ma'am, that's Turner with . . . a T."

"Here it is," the broad woman announced with a forced smile. The thin pink lady frowned as if she had just been trumped in bridge. "He's in ICU. You'll need to check in with the nurses before going in. There's an intercom in the ICU waiting room. Just push the button and a nurse will talk to you."

"What did you say your name is?" The thin pink lady picked up a black felt-tip pen and a sticky-backed name tag.

"Madison Glenn."

"That's a lovely name, dear," the broad woman said.

"Our mayor's name is Madison Glenn," the thin one announced. "Did you know that? You have the same name as the mayor."

"Imagine that," I replied.

"She's not going to be our mayor for much longer," the wider lady said. "She's running off to congress."

She wrote down my first name, then stopped. "Not if I have anything to say about it," her partner said. "I'm going to vote for that nice-looking Garret Kinsley. He has kind eyes."

"Mary Jane! You're a Republican. Kinsley is a Democrat. He's going to steal all your Social Security."

"But he has the kindest eyes," Mary Jane countered. "I trust a man with kind eyes."

"Excuse me," I said. "My name tag."

The larger woman looked at me, then cut her eyes to her friend. "Some women lose all common sense when they get old."

There was no reply to that. "My name tag," I said again.

The thin woman frowned at me like I was a nettlesome child interrupting an adult conversation. "What did you say your last name is?"

"Glenn." I started to tell her that I spelled it with two *n*'s, but was afraid of where that would lead.

"That's right, just like the mayor."

I didn't argue.

With my name badge glued just below my shoulder, I marched down the corridor and took the elevator to the fourth floor. My time was tight when I arrived; it had been made worse by the kind pink ladies.

The ICU unit was behind closed doors. Just as the volunteer had said, there was a waiting room with an intercom and a white button. A sign attached to the wall gave warning that the ICU was off-limits and admission required permission from the nursing staff. I pressed the button. A moment later a tinny voice erupted from the small speaker.

"Yes?" A woman's voice.

"Madison Glenn to see Doug Turner."

"Are you family?" the disembodied voice asked.

"No . . . , a friend."

"I'm sorry, ma'am, but visits are restricted to family and—"

The voice cut off. I was afraid this would happen, but I felt compelled to try. I started to leave, when the distant voice returned. "Okay, ma'am. Come in."

I stepped from the waiting room to the wide double doors that separated the controlled environment of the Intensive Care Unit from the rest of the hospital. A three-inch-square metal panel was fixed to one wall. Red letters on its surface read: Press to Open. I reached for it, but the doors swung open before I could lay finger to the button.

I started forward and stopped when I noticed a tall, good-looking man in a white smock standing in my path. He was my age, sported sandy blond hair and deep brown eyes. There was a glint in the eyes and an easy smile on his lips.

"What's the password?" he asked.

"Um, Vote-for-Maddy?"

"That'll work." He stepped forward and gave me a hug.

"I take it I have you to thank for getting me in here."

"That's true, and your debt to me continues to grow."

He looked good to me. Seeing Jerry Thomas was a tonic. His smile was the best thing I had seen all day.

Dr. Jerry Thomas was several steps beyond a good friend. A pediatrician, he frequented the hospital as well as running a medical office on Castillo Avenue. His humor was sharp, his kindness boundless, and his heart as expansive as the sky. We dated in high school, but as with most such relationships, it evaporated under the heat of growing up. The tides of life forced us to drift apart. He married and seemed happy for the first few years, but it was one-sided. His wife, unable to endure the long hours required of a young doctor, left him for another man with more time and money. I had married Peter and was blissfully happy until his murder. Over the decade since those events Jerry and I remained friends. He pressed the relationship, trying to lay spark to the kindling of love. I resisted at every turn, but Jerry is nothing if not an optimist.

Early this year things began to change. I had come close to losing everything including my life. I was flailing in circumstances far out of my control. Standing there to catch me was Dr. Jerry Thomas.

Something inside me began to thaw.

We see each other on a regular basis and the bond continues to grow. I don't know what the future holds, but I've allowed for new possibilities.

We walked to the nurse's station. A semicircular bench marked off the area. Several men and women dressed in white smocks moved throughout the ICU, ducking in and out of small rooms with glass partitions that separated the work area from the patients' rooms. A doctor in the same style of smock sat at a desk, filling out a form.

"Do you have any information on Doug Turner?" I asked Jerry.

He shook his head. "No. I didn't even know he was here until I heard your voice over the intercom. But I know who does. Dr. Tucker, do you have a moment?"

The man in the white coat who had been filling out the form turned, then rose. "That's about all I have."

"Dr. Tucker," Jerry said, "this is Mayor Madison Glenn. She's a friend of Doug Turner."

He looked me over, then gave a nod.

"Pleased to meet you, Doctor." I offered my hand. He gave it a brief shake.

"I'm afraid Mr. Turner isn't up for visitors yet."

"Is there anything you can tell me, Doctor?"

He looked at Jerry, who said nothing. Physicians are reluctant to talk about their patients with anyone other than family members. "First, the good news," Tucker said. "His spinal cord shows no damage, and there's no indication of paralysis. He was wearing a seat belt, which kept him from being ejected when the vehicle rolled. Mr. Turner has, however, received several head injuries, a broken clavicle, a broken forearm, and a fractured ankle. There are some internal injuries, but those should heal normally. Our greatest fear is damage to the brain. That's still being assessed. We have him heavily sedated to limit his movements."

"May I see him?" Everything inside me was twisting into a knot.

"I'll walk you to his cubicle, but I must insist you stay outside. He's unconscious." Without waiting for a response, he crossed the distance from the nurse's station to one of the cubicles. The number above the door read 4003.

Once at the door, he stepped aside. I felt Jerry close to my left, his hand on my elbow. I looked in.

Doug was motionless on the bed. A thin white sheet covered him from his stomach to midthigh. One arm was in a fiberglass cast, as was one foot. His bare chest was blotched with blue bruises. His face was swollen twice its normal size. I could not recognize the man on the bed. I had to take Dr. Tucker's word for it that the swollen, battered, and bruised body belonged to the *Register*'s ace reporter.

The temperature around me rose at an alarming rate. My face began to burn, and the normally unconscious act of breathing now required my full attention. Something was happening to my legs: the knee joints were morphing into Jell-O. I felt Jerry's hand tighten on my elbow. A hand seized my other arm.

"Okay," Jerry said. "That's enough for now."

I was turned and led from Doug's ICU cubicle. As I walked away, the heat that came upon me as if from an oven door dissipated, and my breathing returned to normal.

"Do you need to sit down?" Tucker asked.

I shook my head. "No. I'm fine. Really." I caught Tucker exchanging a glance with Jerry.

"I'll take her for a walk," Jerry said. "Thank you, Dr. Tucker."

Tucker grunted and returned to his files.

Jerry walked me from the ICU, his hand still clamped like a vise on my elbow. I felt like a little old lady. We passed through the doors and into the waiting room. Thankfully, it was still empty. He directed me to a chair and made me sit. I started to protest, but before I could open my mouth, my fanny met one of the well-worn chairs.

"Stuff like that is always hard to see."

"He didn't even look like the Doug I know."

"The swelling does that. I've sent patients in for brain or face surgery and when they come out, I wonder who they are. In a few days, Doug will look like Doug."

"How did you ever get used to seeing such trauma?" I took a deep breath.

"No one gets used to it." Jerry took the seat next to mine. "Doctors just learn to expect it and deal with it. Fortunately, I don't have to deal with such things very often. Pediatrics is vastly different than emergency medicine. Still, we have our own set of challenges."

I forced my attention from myself to Jerry. I was just now putting together the fact that my pediatrician friend was *inside* ICU. Jerry is like fancy ice cream, uniformly sweet, and filled with little surprises. He was quick with a joke, self-deprecating, sacrificial, and willing to invest himself in those he loves and admires. But the thing that has most impressed me about Jerry is his commitment to his work. Pediatrics was not the glamour discipline of medicine, nor was it the cash machine of other specialties. Dealing with children—sick children—day in and day out required a sturdier soul than most possessed. Jerry had once told me that most of his day was spent with runny noses, hurting tummies, and sore throats; but there were those days when he wanted to "burn his license." Those days included telling parents that little Johnny had leukemia, or bone cancer, or some disease that would keep the child from having anything close to a normal life. I had a feeling that this was one of those days.

"Why were you there?" I nodded to the double doors that kept the heartrending sights on the other side.

"Doing follow-up on a surgery. A six-year-old boy, one of my patients, was hit by a car this morning. ER did a great job, and the surgical team did the impossible. There's nothing for me to do but monitor his condition and, I hope, guide the recovery."

"You hope?"

His eyes shifted from me. That was all the answer I needed. Jerry didn't think the little boy would live.

"How are you doing? You okay?" I took his hand.

He shrugged. "I'm thinking of taking up cabinetmaking."

"The world of medicine would be sorely wounded if you did."

"I'm not so sure. At times I love my job, but days like this make me wonder if I'm the man to do it."

"You've been doing it wonderfully for years."

"Some doctors can flip a switch and leave all the misery in the hospital rooms, but I've never been able to do that. I take it home with me. Images come to me in my dreams." He leaned back, closed his eyes, and rubbed his temples. I could tell he was beat, and it wasn't even two o'clock.

"Did you know that more and more doctors are leaving the profession? Seventy- to eighty-hour workweeks, malpractice insurance premiums that can top a hundred thousand, less respect, and more paperwork."

"You're not seriously thinking of leaving," I said.

"Actually, I'm tired of thinking." He sat up, raised my hand, and kissed it. "Not to worry, just the weariness speaking. You know, this may be the first time a politician paid a visit on a reporter."

The famous male change-of-subject defense. "You know what you need? You need to have pie with a famous Hollywood star."

"What did you do? Land a movie deal?"

"Not me. Catherine Anderson. She's staying with me tonight."

"So you've started taking in homeless movie stars. I recognize the name."

"She's my cousin, and she's in town for a few weeks—"

"Wait a second. Catherine Anderson is your cousin?"

"That's right. On my father's side."

He wrinkled his brow. I figured he had heard about the murder at her home.

"I guess you heard about the murder," I said.

"Murder? What murder?"

"There was an article in this morning's paper and the late news ran a short piece on the television. I didn't watch television this morning, but I imagine it got more play there."

"I was here until nearly two this morning. I went home, grabbed a bite to eat and a few hours' sleep, then came back. I haven't seen the paper or watched the news. Who was murdered?"

I filled him in. His face darkened with concern, but I assured him both Catherine and I were fine. "So how about it. You want to come over for dessert? Say eight o'clock?"

"I should be able to break away for a bit and a bite."

I rose and said, "I'll see you then." I gave him a brief hug and left.

He walked me to the elevator. "Be careful."

"I'm always careful."

"Yeah, right."

I waved as the elevator doors shut. Jerry looked worried. I wondered if I should be worried too.

chapter 11

My meeting with the Community Development Department was short and sweet. We discussed the level of new construction along the coast and in the southern part of the city. New housing meant an increase in revenue, but it also meant a greater burden on schools and city infrastructure. They presented two reports, which I listened to with interest, then took printed reports back to my office. I had fifteen minutes to spare before plunging into the next meeting. I used the time to freshen up.

At two minutes before three, I entered the conference room and found it full. I stepped to the head of the table and took my seat. The table was long and wide and covered in a worn simulated maple veneer that showed its age. The conference room is where the council held its closed-door meetings, but it had little to commend it. The walls were a dull white and adorned with a few easy-on-the-eyes prints of serene landscapes. A sand-colored, low-pile carpet covered the floor. Overhead, fluorescent fixtures oozed their peculiar shade of light. I was thankful for the windows behind me. Natural light was always better.

At just twenty-by-twenty, the square room was too small for the table, five council members, the city attorney, city manager, and city clerk. There had been several heartfelt discussions about enlarging the room, but I had managed to keep the reins pulled back on city spending. I'd lost a lot of friends in city government because of it.

Seated at the table to my right was Tess Lawrence. Prior to becoming deputy mayor, she always sat as far from me as possible. Next to her was Jon Adler. My mother taught me to find the good in people and praise it. Jon was my greatest challenge. He was as warm as an ice cube and possessed an extraordinarily powerful gift of getting under my skin. He was more irritating than a blister and just as welcome.

Maybe it was his career as defense attorney that made him so argumentative. Maybe it was because he was so insecure and needed constant attention. Maybe he was just a selfish jerk. Whatever the reason, he would argue with anyone, at any time, about anything. I had yet to hear him offer an original idea. Instead, he would wait to hear what others said, then take the opposite side. I'm convinced the pinch-faced man would argue with his mother about who gave birth to him.

On the opposite side of the table sat Larry Wu. Larry was the anti-Jon. A middle-aged man with an Asian face and subtle Texas accent, Larry brought heart to the council. He was a dogged campaigner. I know; he was one of the mayoral candidates I beat out for the seat. So was Jon. With Larry, however, I felt guilty about winning. He was gracious in defeat and has been one of my greatest supporters. He's even done some work in my congressional campaign. I could use a few more Larrys around city hall.

To his left sat Titus Overstreet. Titus was one of my favorite people. He seemed to stand taller than his six-foot-two frame, and his ebony face was quick with a smile. A former high school basketball star, he knew he didn't have the height or talent to make the team of any major university, so he pursued the best education he could get. He took an MBA and ran a public relations business when not wrestling with city business. He is a clothes horse, always dapper. It was hard to look good standing next to him.

However, Titus was thinner these days and a little less active. The beginning of this year brought news of colon cancer, surgery, and chemotherapy. Now, with over three-quarters of the year gone, he was doing well, but he had lost a step.

Sharing the end of the table were City Manager Russell Elliot and City Attorney Fred Markham. To one side of Fred was City Clerk Dana Thayer. As usual, she had her gray-kissed dark hair pulled back into a bun and wore a pair of reading glasses perched on the end of her nose. She could be the poster child for 1950s librarians.

"Hello, everyone." I took my seat and spread out my notes. "It's good to be back."

"It's good to have you back," Larry said. Titus nodded. Tess sat motionless, and Jon smirked. I felt loved.

"I called this meeting to share with you some of the more interesting items of this year's governor's meeting with California mayors. Initially, that is all I had planned to discuss, but we should address something that may or may not become an issue."

"I hope it was more exciting than last year," Jon said. "I'm still trying to overcome the terminal case of boredom it caused."

"Now you know how we feel when we listen to you," Tess snapped. Tess and Jon had been political pals for years. Jon looked at the relationship as an advantage; Tess saw it as something to endure to balance the council. For years, she was afraid I'd somehow cement constant agreement and turn the council into a rubber-stamp committee. It was a wasted fear. Titus and Larry are consistent supporters, but both have no compunction about disagreeing with me or voting against something I support. I respected them for their integrity.

"Ease up, Tess," Jon said. "I was just joking."

I decided to ignore Jon and press on. "Much of the discussion centered on the problems created by Proposition 65. As you know, that 2004 proposition changed the way money flows from city to state and state to city."

"To our benefit," Jon said.

"Yes," I agreed, "but there were some unforeseen hitches."

Over the next twenty minutes, I filled them in on the lively discussion in Sacramento and what the other mayors were saying. When I was done and everyone had their say, I moved on to the next issue.

"I imagine each of you has heard about Doug Turner's accident."

"If a reporter crashes in the woods and there's no one there to hear, does he make a sound?" Jon laughed at his joke. He was the only one who did.

Titus closed his eyes and I could see he was struggling to keep back hot and barbed words. Larry just shook his head.

"Oh, come on, guys," Jon said. "We've de-evolved into a bunch of old fuddy-duddies. It's not like Turner was a friend. I don't think he ever wrote anything positive about me."

The room went silent. I weighed the price of shooting off my mouth. Be quick to hear, slow to speak and slow to anger. It was a Bible passage I had committed to memory. James 1:19. It was becoming a life verse for me. I repeated the words again in my mind. I noticed that many of the verses I committed to memory had to do with holding my tongue.

"Do you know what, Jon?" Titus leaned over the table. "Every time you open your mouth, you make an argument for the return of prefrontal lobotomy surgery."

Apparently, Titus didn't know the Bible verse. I scolded myself for finding his comment funny—and accurate.

"Did you think of that all by yourself, or did you have help?" Jon shot back.

Jon has never been witty.

To his credit, Titus didn't take the bait. I glanced around the room and saw four members of the council who could not be more different. They each had their agendas, policies they thought important. If I won the congressional seat, I'd be just one of four hundred and thirty-five such personalities.

"Mr. Turner's accident has brought another problem to the forefront," I said. "Mr. Turner's car went off the road and over the embankment because the guardrail had been removed. I met Tess and Fred and Russell earlier today. They have begun an investigation of the problem. Tess?"

Tess gave me a nod and said, "After our initial meeting with the mayor, Fred, Russ, and I put our heads together and divvied up the work. Why don't you start, Russ?"

The city manager took a deep breath. "I took a stroll over to public works and met with the director. I learned that over the last three months, close to twenty road signs have been stolen, many of them stop signs."

"Twenty?" Larry said. "That's a lot of signs. Why haven't we heard about this?"

Russ looked embarrassed. "The director thought he had it under control. Usually when a sign, especially an important sign, is stolen, some citizen in that neighborhood reports it, and it's replaced within twenty-four hours."

Titus shook his head. "Not good enough. A great many accidents can happen in twenty-four hours."

"Well, I agree with you," Russ said, "and I—*mentioned*—it to the director."

I knew what that meant. Russ was a gentle guy, but he had an explosive side. I guessed that the director of public works discovered that.

"What other kind of signs?" I asked.

Russ cleared his throat and recited from memory, "Ten stop signs, five yield signs, two dip signs, and two slow curve signs. Nineteen in all."

"What?" Jon inserted. "No 'Elect Glenn for Congress' signs were taken. I'd think those would be the first to go."

Tess lowered her head, and I saw her jaw clench. "So help me, Jon, one more crack out of you, and I'll slap you so hard your ancestors will scream."

"That, my dear, would be assault and battery. You would go to jail." Jon leaned back and smiled as if he had just declared "checkmate" in a chess game.

"It would be worth it," Tess said.

The smile from Jon's face disappeared.

"To continue," Russ said, "things have escalated. It's not just signs anymore. Four fire hydrant caps are missing, three segments of guardrail, and—get this—a manhole cover."

"Aren't manhole covers really heavy?" Larry asked.

Russ said they were. "Workmen use a rod with a hook to pull the cover from the hole. It's one thing to drag it out of the way; it's quite another to lift it. It's not a one-man job."

"Why would anyone want to do this?" I asked.

Tess spoke up. "I've been in contact with the police, and they feel that it's a group of kids, probably high schoolers."

"You're speaking in the plural," Titus said. "What makes the police think more than one person is involved?"

"They have some evidence," Fred explained. "In a few cases, including the one involving Mr. Turner's tragic accident, footprints were found in the soft dirt. The prints were of different sizes and sole patterns. The size of the footprints indicates adults or older teenagers."

"Could this be gang related?" Larry said.

"Possibly," Fred replied. "There are many gang initiations, most of them far worse than stealing road signs, and they involve some form of direct violence. I can say that no gang tagging has taken place."

Tagging was another name for graffiti. I thought of my short visit to the site of Doug's accident. I didn't see anything spray painted on the road or the remaining guardrail.

"You know," Jon said, "we look awful liable here. Turner could sue our socks off if he can show negligence on our part. And if this continues and someone else is hurt . . . well, it could get very expensive. The city's insurance may cover it, but we stand to lose our good insurance rating. That will cost thousands of dollars more in premiums."

"Jon is right," Tess said. "It is very important that we catch the people who are doing this. If we can find the perpetrators, they will face criminal charges. It's no longer a prank; it is reckless endangerment of the public."

"The law would allow us to be recompensed for the cost of the signage and repairs," Jon said. He was getting excited at the prospects. "We could drop the whole thing right on the pointed heads of whoever is doing this."

Tess added, "I've contacted all the high schools in the city. As you know, we have three high schools, three standard schools, two continuation schools, and one alternative school. I also contacted the school boards in the areas outside our borders."

"Private schools?" I asked.

"It's not likely that our troublemakers are from one of the private schools, but I put in a call to them anyway."

I looked at the city manager. "Are we liable, Russ? Could we have kept this from happening?"

Russ lowered his eyes and frowned. I didn't like the look.

"It doesn't matter," Jon said before Russ could open his mouth. "We need to be prepared for a little legal kung fu to make certain that blame doesn't fall on us but on the hoods that did this."

"I'm asking Russ, Jon," I said, dragging out each word. "I'd like to hear from him."

"I'm not a lawyer," Russ said, "so I'll leave the determination of liability up to Fred and others but . . ." he trailed off.

"But what, Russ?" I pressed.

"It's amazing how you never think of these things until there's a problem." He released a humorless chuckle. "The signs could have been installed to make it much more difficult to remove them."

"How?" I asked.

He took a breath. "Street signs in the city are attached to four-by-four wood posts with a pair of carriage bolts or to what is called a U-channel post. A U-channel is a metal post."

"I've seen them," I said. "So what's the problem?"

"Many cities, the county, and the state use the same basic system but they use different fasteners. With a simple carriage bolt system, all it takes to remove the sign is a wrench to remove the bolt's nut and maybe a hammer to drive the bolt back out of the support. There are several other ways of doing this, all of them much more difficult to remove."

"Such as?" Titus asked.

"Star bolts that require special tools to remove, pyramid nuts that can only be removed by a special wrench or expanding blind rivets. There are a dozen choices. The problem is, most of our city signs are simple carriage bolt and nut systems. Anybody can take one off. For that matter, to make it more difficult to remove signs, some crews just take a hammer to the threads of the bolt after the nut is tightened."

"Uh-oh," Jon said.

"What?" Tess asked.

"It's simple. A good lawyer could cite cities and counties that use the devices Russ describes and it will make us look careless. We don't want to look careless."

"Why hasn't public works been using the bolts and nuts you described?" I asked.

"Because it's easier to repair or change signs with the system we use, but to be fair, Mayor, we've never had a problem before."

"The good news is that no one has been hurt because someone drove through an intersection because a stop sign was missing," Larry said.

"True," I said, "but Doug Turner is in ICU because a guardrail was stolen. What about the guardrail, Russ? Could we make those safer?"

He studied me, then the others. "Yes."

"Let's not forget any system can be beaten," Jon said. "A recip-rocating saw with the right blade could make short work of any bolt."

Somehow, that didn't make me feel any better.

chapter 12

I settled into my office chair and let the cool, padded leather do its job. I had been seated most of the day, exchanging the car seat for a seat at the head table of the chamber luncheon, and then sitting through two meetings, but sitting in my office chair was different. I felt most in control when sheltered behind my desk and nestled into a chair that fit my body as if it had been custom designed to match spine, shoulders, and hips.

The clock read four, and I was ready to call it a day. The travel, a week of meetings, the pressure of campaigning while running a city, and the stress of swimming with a dead man began to weigh on me like a lead sweater. I shook off the weariness and examined tomorrow's schedule. The only pressing thing I had on the agenda was a campaign meeting with Nat.

Floyd poked his head in the office. He looked like his best dog had just died. "I wanted to thank you for buying lunch for Celeste and me." His words flowed like cold honey.

"My pleasure. How did it go?" I was pretty sure I knew.

He shrugged. It was pitiful.

"Come in, close the door, and sit down." He did but once seated he looked at his shoes and not at me. "I assume it didn't go all that well."

"She's mad at me."

"So has she been dating another guy?"

He shook his head. "She said no. You were right. When I called that time and she said she was too busy to talk, she was helping her mom with something."

"See. Just as I figured. So why is she mad at you? What happened?"

"I don't know. We were just talking and then she got up and stormed off."

Not good. "Floyd, what were you talking about?"

"Just stuff."

"Uh-huh. What kind of stuff?" I pressed.

He shuffled his feet. "I was just telling her about things. You know, about meeting Catherine Anderson, and having dinner at your place."

I knew where this was going. "Tell me what you told her."

Some more shuffling. "I don't know why she got so mad. I told her how neat it was to meet someone special like Catherine and how beautiful she was and how I couldn't take my eyes off her."

"Oh, Floyd." I raised a hand to my forehead and fought the urge to say what I really thought. Floyd is a young man of pure heart and not even a tinge of guile. "And you can't figure out why Celeste is angry?"

"No. It doesn't make sense. Everything I said was true."

It wasn't that Floyd was not bright; he was. It's just that his bulb flickers from time to time. "Floyd . . ." *How do I begin?* "Floyd, you made the effort to call Celeste, to invite her to lunch and not just any lunch, but a meal at one of the best restaurants in Santa Barbara.

That's pretty special to a woman, especially a young woman like Celeste."

"Yeah." His face was a blank canvas.

"Yeah? Floyd, you spent your time with her talking about how enamored you were with Catherine."

"I thought Celeste would be interested." I could imagine the fog thickening in Floyd's brain.

"How often did you date in high school?" I asked.

"Not much ... never."

"And college?"

"A couple of times, but girls just weren't interested in me."

I ached for him. Floyd was a faceted diamond. In the right light he could shine beautifully. Like many highly intelligent people, he was socially awkward and mired in admirable innocence.

I started to speak when the phone rang. Floyd stood and picked up the receiver on my desk. "Mayor's office," he said. He listened for a moment, then said, "Please hold." He set the hand piece back in the cradle. "It's a Mr. Harold Young."

"That's the man who's directing the play," I explained. I raised the phone to my ear. "Mr. Young. How are you?"

"I'm sorry to bother you, Mayor, but I didn't know who else to call."

"Is there a problem?" I looked at Floyd and shrugged. He tilted his head to the side as if doing so would allow him to hear the conversation on the other end of the line.

"Yes ... well, I think so. It's Catherine. She's locked herself in her dressing room and won't come out."

"What happened?" I pressed.

"We had just finished dress rehearsal. I planned a little party, then the dinner theater was going to provide a meal. You remember that I invited you. You're still invited."

"Thank you, Harold, but what happened to Catherine?" Floyd moved to the edge of his seat.

"Like I said, we had just finished rehearsal and resetting the stage. A young man came in and handed something to Catherine. I was on the other side of the theater but it looked like a script to me. Catherine seemed glad to see him and even gave him a peck on the cheek. The guy left and Catherine sat down at one of the tables and started looking over the pages. Five minutes later she lets out a little scream and runs backstage. I've been trying to get her out of the dressing room ever since."

"I'll be right over." I hung up.

"Is Catherine all right?" Floyd stood when I did.

"I don't know. Apparently, something has upset her. I'm going over there now." Floyd cast a woebegone look like a fly fisherman casts his line. I bit. "Want to keep me company?"

"Absolutely. Give me a second to shut down the computer and lock up."

Floyd moved with rare speed, closing the blinds, turning off the computer, putting away a few wayward files, and transferring the phones to the message server. When he was finished, I said, "Come on, Galahad; let's see if we can't rescue a damsel in distress."

My words were light for Floyd's benefit, but there was a sharp-toothed nagging nibbling inside me. I kept my calm mask fixed on my face but caught myself walking faster than normal.

Five minutes later we were in the car.

The parking lot of the Curtain Call dinner theater was bare except for a dozen cars belonging to actors and office staff. Tomorrow night, autos would blanket the lot to its edges. I had never attended a play here, but I knew the place had a stellar reputation, and its plays garnered good reviews in the *Register*.

I parked near the door and exited. Floyd scampered from his seat, rounded my SUV, and hurried to catch me. He looked worried. His appearance matched my gut feeling. We exchanged the pre-evening sunshine for the dim lights of the dinner theater. I led Floyd through the foyer, past the hostess stand, and through a pair of double doors that opened to the dining area.

It had only been a day since I was last here, yet it seemed more like a week. On my first visit, the dining area was deserted except for Harold Young who had been standing near the stage. Now the place was abuzz with a dozen actors and stagehands standing in small clumps of humanity, talking and at times laughing. The long center table that ran the middle of the lowest level was covered in white linen. Bread plates, drinking glasses, butter dishes, and silverware decorated the surface. A hunger-activating aroma filtered through the air. I guessed prime rib. There were glasses filled with wine and bottles of beer here and there. Whatever had upset Catherine had not delayed the party.

"Madam Mayor, I'm here."

Harold stood center stage and waved. He marched across the boards and down the right-hand stairs. A moment later I was eyeball to eyeball with the director.

"Thank you for coming." He looked stressed. "I hated to bother you at the office, but you being family and all . . ."

"It was no bother. The workday was just about over. Tell me again what happened."

"Sure, sure. Um, can I get you anything? Beer? Wine?"

"No, thank you. I'm fine."

He looked at Floyd.

"I'm sorry," I said. "This is my assistant, Floyd Grecian. He and Catherine met last night at my home."

Harold asked if Floyd wanted a beer. Floyd declined.

The director seemed disappointed. "Nothing has changed since we spoke on the phone. Catherine got what I think is a script, looked through it, got up, and ran backstage in tears. I can't get her to open the door or to talk to me. Neither can any of the actors."

"Is there a key to the room?" I asked.

"I'm certain there is. The stage manager should have one."

"Okay, let's get that. But let me talk to her first. It would be better if she opens up to me on her own."

"I understand." He turned and scanned the room. "Gill! Hey, Gill. You got a sec?"

A squat, barrel-shaped man broke away from a gaggle of young actors and moved toward us. His head was covered with thin, dark hair, and his face bore the wrinkles of at least four decades of life in the sun.

"This is Gill Dysert, the Curtain Call's stage manager. Gill this is Mayor Madison Glenn and . . . and . . ."

"Floyd Grecian," I filled in.

"Yeah, Floyd Grecian, the mayor's aide. Mayor Glenn is related to Catherine. She wants to know if you have a key to the dressing room."

"Yup. I got it right here." He patted the right front pocket of his loose-fit jeans.

"I'll show you where she is," Harold said.

We followed him through the dining area and up the short rise of stairs that led to the stage. The stage area was set up like the living room of a New York apartment. A sofa, coffee table, and love seat dominated center stage. At the back a plywood and two-by-four wall ran the length of the stage. It had a door that looked like it swung on real hinges and window that could be opened. The window had no glass, just the frame and white mullions. Beyond it was a backdrop of a cityscape.

Harold led us to the right, through an area defined by black curtains. He pushed the drapes aside and held them as we crossed from the world of imagination to the world of production. The stage out front had been neat and orderly; backstage looked like the aftermath of an earthquake. I adjusted my thinking. While there was indeed a clutter of furniture, costumes, lights, ropes, and several things I couldn't identify, there was a logical arrangement to it. What had first struck me as a packrat's garage had a system underlying it. I would have loved a formal tour, but I was there for a different reason.

Behind the backdrop was an open space about the same size as the stage. I could imagine actors lining up, listening for their cues, and stagehands at the ready to lower a curtain or raise a backdrop. Out front was illusion; back here reality. There was sadness to it, like learning a magician's trick; once known, it ceases to impress.

Another black curtain divided the backstage from rooms just a few feet farther on. A wall ran the width of the building, marked off by several doors. In the middle of the wall were two doors. One read Men and the other Women. Not much guesswork needed there. To the right of the women's restroom was another door with a sign: Dressing Room 2. Harold stopped a foot away from the door.

"I was expecting several rooms with stars on them," I admitted.

Harold gave a polite but knowing smile. "This is dinner theater, Mayor, not Broadway. The men dress in that room over there." He pointed at Dressing Room 1.

I studied the door to Dressing Room 2 as if doing so I could peer through and see all that Catherine was doing. The others were staring at me, waiting for me to do . . . what? Materialize on the other side of a locked door?

I gave the smooth surface three or four raps with my knuckles. "Catherine, it's Maddy."

Nothing.

"Catherine, I know you're in there. I know you're upset about something. Now let me in so we can talk."

"No. I'm fine. Go away." Her voice was muffled, but I could hear enough to know she had been crying.

"Catherine," I said firmly, "you need to open up."

"I don't want to."

"Actors can be so temperamental," Harold said. "I can't tell you the number of times I've had to—"

"You're being childish, Catherine." I didn't want to hear about Harold's other adventures with the sensitive thespian set. I wanted to get into the dressing room and find out what had set off Catherine. There was no response.

Gill moved forward with the key, but I stopped him with a raised hand. "Not yet," I whispered. "It would be better if she opened the door herself."

"I don't understand," Floyd said.

"That's because you're not a woman." I knocked on the door again. "I'm not going away, Catherine. I can be as stubborn as you."

"Ain't that the truth," Floyd said.

I cut him a harsh glance. He backpedaled. "I'm just agreeing with you, Mayor. That's all."

"I'll take care of you later." I winked at him.

"What now?" Harold asked. "She's acting like a teenage girl."

"She hasn't been out of those years for very long," I said. "And she's had a rough couple of days."

"So you think we should be patient." Harold rubbed his chin.

"No, I think if she wants to act like a high schooler, I should approach her as such."

Harold began, "What do you mean—"

I banged on the door with my fist hard enough to make the locked doorknob jingle. "You listen to me, young lady," I shouted.

"I'm coming in there. I have the key. Now you can open this door yourself and allow me in, or I'll open it myself and everyone out here will come in with me. What's it going to be?"

I've never had children, but I have been a child and a rebellious teen. I used the same tone on Catherine that my mother used on me. The imitation was spot-on. Mom would be proud.

I heard a sniffing sound near the door. I waited. I had played my trump card, now there was nothing to do but wait for Catherine. If she didn't respond, then I'd have to use the key, but that had the feel of invasion.

Another sniff. My gaze drifted to the doorknob. It moved, then stopped. *Come on, come on, Catherine.* The knob turned some more, the door opened an inch, but that was all. Catherine had unlocked it, unlatched it, then stepped away. It was as much of a concession as I was going to get.

Pushing the door open, I crossed the threshold. Three sets of feet shuffled behind me, moving closer. I stopped and turned. "Thank you for your help, gentlemen." I took another step back and closed the door in their faces.

I locked it.

chapter 13

Her eyes were red, her stage makeup marred by running tears. She stood across the room, near a long counter with a series of mirrors above. Lights lined the perimeter of the mirrors. The dressing room was wide but narrow. Costumes hung on metal racks along the wall with the entry door. Folding chairs were strewn about as were stylish duffel bags with brand names on them, no doubt the personal items needed by actors. The floor was bare concrete. Posters and photos of previous plays covered the walls. *Man of La Mancha, 42nd Street, Dial M for Murder*, and a dozen more.

I wondered what words would be useful; what phrases would kick-start a meaningful conversation. Speech making is second nature to me. On more occasions than I can count, I have been called to give an impromptu discourse to one group or another. The words flow easily. For some reason, I was tongue-tied.

Catherine looked as frail as an ice sculpture. Her face was pale, but much of that was due to the heavy stage makeup she wore. In her hands was a tissue which she turned over and over. On the counter behind her were several tissues that had endured the same torture.

We stood like cowboys facing off in a quick-draw competition, neither willing to speak first. My family has a history of obstinacy. This could last for a while.

I heard something behind me and I glanced at the door. I raised a finger, turned, unlocked the door, and snapped it open.

"Go away," I said. I smiled, then closed and locked the door again. I heard muffled footsteps moving away. I shook my head. "Men! They have to be told everything and then be made to think it was their idea."

Catherine lowered her head but I heard a soft chuckle.

Silence rose again but this time I wouldn't tolerate it. I crossed the room, set my purse on the counter, and took Catherine in my arms. It was the most eloquent thing I could think of to say. She stood stiff as a board but then softened as the facade crumbled. She didn't cry, and I wasn't surprised. My guess was that she was cried out. For now, the reservoir of tears was dry and that was fine with me. I hate it when other women cry in my presence. Something about it affects my vision, and things get blurry.

A moment or two later, maybe it was a minute, I couldn't tell, we parted. I pulled up one of the folding seats and lowered myself into it. Catherine did the same.

"Okay, kid, dish it," I said.

She dabbed at her eyes. "I got my new script today."

She looked to the makeup bench. I followed her gaze and saw a thick stack of canary yellow paper, three-hole punched but held together by two brass fasteners.

"Did they write you out or something?" I couldn't imagine anything in a script that would cause such a reaction. Maybe they had reduced her part or—"Wait, they're not asking you to do something . . . inappropriate, are they?"

"No, no. It's worse than that."

What could be worse than that? "I don't understand."

She pulled the script close, touching it like it was covered in green slime. She paged through the papers, then handed it to me. "It's the end of act one; it's the plot point."

I didn't know what a plot point was but I looked at the page. It read:

```
INT. THE FRONT ROOM OF LACY'S HOME—AFTERNOON
    The room is sparsely furnished. Curtains hide a
    window wall. Lacy starts up the stairs. Her woman
    friend MADDY remains on the first floor.

                    LACY
        Six bedrooms, an office, a rec room, a
        media room, and a den, plus the usual
        kitchen, breakfast nook, dining room, and
        five bathrooms.

                    MADDY
        And you plan on living here alone?

                    LACY
        I hope not.

                    MADDY
                (Smiling)
        Oh? You have a husband-to-be waiting in
        the wings?

                    LACY
    Lacy picks up the remote and points it at the wood
    blinds over the windows. She pushes the button and
    the blinds open. Light streams in.

        No, Maddy, I don't. Not that I haven't
        been asked. In fact, I get about twenty
        proposals a week from love-struck fans.
```

                    MADDY
If not a husband . . .

                    LACY
I'm hoping to convince Mom and Dad to
move back to Santa Rita. It's one reason
I built my home here. They're not getting
any younger and I would love to have them
around.

                    MADDY
You're a good daughter. Not many people
your age would want to have their parents
around. It would cramp their style.

                    LACY
I don't have a style. I'm just a very
fortunate actor. No one knows how long
fame will last. This time next year, I
may be a used-to-be.

                    MADDY
Somehow I doubt that.

                    LACY
          (Looking around, frowns)
I wonder where Ed is. We've made enough
noise to wake the dead.

                    MADDY
Bathroom? Or the media room?

                    LACY
There's nothing in the media room.

Lacy sets the remote down.

I'm going to take a quick look around.
I'll be right back and we can continue
the tour, then I'll buy your dinner.

MADDY

And I'll let you.

Maddy picks up the remote and studies it. After a moment she opens the drapes. The wall of curtain pulls back to reveal tall and wide windows over-looking the ocean and a wide and deep backyard.

LACY
(Screams)

MADDY

What? What? What is it?

LACY
(Points out window with shaking hand.)

Maddy races up the stairs and looks out the window. She gasps.

EXT. LACY'S BACKYARD POOL
A body in chauffeur's uniform floats facedown in the pool. Clouds of blood billow in the water.

MADDY
(Softly)

Ed?

LACY

Yes.

MADDY

Call 9-1-1.

Maddy races down the stairs toward the window wall and door. Lacy is frozen in place.

MADDY

Call 9-1-1 now!

Maddy runs outside, kicks off her shoes, and
plunges into the pool. She swims to the dead man,
grabs him, and tows him to the shallow end of the
pool.

The last half of the page was blank.

I felt sick. Thoughts raced through my head at such speeds they collided, leaving me unable to pull a cohesive notion together. I said nothing, knowing that if I tried I would do little more than babble like a two-year-old.

I was holding an account of what had happened at Catherine's home yesterday. It was as if someone else had been in the room.

"How could anyone know this?" I asked.

"I don't know," Catherine said. "Someone was watching us."

That sent a cascade of ice water down my spine. "It has my name but not yours. It says Lacy, not Catherine."

"Lacy is the part I play. It's my character in the movie."

She was tearing up again, and she would get no criticism from me. There was a grapefruit-sized knot in my belly. No wonder Catherine had been so upset.

I closed the script and looked at the title page. Like the rest of the pages it was canary yellow. The title page read:

A LONG WAY FROM NOWHERE
Original Screenplay by
Anita Gorman

The words were centered on the page. In the lower right-hand corner was a list of dates tucked next to the right margin:

August 30, 2006
REV. 9/15/06 (BLUE)
REV. 9/30/06 (PINK)
REV. 10/1/06 (YELLOW)

"Every revision gets a different color paper?" I was doing what I always did when stressed—I analyzed.

"Yes. Scripts get changed throughout the whole movie-making process. After a while there are dozens of scripts floating around. By changing the color the actors know which is the latest version. There's nothing worse than showing up having studied the pink script only to find out everyone is reading off the yellow."

"Who is Anita Gorman?"

"She's hot property. Her last two scripts did super at the box office. Both were Academy Award nominees. She's the best."

"Do you know her well?"

"No. I've met her at script meetings. She seems pretty together and has been nice to me."

"Would she write something like this? I mean, these pages weren't in the original, right?"

"Of course not."

I flipped through the pages. The offending ones were formatted like the rest. "Whoever did this knows something about scripts. I wouldn't know how to format a screenplay."

"Producers and directors are very fussy about that. Each page is supposed to represent about one minute of screen time."

I looked at the last page. "One hundred and twenty pages. Two hours?"

"About. Things change in the process but that will be close. Comedies are about ninety minutes and dramas around two hours."

"Is anything else different in the script?"

"I don't know. That was as far as I got."

"I can understand that. Who brought the script to you?"

"Andy Buchanan." She raised the tissue to her face and blew her nose. "He's the director's son. He's sort of an assistant-assistant director. He's just out of film school."

"Did he come with the new limo driver?"

"The new driver hasn't shown up yet." She sniffed again.

I started to ask another question when there was a loud knock on the door. I jumped from my chair, my heart in overdrive.

"Catherine, baby. It's me, Franco. Open up."

Great. Frankie the Ego.

He knocked again.

Catherine looked at me with fearful eyes. "I'm not ready to be seen by others yet."

"I'll take care of it." I walked to the door, unlocked it, and opened it just a foot. There was Frankie Z., the man who had sat in my home and insulted me and my city without batting an eye. I spoke before he could. "Catherine is fine. We'll be out soon."

"I want to see her."

"Not now."

"Listen, lady, I said I want to see her."

"And I told you no—man."

He started to push his way in, but I had placed my foot on the door in a reverse door-to-door salesman trick. He reached through the opening.

"Before you touch me, pal," I said with concrete resolve, "I need to remind you that the entire Santa Rita police department works for me." It was hyperbole but true in its essence.

He withdrew his arm.

"You may wait with the others. Have some dinner."

"When will you be out?" I saw his jaw tighten.

"When we're good and ready, Frankie." I closed the door and quickly turned the lock.

I walked back to Catherine.

"I should have let him in," she said.

"Nonsense. The guy needs to learn a few manners."

"He is a little brusque, but he's been good to me."

I placed my hands on her shoulders and turned her in her chair until she was facing the mirror. "I'm glad to hear that, but he irritates me, and when I'm irritated I like to share it with others." She smiled. "Why don't you clean that stuff off your face? It looks like you put it on with a trowel."

"Stage makeup never looks right up close, but it keeps the theater lights from washing out the actor's expression."

"Well, you start scrubbing, and I'm going to make a call."

"To whom?"

"Detective Judson West. He needs to know about this script. I'll admit that it has me a little on edge, and I'd feel better if West were involved. Besides, it's tied to a murder he's investigating. We have to tell him."

"I understand." She began to wipe off her makeup. "I'm sorry you've gotten involved. Maybe I shouldn't have come back."

"This is your home, and no one is going to run you off." I pulled my phone from my purse and dialed. "Besides, you promised to raise millions of dollars in my last fund-raiser."

"I said I'd show up if it would help. I said nothing about dollar amounts." She grinned.

"No, I distinctly remember hearing the phrase 'millions of dollars.' Maybe it was 'billions of dollars.'" She laughed.

A few seconds later, I had West on the phone. I gave him a thirty-second summary.

He was not happy.

chapter 14

We walked into the dining room just as the meal was being served. The actors and behind-the-scenes people were seated along the long table. Wine glasses, tumblers of water, bottles of beer, and sodas formed a forest of glassware. Before each of them was a plate of London broil—I had been wrong about the prime rib—garlic mashed potatoes and asparagus spears with hollandaise sauce. Salad bowls were being gathered by the servers to make more room. A basket of rolls was set before each group of four.

To Catherine's credit, she walked in with her eyes dry and her head held high. Everyone turned our way as we entered, but no one said anything or fired any questions. It's a rare thing to find a group of people who know when an event is none of their business. Of course, there is always an exception. Franco sprang from his seat.

"Catherine, baby, are you all right?"

"Did everyone get to meet Franco Zambonelli?" Catherine said, diverting Frankie Z. "Take a good look at these guys, Franco. Some may be your clients soon. They're all wonderful actors."

The group gave a happy rumble.

"Let's sit down," she added and took Franco by the arm. Soon we were all seated. Harold eyed Catherine and me. I gave him a slight nod. It was reassurance enough. He dove back into his meal.

I hadn't planned on staying for dinner, but West didn't want us to leave. Nor did he want us to talk to anyone about the script. He officially gagged us. Before coming out, I made a side trip to the kitchen, a much larger affair than I imagined, and asked one of the cooks for a large Ziploc baggie. He had one and was kind enough not to ask why. I slipped the script into the bag and carried it with me to the dining room, being careful to set it on my lap. I wanted to know where it was at all times.

I caught Franco studying me, then Catherine. To him, I was an interloper. To me, he was a pain. His expression said he knew he was out of the loop but that he was in the wrong place to talk about it. Barring the door to him may have cost me a few points on his admiration meter, but somehow I didn't care.

Fifteen minutes later, Judson West walked in. I had just finished my salad and Catherine had finished pushing hers around with her fork. I didn't count, but I don't think she ate more than three or four bites.

"Good evening, Madam Mayor," West said as he stepped to my side. I glanced over my shoulder and saw him towering like a redwood tree. "I wonder if I could bother you and Ms. Anderson."

I excused myself from the table. Catherine did the same. Holding the script in the plastic bag, I rose. I noticed Harold studying West, but he said nothing. Franco, however, blurted, "Who are you?"

"I work with the mayor," West said. He withdrew my chair for me.

"What's that got to do with Catherine?"

"She has some information for me," West said and offered nothing more.

Franco was becoming agitated. "If it concerns Catherine, it concerns me."

"Sit down, Franco," Catherine said sweetly. "I just want to talk to Mr. West for a moment."

That didn't work. Franco rose. "I'm not sure I like your attitude, West."

I glanced along the table. No one was eating. No one was moving. West pulled back his suit coat, revealing a shiny bronze badge. I also noticed that he pulled the coat back far enough to reveal his gun. Franco blanched and oozed down into his chair. West has a way of smiling that is unsettling, a smile that has its origins someplace other than the funny bone.

"Ladies," West said and motioned for us to follow him from the land of tables to the land of booths, the more expensive seats. I slid in the U-shaped booth. Catherine took the place to my left and West to my right.

"Is that it?" He nodded at the plastic-sheathed screenplay.

"Yes." I pushed it across the table toward him.

"Whose idea was the plastic bag?"

"Maddy's," Catherine said. "I wasn't at my best."

"Who's handled it?"

"I have," Catherine answered, "and Maddy too. Oh, and the guy who delivered it."

"Tell me about him." West studied the script, and I could see that he was dying to open it. He looked over at the feasting actors. They had been watching us, but as soon as he directed his gaze their way, they decided their meals were more interesting. Only Franco maintained his stare.

"His name is Andy Buchanan. He's the director's son."

"Can you describe him?" West pulled the still-wrapped script closer.

"Of course, I just saw him an hour ago."

West gave a genuine smile. "I mean, would you describe him to me?"

"Oh. Sorry." Catherine blushed. "He's a couple of years older than me, maybe twenty-seven or twenty-eight. He's three or four inches shorter than you."

"Hair? Eyes?"

"Thick brown hair, naturally curly. I think his eyes are blue."

"White?"

"Yes, white. Why are you asking these questions?" Catherine asked. "You don't suspect him, do you?"

"Is there some reason I shouldn't?"

Catherine looked shocked. "He's . . . he's the director's son. Why would he torture me this way? And I know he wouldn't kill Ed."

"How do you know that?"

"He's a good kid. What would his motive be?"

"I don't know, Ms. Anderson, but he did have possession of the script prior to you. I've arrested a lot of good kids. Some aren't as good as they appear."

Catherine bit her lip. Before West could ask another question, a server appeared with a wide round tray on one hand and folding metal stand in the other. With a practiced motion, he set the stand down, opened it, and then lowered the tray. Three plates of food waited to be lifted to their final resting place. Within seconds, all three plates were plunked down in front of us. A basket of bread and a small silver tray of butter followed. He also laid down linen napkins and silverware.

"No, thank you," West said. "I didn't come to eat . . . Is that London broil?"

"Yes, sir," the waiter said.

West leaned over and took a sniff. His eyes widened. "Well, okay." He slid the script from the table and set it on the seat next to him.

West began to cut the meat, Catherine stared at the food, and I did something that still seemed new to me: I closed my eyes and offered a prayer of thanksgiving. When I opened my eyes, both West and Catherine were staring at me. I said nothing.

"Why was he delivering the script here?" West slipped a piece of the beef into his mouth. "Hey, this is really good."

"The one I brought with me was missing. I have a script meeting tomorrow, so I called and asked for another." Her hands rested in her lap.

"Remember, I called you to ask permission to go by her house to pick up the script," I said.

"I remember. What does young Mr. Buchanan do for the movie biz?" West tasted the potatoes.

I tried a bit of the food. West was right, it was wonderful.

"Like I said, he's the director's son. He's on the learning ladder. You know, working his way up. He runs errands, gets coffee, and carries messages. He also gets to hang out on the set and watch how it's done."

"You told me he just finished film school," I said.

"That's right. In New York. He was a party animal the first few years but then settled down. Chuck says he has a lot of talent."

"Chuck?"

"Charles Buchanan. He's the director and Andy's dad," Catherine explained.

West continued to question Catherine, and I sat listening and consuming the meal before me. West ate during the answers. Catherine didn't touch her food.

"So, what happens now?" Catherine asked.

"I take the script to the lab guys and see if they can tell me anything. At the very least we should be able to lift some prints. I'll need a set of your prints, Ms. Anderson."

"Why?" She leaned back.

"You touched the script. We need to be able to distinguish your prints from any others on the paper and those found at your home."

"Maddy touched it too. Will she have to be fingerprinted?"

West cut a glance at me. "Actually, we have her prints on file. She was fingerprinted last year to help out with a case."

"It doesn't take long," I said. "It's kind of interesting, really."

The server returned and removed my plate and West's. He reached for Catherine's and stopped when he saw it was untouched.

"Was there something wrong with the food, ma'am?" the young man asked.

"Oh no. It was fine. I'm just not hungry."

"May I bring you something else?" he offered.

Catherine declined. After he left, she looked at me. "I'm still a little upset about the script. I can't eat when I'm upset."

"I understand," I said. "Oddly, I sometimes eat more when I'm nervous or frightened."

West brought us back. "I'm concerned about your safety, Ms. Anderson. Clearly, some nutcase is drawn to you. It took a lot of work to arrange that scene in the script. I'm even more concerned that he knew exactly what was said in your house. Did you search all the rooms looking for your chauffeur?"

"No. I looked in a couple but then saw . . . I saw the pool."

"Are you saying the guy could have been in the house with us?" That thought upset my dinner.

"He had to have heard your conversation one way or another," West said. "That's one way."

"How do we know it's a he?" Catherine asked.

"We don't," West said. "It's just shorthand. Most crimes are committed by men, although women do their fair share. I'm not ruling anyone out; male, female; young, old; rich, poor. Right now, everyone is a suspect." He looked at me. "Well, almost everyone." He winked.

"What should I do?" Catherine asked. "I don't want to hide away."

West leaned forward, his expression serious, his eyes fixed on Catherine. "I want you to become a little paranoid. Limit your trust to those you know very well, and I mean *very well*."

"But I deal with people I don't know all the time." She looked at the others. "There isn't an actor here I've known more than a few days. I know Harold and Franco, but the others are strangers."

"I'm not so sure about Franco," West said.

"He's a good man." Catherine seemed offended.

"Perhaps he is, but he strikes me the wrong way," West said.

"Maybe you strike him the wrong way," Catherine flared.

West pressed his lips into a thin line. "I strike many people the wrong way, Ms. Anderson. It goes with the job. I'm just trying to get you to understand the danger you may be in. There's been a murder at your home and someone is playing mind games. Just be extra cautious and limit your trust to as few people as possible until we get to the bottom of this. For example: are you thinking of getting another chauffeur?"

"I don't *get* a chauffeur, Detective, one is provided for me by the production company."

"Are they providing another?"

"Yes. Of course."

"Who will it be?" West folded his hands and waited.

"How should I know?" Catherine snapped. "I told you, the production company provides the driver."

"So you're going to allow a stranger to drive you around, even after the last chauffeur was killed?"

"What's that got to do with—?" Catherine stopped. "You're thinking that someone may have killed Ed because they wanted him out of the way so they could take his place."

"It's a possibility," West said.

I had not made that connection. It made bone-chilling sense.

"But the production company is already sending out a new chauffeur. He should be here anytime."

"Stay away from him. If you want, I'll talk to the new guy and do a background check on him and the company he works for, but until he's cleared, don't get in the car alone with him. My suggestion is you send him home and arrange for your own driver."

"Wouldn't that be insulting to the production company?" she asked.

"I don't care," West said. "I'll tell you what: Tell them I insisted on it and although you're unhappy about it, you feel compelled to follow my advice. Blame me. I have broad shoulders. They can yell at me all they want."

"Okay," Catherine said. I could tell she was unhappy about it.

"It makes good sense," I said. "I think you're wise to follow it."

She looked crestfallen, and I knew it wasn't from not having a chauffeur. Her life was changing against her will, and she was having to face being the center of unholy attention.

"I have a script meeting tomorrow," she said. "If I don't have a driver, I'll need to rent a car."

"Let me take you," I said. "It will be fun. I can sit in the corner and be as quiet as a mouse." I didn't want her to be alone. The more I watched her, the more fragile she seemed.

"But what about your work?"

"The day is fairly light, and Floyd can rearrange things. There's no problem."

She gave a barely perceptible nod.

West said, "I suggest that you stay with Maddy for a while, or at least stay away from your home."

I squashed a smile. Judson West seldom used my first name, let alone my nickname, when others were present. "I know it's still early in the investigation, but have you learned anything yet?"

"A few things, but not much. We're facing a difficult situation because the house and grounds are so new. We found footprints outside, but there were dozens of them. So many workers, especially landscapers, have been over that dirt that identifying which sole print doesn't belong is going to be tough. Most impressions were left by work boots, but there are at least four sets of prints made by sneakers. We've taken casts of the impressions and plan on comparing them to as many workers as we can find, but that is going to take some time. And we can't dismiss the work boot prints either. For all we know, the killer wore work boots. Or the killer may be one of the workers."

"You went to the autopsy today, right?" I asked.

"Yeah. It was pretty straightforward. One shot to the head with a .38 caliber Glaser blue-tip, close range. The victim died quickly."

"What's a Glaser blue-tip?" I asked, uncertain I wanted to know.

"It's a bullet filled with metal fragments. Once it enters the victim, the fragments scatter causing all kinds of damage. It's called a blue-tip because the end of the bullet is blue."

Catherine made a noise and raised a hand to her mouth.

"I think I'm done asking questions," I said.

"We're running a DRUGFIRE search on the blue-tip copper jacket." West must have seen my blank stare. He explained. "DRUGFIRE is to ballistics what AFIS is to fingerprints."

That didn't help.

"AFIS is the Automated Fingerprint Identification System. It's a national database of fingerprints. We can electronically trace a fingerprint of a criminal, victim, or whomever. DRUGFIRE does the same thing with ballistics. So a bullet removed from a murder victim in Florida can be matched to one found in a victim in Oregon. You get the idea."

I got it and Catherine's face said she got it too.

He slipped from the booth, taking the script with him. "I need to get going. I'll keep you posted on what I find out about the script."

I thanked him and watched him leave. The moment he was out of the dining area, Franco scooted to our booth.

"What did he want?" he asked.

Catherine looked at him, then at me. "I think I'm ready to go," she said. The words were just a few decibels above a whisper.

"Wait," Franco said. "I want to know what he said."

"With all due respect, Mr. Zamboni—" I started.

"Zambonelli."

"Sorry. Mr. Zambonelli. With all due respect, if Detective West wanted you in on the conversation, he would have invited you." I worked my way around the booth until I was standing next to the publicist. Catherine did the same.

"Look, lady, I don't know who you think you are—"

"I know exactly who I am, Mr. Zambonelli—and it's not 'lady,' it's Mayor Glenn."

He laughed. "You may think you're something special, lady, but I deal with the biggest names in Hollywood and New York. I bring down more money than you can count in that pretty little head of yours—"

"Franco?" Catherine said.

"Yeah, baby?"

"Shut up. Go home. I'll let you know if I need you."

"Oh, come on, Catherine. I'm just looking out for your interests."

"I'm leaving now, Franco. I'm going home with Maddy and getting a good night's sleep. Tomorrow she will take me to the script meeting, then we'll come back and have a great opening night here."

"Catherine—"

She didn't wait for the rest of the sentence. Instead, she walked to the long table, whispered something in her director's ear, said a few good-byes, then started for the door.

I motioned for Floyd to follow, and we left the Curtain Call behind.

chapter 16

We dropped Floyd off in the city hall parking lot, and I began the drive home. I was looking forward to being in familiar surroundings, wrapped in familiar smells, and cocooning myself away from the outside world. Catherine sat like a stone in the passenger seat.

"Do we need to swing by your house for anything?" I asked. It was my third attempt to start a conversation.

"No. I brought a few extra things last night." She gazed out the window. "I don't feel good about going to the house."

I guess not. "You're welcome to stay with me as long as you like."

"I suppose I'll have to face it someday."

"Living in your new home? Yes, you will and you'll handle it just fine. The key is not to rush things." To avoid traffic I steered the car along the surface streets. I wanted the decompression time for me as well as for Catherine.

"Maybe," she said. "Maybe I should just sell it. I can't get the image of Ed's body out of my mind and now knowing that someone was listening to us—it creeps me out big time."

"Well, it's good to know you're normal. If you felt any other way, I'd be worried about you."

"I'm not so sure normal is all that good."

"I think it is." I glanced at her. She was holding up, but looked as if she were standing on the precipice of a breakdown. A murder at her home, being spied upon, tormented in a script, opening a new play in a day, and getting ready for a big Hollywood movie—she had every right to teeter.

"Dr. Jerry Thomas is coming over tonight."

"I don't need a doctor," she said.

I laughed, and she tossed me an annoyed look. "I'm sorry. I'm not laughing at you. Jerry's a dear friend. We go way back. We were friends in high school. He's a pediatrician, so even if you did need a doctor, he wouldn't be the one to call."

"Oh," she said and returned her gaze out the window. "Is he your boyfriend?"

I paused on that question. I had lived alone so long and put off Jerry's advances so many times I found it difficult to own up to our relationship. "Yeah, I guess you could say that. How'd you figure that out?"

"Your eyes light up when you talk about him."

"I didn't know I was that obvious."

"Detective West's eyes light up the same way when he talks to you. I think he has a thing for you."

She was perceptive; I had to give her that. "He does, but I don't think it could work out. We're very different people."

"Is that bad?"

"No, I suppose not. It's odd, really."

She looked at me again. "What's odd? Having men interested in you? You're a catch, Maddy."

"So is a catfish," I said with a smile. "I meant the whole thing with Jerry and West is odd. West is the dashing one, but Jerry is steady. Both are brave. You'd expect that from a detective but not a pediatrician." My thoughts drifted back to January when Jerry risked his life to save mine.

"Life is full of surprises." Her words were morose. I couldn't disagree.

"Tell me about scripts," I said, as I pulled to a stop at one of the many stoplights that dot our city. "How could someone change pages like that?"

"I don't know."

"Tell me how the system works," I insisted.

"A script is bought or a writer is hired to produce a script," she said. "Some scripts are adaptations of books, others are original. Once the script is finished, revisions begin. Some writers hate Hollywood. In college, a successful screenwriter spoke to our drama class. He said the biggest mistake a writer could make is falling in love with his own work."

"Because it's going to get changed?"

"Yes. Sometimes the screenplay will be given to another writer who then reworks the whole thing only to have some other writer rework that. The screenwriter called it writing by committee. He said the first thing they do is tell you how wonderful you are, then how fabulous the work is, then they begin to pick it apart, page by page."

"That's why there were so many revisions listed on the title page," I said.

"That was nothing. My last picture had fifteen revisions in the last three months. I imagine this script will be changed at least a half-dozen times."

"So, there are lots of scripts of a movie floating around."

"Not floating around. The production companies like to keep scripts a secret until the movie comes out. They like to know where every script is. These things have a tendency to end up on the Internet. That's why I was so upset when mine went missing."

This was too weird and weird worried me. Someone had broken into Catherine's house, despite a state-of-the-art security system, and stolen a script, forcing her to request another, then somehow, changed the contents to reflect events and conversation that happened the day before as well as kill someone. How could that be done? No wonder West's first suspicion fell on the delivery boy.

I chewed on those thoughts as I pulled into the garage. Two minutes later we were in the house, and I was glad for it.

Jerry arrived just before eight. A tweed sport coat with patches on the sleeves had replaced the doctor's smock. He looked positively professorial. I greeted him with a kiss to the cheek and a wide-open door, something I closed and locked once he was inside. I introduced him to Catherine, who was seated on my sofa. We had been drinking tea and watching wood burn in the fireplace. I had turned on an easy jazz station and a miasma of music wafted through the living room. Jerry was carrying a pink box with the words Benny's Bakery.

"Thanks for picking this up," I said as I took the box.

"When you invited me for pie, I didn't know I'd have to buy it." He looked tired. The skin beneath his eyes was dark, his lids drooped as if he was ready to doze off on his feet, and his shoulders were rounder than normal.

"At least I didn't ask you to bake it," I said. I walked into the kitchen.

"What, you don't think they taught me basic baking in med school?"

There was an image: med students in smocks, stethoscopes around their necks, dipping a thermometer into a cherry pie. I opened the box and found a brown pumpkin pie staring back. October was a good month for pumpkin pie. I served up three pieces on plates, set them on a serving tray, and returned to the living room.

"What can I get you to drink, Jerry? I can make coffee."

"No coffee for me. I'm beat, and I don't want anything to interfere with my eight hours of coma. How about some milk?"

I retrieved it and returned to my seat on the sofa. Jerry dug into his pie as if it was the first food he had had all day. Catherine held the plate in her hand and cut off a tiny morsel with her fork. She raised it to her mouth and gently pulled it from the fork, making certain her teeth didn't touch the metal. I caught Jerry watching her.

"How's the little boy?"

Jerry gave a weary frown. "The same. He spiked a fever so we started another course of antibiotics. Tonight will be crucial. His parents are beside themselves. No parent should have to go through this."

"Boy?" Catherine said.

"One of Jerry's patients was hit by a car this morning. He's . . . did you say seven?"

"Six. He's busted up pretty bad." I saw his eyes mist. "But enough of that. He's in good hands for the evening. Tomorrow should be better. I checked on Doug."

I hoped he had. "Good news?"

"No change. He's still stable, but his doctors are remaining noncommittal. They're doing everything they can but there are limits. His editor came by today. I happened to be in ICU when he showed up."

I poked at my pie and tried to spin the news into something good. No change meant he hadn't gotten worse and hope was still alive. I thought of him lying alone in a hospital bed, oblivious—I hoped—to pain and the danger he was in. I thought of the injured child Jerry was helping treat and of Ed Lowe dead in a pool and of a script altered with the clear intent of terrifying—it was an evil world. That thought chewed on me like I had been chewing on the pie. I'm an optimist confined in a straightjacket of reality. I tend to see the good in people and in situations, but I am also quick to recognize darkness. I tried to stay away from the latter. Negative thoughts stick in my mind longer than I like. Yet here I sat, stewing in the knowledge that Doug Turner hovered over the pit of death because someone thought it would be humorous to remove a roadside guardrail.

My fledgling faith had caused me to look at life differently. At first, it changed the way I saw myself. I was no longer just one drop of female humanity in a sea of people; I was a child of God. It was still a difficult concept for me to embrace. I had never been opposed to faith; never argued against any religion; never considered the needs of my own soul. Truth is, I just never thought about it, not even after two carjackers killed my husband. Peter's death had crushed me like a soda can under the grinding tracks of a tank, but I had consoled myself with the knowledge that people endured such things every day; that it was the way the world was and no one could do anything about it. It wasn't much consolation.

"What kind of accident?" Catherine set down her pie plate. Half of the slice remained untouched. "The boy, I mean. You said he was hit by a car?"

"Yes," Jerry said. "He was walking to school. A car ran a stop sign and hit him. To make things all the more poignant, the woman who hit him was taking her children to school. Her kids saw everything."

"That's horrible," Catherine said. "How could the mother be so careless?"

"It may not be all her fault," Jerry said. "This afternoon the accident investigator came by to check on my patient's condition. We talked for a few minutes. Turns out, the stop sign was missing. The poor lady didn't stop because there was no sign telling her to. Still, she could have been much more careful."

The comment was punishing. Every word landed with the power and precision of a boxer's glove. "What?" I said, uncertain I had heard it correctly. He repeated it but I was no longer listening.

The city now had its second casualty. I lost my taste for pie.

chapter 10

No one would ever confuse Hollywood with Santa Rita. I was doing my best to guide my SUV through streets made narrow by cars parked along the curb, delivery trucks which, unable to find places to park, stopped in lanes to unload their wares. Men and women dressed in business attire marched along the sidewalk with clear purpose; others dressed in oddly matched clothing stood on street corners. The streets of downtown were an amalgamation of the expected and the outlandish. Tourists mixed with street people; executives waited at the same lights as the down-and-out.

Overhead, the sun shone down with indifference, casting its glow without prejudice on rusted Pintos and highly polished Rolls-Royces. There was a quality in the air that made it feel as if I had driven through Lewis Carroll's looking glass. I looked at Catherine, who glanced around the setting.

"This is one weird town," she said.

"I was going to say that, but I was afraid you'd take offense." I steered around a man standing in the street shouting something about mind control and Fritos.

"This isn't home, Maddy," Catherine said. "It's just one of the places I show up to do business. Take the next right."

I did. We had left my home at a few minute's after six this morning which allowed us enough time to pick up a couple of lattes before working our way down the 101 freeway. After Detective West's warning, and at his urging, Catherine called her production company and told them that she would arrange for her own transportation. I heard her say in a firm voice, "Because the police say it's what I should do." That had ended it.

The drive from Santa Rita had been better than I expected. The 101 choked up in several spots as we approached the LA basin, but traffic kept moving. It was not as bad as it could be, but not as nice as I would have liked. Still, we made it well before the ten o'clock meeting.

At Catherine's direction, I pulled into an underground parking structure where I was stopped by a guard next to a yellow-and-black arm of an automatic barricade. I rolled my window down.

"May I help you, ma'am?" A middle-aged guard gave me a suspicious look as if I had mistaken his parking garage for a discount shoe mall.

Catherine spoke before I could. Leaning my direction, she said, "Catherine Anderson to see Stewart Rockwood and Charles Buchanan."

The guard leaned closer and peered through my window. I thought he was going to stick his head in. "Oh, sorry, Ms. Anderson. I didn't see you. I was expecting a limo."

"That's all right. This is Madison Glenn. She's a relative."

The guard straightened, reached for a clipboard, and made some notes. Then he pressed a button and the barricade arm rose in a jerky motion. I pulled in.

"Where do I park?"

"Just go to the far wall, there are plenty of spaces there. We'll walk the rest of the way." A few moments later we were in an elevator headed to the eleventh floor.

"Is there anything I should expect?" I asked as the elevator cab rumbled up.

"What do you mean?"

I smiled. "Sorry. It's the kind of question a person like me asks. If you attend enough meetings, speak at enough gatherings, you get in the habit of asking what to expect so you can be prepared."

"Ah," she said. "Not much to expect. This is another read-through. We'll sit around a big table and go over any changes. Then we'll do a dry read—you know, not much acting, just reading to see if the dialogue is realistic. Then people will make suggestions, and the screenwriter will write them down and maybe make changes. It's all pretty dull."

The elevator opened to a private lobby. A woman with red hair that was threatening to go orange and who couldn't be more than a year older than Catherine greeted us.

"Hi, Lindsey," Catherine said and walked to the large desk that anchored the room. She gave the young lady a peck on the cheek. Lindsey returned the favor although I doubted that real lips touched real cheek.

"You look great," Lindsey said, running her eyes over Catherine.

Catherine was wearing well-worn jeans and a sloppy T-shirt two sizes too large for her. I wondered what the receptionist saw that I didn't.

Lindsey's countenance changed so quickly I expected my ears to pop. "I heard about your chauffeur. That is like so horrible. How are you managing?"

"Maddy has been a big help." She turned to me. "Lindsey, this is my cousin Madison Glenn, but everyone calls her Maddy. She's the mayor of my hometown. I'm staying with her for a couple of days until ... until things smooth out."

"Mayor?" Lindsey said. "That is like so cool." She shot her hand out to me.

It's like so cool to meet you. Out loud I said, "My pleasure." She shook my hand with a grip so loose I thought of a dead fish.

She returned her attention to Catherine. "Um, do Chuck and Stewart know . . . ?" She cut her eyes my way.

"Yes," Catherine said. "Are they in there?"

"Sure are. Go on in. You want a soda or something?" Catherine said no. Lindsey looked at me. "May I get you a cup of tea, ma'am? Or a bottle of water?"

Ma'am. Coming from someone her age, it made me feel old. "The water will be fine."

I followed Catherine down a short, wide, white hall and into a conference room. The place was twice the size of the one in Santa Rita's city hall, and a rush of envy rolled over me. The far wall was made of narrow, floor-to-ceiling windows marked off by bronze jambs and chrome miniblinds. The conference table looked to be made of some exotic hardwood I couldn't identify and had a sheen on it that could blind. It was long enough to land aircraft.

We stepped in, and my feet settled on a thick pile, dark copper-colored carpet. Paintings hung in simple frames on ivory walls. It took a moment, but I realized the paintings were stylized renderings of movie posters. I had a feeling the interior designer made more per year than I had in the last decade.

Several people were in the room and were already seated at the distant end of the table. Catherine marched forward and I followed in her wake. They stood as she approached and a chorus of greetings bubbled from the group. There were four and Catherine introduced them as Charles Buchanan, the movie director; Stewart Rockwood, the executive producer; Patty Holt, Buchanan's aide; Andy Buchanan, the producer's son and what Catherine had described yesterday as the assistant-assistant director.

Rockwood was the first to hug Catherine. Money has its privileges. "I'm so sorry to hear about the tragedy at your house. You must be mortified."

Rockwood was a thick man. Not muscular, just thick. His hair was just the right mixture of brown and gray and cut to the perfect length. It took me a few seconds to realize it was the kind of hair one put on a Styrofoam bust each night. He wore a striped dress shirt open at the collar, dark slacks, and a tan sport coat. I judged him to be in his early forties.

"It's been difficult," Catherine said, breaking the hug. She had to try twice.

"Of course it has," Buchanan said. "Death on your doorstep has to be unsettling. Hey, 'death on your doorstep.' That'd be a good movie title." Buchanan was the same height as Catherine, thin, with a shaved head and a short, narrow patch of hair that hung below his lower lip. It had been dyed yellow. "Let me get you a chair." He pulled out the padded desk chair he had been planted in when we arrived and helped her to it as if she were eleven months' pregnant.

Lindsey walked in with a bottle of water and handed it to me. I thanked her and returned my attention to the drama around the table. Of the four who were in the room when we arrived, two stood off a short distance; both were young, about Catherine's age.

Andy Buchanan, Catherine had told me, was a year or two older than she, but he looked younger. Maybe it was the earrings, or the wrinkled black T-shirt with the picture of a flaming pile of bones, or the baggy jeans that did their best to cling to his narrow hips. Where his father's head had been sheared of all hair, Andy had a crop of brown, curly hair that reached out in every direction.

Patty Holt stood by her chair, which was just to the right of Rockwood's. A small laptop computer rested in front of her. She was five foot six or so, mousy hair, lipstick two shades too dark for my tastes, and wore narrow glasses perched high on her nose. Behind those glasses rested the bluest eyes I had ever seen.

A noise to my left caught my attention. Several more people entered the room, and they did so with flare. Leading the pack was a young man whom I immediately recognized. William Vetter was Hollywood's newest young hunk. I had recently seen him interviewed on *Larry King Live*. I learned that he was thirty-one but could pass for twenty-three if needed, or older with the right makeup artist. He had made six movies in five years and each had led the box office for the first three weeks following its release. He was six feet of body, finely crafted by a personal trainer, and had a face genetically designed to melt hearts. On-screen he exuded confidence, certainty, and a keen self-possession. Seeing him in the flesh was disappointing. He hadn't shaved in days, his hair was tussled, and he wore flip-flops instead of shoes.

The others were actors, assistant directors, and others with titles I didn't recognize. The only other person of note was a dignified woman in her early thirties. She wore a comfortable-looking brown pantsuit. Her hair was the color of straw, her eyes hazel, and her build unremarkable. I learned her name was Anita Gorman and that she was the sole screenwriter on the project.

Catherine stood up. "Before we begin, I'd like to introduce someone to you all." She looked at me. I smiled and felt like I was on display. "This is my cousin, Madison Glenn—That's Mayor Madison Glenn. She's my guest today."

"Mayor?" Young Vetter said loudly. "What city?"

"Santa Rita," I said.

The actor smirked. "Never heard of it."

"It's up the coast. Just south of Santa Barbara," I said.

"Oh," Vetter said, then snickered.

The others said hello, nodded, or gave a little wave, then took seats around the table. I was left standing. I started to move when Rockwood stopped me.

"Mayor, I wonder if I might trouble you for a moment." He waved me over. As I approached I saw him punch a button on a small box positioned in front him. "Lindsey, do you have the documents ready?"

"Yes."

"Please bring them. We're ready to get started." He smiled at me. "This will only take a moment."

Lindsey plowed into the room taking unnaturally long steps. She handed two sheets of typed paper to Rockwood. Catherine leaned over and whispered something to the producer. In turn, he motioned for Lindsey to step closer and said something I couldn't hear. Lindsey nodded and left only to return a few moments later holding a bound stack of paper. I recognized the color. Lindsey was holding a script. I glanced along the table and realized that Catherine was the only one who didn't have a script before her.

Rockwood reviewed the documents, then handed one to me. "Yes, this will do." As I took it, he reached for the script and Lindsey relinquished it. Without a word he placed it in front of Catherine. She gave it a wary glance, then turned to the spot where the offending pages had been. She gave a sigh of relief. A clean script.

"What happened to *your* script, Catherine?" Vetter asked.

"Never mind that," Rockwood said.

"What am I looking at?" I asked as I began to read.

"It's an NDA—a nondisclosure agreement. It simply means that you cannot discuss anything you hear in this room with anyone else. That means nothing about the script, the planning, the discussions, the participants, or anything else. Having you here is rather unusual, but considering what Catherine's been through, I can understand her need to have a family member close by."

I glanced over the document. As mayor I see more legal documents than I care to and have developed an eye for the tricky parts. This was straightforward and to the point. It could have been summed up in a line: talk to the media or our competitors about this and we'll sue you and everyone you've ever met.

I signed it but held on to it for a moment. "I wonder if I might trouble you for a chair?"

"Of course." Rockwood looked at Lindsey who just nodded, took the papers, and scurried from the room. A few moments later she wheeled in a chair similar to the ones the others sat in. It was as large as my desk chair and twice as comfortable. I spent a minute wondering if I could fit it in the back of my SUV.

Rockwood leaned back in his chair. "The show's all yours, Chuck."

The director thanked him and said, "Okay, people, we are using revision October 1, yellow. There have been some revisions in act one and act two, mostly dialogue issues. Let's start at the top and do a quick read through to see if everything is holding together. Catherine and William will read their parts. Andy and Patty will voice secondary male and female roles. We're still trying to cast our antagonist, so I'll fill in on that for now. As usual, Anita will do narration."

The meeting started, and I learned four things. First, I learned that some actors are lousy at reading aloud; others excelled. Second, a whole meeting can dissolve into an argument about a single line of dialogue. Third, Anita was a woman of iron to endure the constant nit-picking of her script.

Last, I learned that Catherine was right. This was boring.

Twenty minutes later my mind traveled back up the 101 to Santa Rita where I thought about a reporter in a coma and a broken six-year-old struggling to survive being run over by a car—two accidents that never should have happened.

chapter 17

After ninety minutes of give-and-take, Buchanan called for a break. Judging from the scripts on the table, they had made it about halfway through the screenplay. Almost everyone left the room. Only Rockwood and Catherine stayed behind. I approached as they rose from the table.

"Enjoying the exciting side of movie making, Mayor?" Rockwood asked.

"It's been interesting," I said. "Where did everyone go?"

"The smokers are headed outside for some quality time with their cigarettes, some are making phone calls, and others are headed to the next room where the food is. We had a caterer come bring a few things in. Hungry?"

"No, but thanks." I looked at Catherine.

She glanced around the room, then fixed her gaze on Rockwood. "We need to talk." Her words were blunt and emotionless.

"Sure, kiddo. What do you want to talk about?"

"It's about the script you sent me. There was something wrong with it. That's why I needed another one this morning. I couldn't bring the one you sent."

"What was wrong with the script I sent you?" He tilted his head to one side.

"It had additional pages." Catherine's words were soft as cotton.

Rockwood blinked several times, looked at me, then back at Catherine. "I don't understand. It had extra pages?"

"Pages had been inserted into the script, and they described things that happened in my house … they described … they described Ed's death." Her lower lip quivered for a second, then became taut. She was fighting back the emotion. I moved closer to her side.

"How can that be? It can't be. I personally sent that script to you."

"Catherine's right, Mr. Rockwood," I said. "I saw it myself. The pages looked like the others in typeface and paper color. The only difference I could see was that they had no page numbers."

"I wish you had brought it to me," Rockwood said with a frown. "With all due respect, Mayor, scripts are my bailiwick, not yours. I would be in a better position to judge than you."

"I'm certain you are, but the police took possession of the manuscript."

"That's why I couldn't bring it with me today. They still have it."

The revelation seemed to unsettle the producer. Rockwood lowered his gaze and worked his lips before speaking. "I wish you had told me sooner." He paused, then raised his head. A smile revealed beautifully capped teeth. "You did the right thing. Of course, the police have the script and they should. I suppose they're trying to get fingerprints."

"I suppose," Catherine said.

"Mr. Rockwood, Catherine has told me a little about how important scripts are and how they need to be protected. Asking me to sign the NDA just brought the point home. How could someone obtain a script and insert pages, then arrange to have it delivered to Catherine?"

"Who actually delivered it?" Rockwood asked.

The question surprised me. "You don't know?"

"No, why should I? I don't know how your office operates, Mayor, but this business is like running through a minefield. I don't handle details. I have people for that. I'm the Big Picture guy. I find projects I want to do then start hiring people to do it. If someone needs a document, a check, whatever, I usually assign someone to make it happen."

"So when Catherine asked for a new script . . . ?" I prompted.

"I told Lindsey to make sure she got one. After that, I don't know what happened. I have a full plate. I can't be worried about details."

"I just thought you should know," Catherine said. "I don't know what happened to the first script, and then I show up without the second—I'm afraid you're going to start thinking you hired a ditz."

He laughed. "A ditz, eh?" He put his hands on her shoulders and pulled her close, planting a big kiss on the top of her head. "There are a lot of ditzy people in this business, but you're not one of them. Everyone who knows you speaks highly of your personality, talent, and intelligence. Don't ever demean yourself, kid. You are one of the bright lights in an otherwise dark business." He let her go.

"I understand you let the second chauffeur go," Rockwood said. "That didn't go over well with the limo company."

"That was my idea." The voice came from the door behind me. I turned to see Judson West crossing the threshold. "I cleared them to pick up the limo Lowe had been driving. They have no room to complain."

A young man with chiseled features and pale eyes accompanied West. He wore a tan sport coat over pleated slacks and a crisp white shirt, no tie. On his belt was a shiny badge. West was as dapper as ever in a black shirt, light brown tie, black suit coat, and gray slacks. He carried a laptop tote bag.

"Who are you?" Rockwood snapped.

Lindsey pushed past West and his buddy. "I'm sorry, Mr. Rockwood. I told them you were busy."

"And we didn't listen," West said. I've known West long enough
and seen him in action sufficient times to know he doesn't like to
stand on formalities. "I'm Detective Judson West of the Santa Rita
Police Department; this is Detective Brian Duffy, LAPD, Hollywood
division."

"That's all right, Lindsey," Rockwood said, then to West he said,
"Are you here to talk to me?"

"Yes, to begin with." West's eyes covered the producer from top
to bottom as if he could absorb the information he needed by mere
scrutiny.

"Will it take long?" Rockwood asked.

"That's hard to say," West said.

Rockwood frowned. "Lindsey, set up my office for a meeting
of . . . what? Four or five?"

"We'd prefer to talk to you alone. There are a couple of other
people we would like to speak to while we're here. I'm sorry if this
disrupts your meeting."

"I understand," Rockwood said. "Chuck is running the thing
anyway. Let's go to my office."

I floated a questioning look at West. No words were spoken,
but he knew what I wanted. I had in the past elbowed my way into
his investigations. Being mayor granted me more patience from
city employees than I would ever get otherwise. He sighed and
nodded.

Just before I reached the door, some of the others from the meeting began filing in. I saw Rockwood take Chuck Buchanan by the
arm and whisper something in his ear. Passing the mantle of meeting leadership, no doubt.

Stewart Rockwood's office was more an interior designer's show-room than a place of business. It was wide, open, and filled with art by an artist I didn't recognize. The walls were painted a trendy latte color, statuettes sat upon what I assumed were custom-made display stands. In one corner was a glass-and-wood desk and side table. Along one wall ran bookshelves devoid of books. More trinkets and objects of art filled the spaces. The carpet was blue and thick. A large table sat in the middle of the room and to the side of it, three leather sofas defined a conversation pit.

"Please come in," Rockwood said, adopting a cheerful air. "May I fix anyone anything?" He moved straight to a wet bar a few steps from his desk.

"It's a little early for drinks," Brian Duffy said.

Rockwood scowled at the LAPD detective. "I was thinking along the lines of juice, water, tea. The image of the hard-drinking, las-civious producer is inaccurate—well, mostly inaccurate. Some of us are pretty nice guys. Law-abiding guys, I might add." He looked at us, quizzing us with his expression. "Nothing then?" He reached beneath the counter and removed a small bottle of orange juice. "Unsweetened," he said as if the revelation meant something.

He moved to the sofas and we followed. "Is this okay, Detective, or do you prefer sitting around a table?"

"This will be fine," West said and sat.

We took seats. I sat farthest from Rockwood and the others. I was trespassing on police business, and I thought it best to be as invisible as possible.

"I can understand you being here, Detective West," Rockwood said and raised the drink to his lips. He downed a third of it in two gulps. "But why is the LAPD involved?"

"Common courtesy," West said. "When you fish in someone else's pond, it is always wise to invite them to join you."

"Ah, jurisdiction is the issue, is that it?"

"Something like that," West said.

"As you know, a man was murdered and his body left in the pool of Ms. Catherine Anderson."

"I do know that, but only because Catherine called and told me." Another third of the drink slipped down his throat.

"Did you know the deceased?" West asked.

"No. We've used several limo companies over the last year. I just place a call and tell them who to pick up and when. At the end of the month I get a bill which I promptly pay."

"So you've never actually met Ed Lowe?"

"I didn't say that, Detective. You asked if I *knew* him. I don't. I have met him a few times and earlier this year when he was the driver for another actress. His employers speak well of him, and I found no fault in his work."

"Can you think of any reason someone would want to kill Mr. Lowe?" West asked.

"I can't imagine why anyone would want to kill anyone else. Violence in movies is one thing, but violence on the street is incomprehensible."

"Yet it happened," Detective Duffy interjected.

"So it seems," Rockwood answered. "May I ask how he was killed?"

West stared at the producer. "He was shot in the head with a Glaser blue-tip safety slug." Rockwood looked puzzled. West filled in the details. "The bullet is filled with small fragments that spread out when they strike their target. It leaves a hole on the outside and a real mess on the inside."

"And it's called a *safety* slug?"

"It's called that because it reduces the risk of overpenetration and ricocheting."

"Overpenetration? Never mind, I don't want to know." Rockwood blanched. "The poor man." He looked at his orange juice and set it down. "I wish I had information that could help you, Detective."

"Perhaps you do," West said. "I overheard Mayor Glenn and Ms. Anderson telling you about the script."

"The one with the supposed extra pages."

"Not supposed extra pages, Mr. Rockwood. They're very real. As I understand it, Ms. Anderson called you and requested that a new script be delivered to her. Is that correct?"

"It is. She called me, told me about the murder and later about the missing script. Of course, I sent her one."

"Tell me how that worked." West crossed his legs as if settling in for a good movie.

Rockwood looked puzzled, then shrugged. "It's not very complicated, Detective. I received the call about the missing script. Catherine was calm but I could tell she was upset. She's such a talented actor that I started to suggest that she just wait until today's meeting. There have been very few changes in her part. So far anyway. This business feeds on change."

"But you didn't make that suggestion. You had a fresh script sent anyway."

"I did. I thought it might provide a little comfort."

"Did you personally send it?"

Rockwood shook his head. "That depends on what you mean by 'personally.' I didn't actually package the thing up. I called Lindsey and asked her to take care of it."

"She's in charge of the scripts?"

"She keeps track of who has what and makes that information available to Chuck and Patty."

"Chuck and Patty?" West pressed.

"Charles Buchanan, the director. Patty Holt is his right-hand girl. Lindsey and Patty keep track of actor schedules, script possession, and a thousand other things."

"Sounds like you keep them busy," Duffy said.

"Movie making is the art of managed chaos," Rockwood said. "To be a success in this business one must manage people well."

"So," West continued, "your aide grabs a script, then what?"

"She doesn't just grab a script, Detective. She would have notified Chuck that she was sending an extra script out. Most likely she spoke to Patty who would also note it."

"Ms. Anderson tells me that an Andy Buchanan delivered the script and that he is the son of the director."

"That doesn't surprise me. Chuck has been putting his son through the paces. The boy has a talent but next to no experience. Like every third person you meet in this town, he wants to direct. His advantage is that he has a father who is well respected in the business."

"So when Ms. Anderson calls him an assistant-assistant director—"

"It means he gets to do the grunt work other directors don't want to do. It's a good way to learn the business."

"There's more than one director?" I asked. West gave me a hard stare. I got the message.

"Yes, Mayor, there's more than one of everything," Rockwood explained. "Have you ever gone to a movie?"

"Of course," I said.

"Have you ever stayed to watch the credits at the end of the show?"

He had me there. "No. I usually move on."

"Typical. Very few people do. Those who do stay know how many people are involved in making a movie. I have two other executive producers, three coproducers, and scores of other employees. While there is one director who is responsible for getting the movie shot, he has assistant directors, and a director of photography. At the end of every movie a list of hundreds of names goes by on the screen. What you've seen here today are just the principle actors and staff."

"But only a portion would be in a position to make changes to a script and deliver it."

And know enough to use the right typeface and the correct color of paper.

"That's true. So now you want to know who would be able to do such a thing. I can't blame you. Unfortunately, almost anyone in the business would know the format to use, but the person you're looking for had to have access to the most recently revised script." He paused and thought. "That would limit it to maybe fifty or so people."

"Fifty?" West said.

"Give or take. Scripts have already gone out to site hunters, costumers, special effects, and various people and businesses in the chain of production." He paused and toyed with the orange juice bottle. "The key, it seems to me, isn't who has a script, but who knew Catherine would need a new one."

"We believe it was stolen to force her to ask for another," West said.

"That makes sense, but . . ." He trailed off. I had a feeling I knew where he was going. "But there is another crucial issue, and I'm afraid it doesn't make me look very good." He studied West. "This is what you've been leading up to, isn't it?"

"Perhaps." West smiled.

"I'm a few beats behind here," I admitted. "Someone care to fill me in?"

"Let me try," Rockwood said. "That is, if you don't mind, Detective West."

"Go ahead."

"The question is, Mayor: why didn't Catherine receive two scripts? I took the call. I started the ball rolling. A script—an altered script—was delivered to her. If someone on the outside was delivering a script, then Catherine should have received two, one from them and one from me. Since only one script arrived, it must—"

I finished his sentence. "Be one from this office."

Rockwood nodded.

"Couldn't the one you sent be intercepted somehow and another substituted?" I asked.

"I suppose it could," Rockwood said. "I'm impressed, Mayor. Maybe you should give up politics and become a detective."

"No thanks," I said.

"Mr. Rockwood," West said. "I'd like to get your fingerprints to compare with those found on the script. I would also like to interview Lindsey, Patty Holt, Buchanan, and his son."

"You're welcome to my fingerprints, Detective," Rockwood said, "but you're on your own with the others. I'm just their producer, not their lawyer."

"I'm sure your cooperation will go a long way to encourage their cooperation," Duffy said with a small smile.

Rockwood looked down at his feet. "I suppose I need to go to the police station for this."

"No need," West said. "I brought a field kit. It will only take a few moments."

"Tell me, Mayor," Rockwood said as he watched West set up, "these inserted pages you saw, where were they in the script?"

"What do you mean?" I asked. His question was odd.

"Were they at the front, in the middle, or toward the end?"

I thought back to what Catherine had said. "Catherine said it was at the end of act one and she called it a plot point."

"Interesting." His tone was dismal.

"What's a plot point?" West asked.

"In a three-act screenplay it is the culmination of events or a significant event that sets act two in motion. Usually there's one at the end of act one and another at the end of act two."

"And that is interesting, but why did you ask?" West said.

Rockwood shrugged. "It's probably just me, but it makes me wonder if there will be a second act."

West stopped cold.

So did my heart.

chapter 10

The script meeting lasted longer than planned. West and Duffy's presence had caused everything to grind to a halt. An exasperated Charles Buchanan finally called an end to the meeting. West spoke to the group for a moment, gathering names and addresses. Catherine and I slipped out as soon as we could. We were already an hour behind our planned departure time and Catherine had to be at the theater early.

Traffic was uncooperative and as thick as mud. I pressed on, doing the vehicular equivalent of throwing elbows. My frustration grew as two cars conspired to move side by side at the same speed, becoming a bone in the throat of forward progress.

"How do you do it?" Catherine asked.

Since leaving Hollywood she had barely spoken. I was giving her time to decompress. I have learned that fears can compound. Even small things in sufficient quantity could press a person to the ground. A ton of feathers still weigh a ton. Catherine didn't have feathers on her mind; her issues were large and hard and unrelenting.

"How do I do what?" I shifted lanes again.

"Remain so together, so confident when things go wrong." She paused, then continued before I could respond. "I visited Mom and Dad last month. My mom had been talking to yours. I know about the attack in your home and about the death of your friend." She looked out the side window. "Yet you keep going forward, running for congress, managing the city . . . taking care of me."

A tiny tear crawled down her left cheek. A black sadness oozed into my soul. I kept my eyes forward, partly because of the dense traffic, partly because I knew that her anguish was contagious.

"I was going to ask you the same thing," I said. "You've gone through all of this with unbelievable strength."

"It's a facade," she said. "I'm a mess, Maddy. What you see, what others see, is just an act. I'm an actor, it's what I do. Inside . . ."

I let a moment pass. We both needed a few seconds of silence to gather our wits. "I think most people are actors, Catherine. I know I've spent a good deal of my life putting on airs. That's not so bad. Sometimes we begin to feel the way we act, not the other way around. Other times the mask we wear doesn't matter. We can fool others, but we can't fool ourselves."

"So you just keep going regardless of how you feel?"

"I used to."

"Used to?" She turned to face me.

I moved to the far right lane where the traffic was slower. I couldn't duke it out with other drivers and tell the story at the same time. I needed the slower pace. Catherine didn't object.

"As you know, my husband Peter was killed in a carjacking. That was a long time ago, but the shock and pain never fully goes away. All time can do is quiet the sorrow; it can never extinguish it." I took a deep breath. "In less than two years I've lost two friends to violence. I wanted to hide from the world."

"But you didn't run away," Catherine said.

"A person can't flee such things. Loss like that is a wound. No matter where I go, the wound will still be there."

"So you just gut it out?"

"Not exactly." I felt awkward, and I was uncertain how she would respond to what else I had to say. I took the plunge. "A little over a year ago I made a decision, and it's changed the way I look at things."

"What kind of decision?" she pressed.

I let a Chevy pickup pull in front of me. Several pieces of lumber cantilevered over the tailgate. "Before Peter died, he started hanging out with a group of businessmen who used to go deep-sea fishing once a month. Peter was born and bred to be a salesman. Having a dozen businessmen confined on a boat was an opportunity he couldn't pass up."

"He worked with his father, right?"

"That's right. Glenn Structural Materials. They make commercial flooring. The businessmen came from banking, restaurants, construction, and the like. Prime targets for Peter. It was the only way you would get him on a boat like that. The only thing he ever fished for were new clients. On his first trip out, he learned that more was going on than fishing."

"Nothing illegal, I hope."

"No, nothing like that. They were holding a Bible study. On the way out and on the return trip, the men studied the Bible."

"That's weird."

"I thought so too when I heard about it. Peter went several times. I knew nothing about what was happening on the fishing boat. Peter never talked about it. He made one last trip with the guys before going to LA where he was murdered. Years later I learned that he had made a decision for Christ, that he had become a believer."

Catherine opened her mouth to speak but nothing came out. I gave her an understanding smile. "I felt the same way when I heard of it. I didn't learn about this change in his life for years. Peter was a believer for less than a day."

I forced my eyes straight ahead and reminded myself that I was driving on a crowded freeway. Talking about Peter still hurt, but I pressed on.

"A friend, Paul Shedd, gave him a Bible. Do you know Paul?"

"No."

"No reason you should, I suppose. He used to be a banker but decided he'd be happier as a restaurateur. He owns the Fish Kettle diner on the pier. Paul has a habit of reading through the Bible every year. As he does, he makes notes in the margins and underlines verses that strike him as important. Every year he gives the Bible to someone he thinks will benefit from it. He gave one to Peter the day he drove to LA, the day he was killed. When the police returned Peter's personal possessions, the Bible was with them. I kept everything in a cardboard box stuck away in a closet. It took a long time for me to open that box. I found the Bible."

"And it changed you."

"It took a little time and a lot of explaining from Paul Shedd, but ultimately I made the same decision for Christ that Peter did years before."

"And so everything is perfect in your life." Her words had an edge to them.

"I don't recall saying that."

"I'm sorry." She closed her eyes and leaned her head back against the headrest. "It's just that Hollywood has its share of so-called Christians. I haven't been impressed."

"What are you expecting from them?"

"What do you mean?"

"You sound disappointed. What are you expecting out of the Christians you know in Hollywood?"

"I don't know. What should I expect?"

"You should expect people who do their best to be godly, but you shouldn't expect perfection. Walking in faith isn't easy. I've learned many take the name but they don't take the challenge."

"So because you have Jesus in your life now, you no longer have problems."

That made me laugh out loud. I apologized and then said, "I can't say that. In some ways, I have new problems because of my faith. Took me awhile to learn this, but embracing faith in Christ didn't turn me into the perfect saint. It's not like flipping a switch. The decision, the prayer, can happen in a minute, but the lifestyle takes practice. I still struggle with my temper, and most of all, my mouth."

"So what's the difference?"

I checked my rearview mirror, buying some time. I felt awkward. Being so new to the faith, I had very little practice at explaining what I had come to believe. "The difference is, now I care. Before I plowed forward and if I hurt someone's feelings along the way I wrote it off as the price of living. Now I try to think about the impact of my words. It's not natural for me and I have a long way to go."

I pulled one lane to the left and pulled around the pickup. "You asked how I dealt with the tragedies I've faced. Well, that's how. I pray. I seek God's will. I try to live like a person who has Christ in her heart. The more I learn, the more sense it all makes."

"But God hasn't protected you from pain. That doesn't seem like a loving God to me."

I understood the sentiment well. I should. I've wrestled with it for as long as I can remember. "Catherine, I'm no theologian. I'm not a preacher. I'm just a woman who has found strength and purpose when I didn't even know I was looking for it. All I can tell you is that my belief in Christ has changed everything for me. Sometimes . . . sometimes experience is the best explanation."

The next fifteen miles passed in silence. Catherine sat as if someone had sewn her to her seat. She didn't fidget, didn't shift, didn't move. Her tears had been replaced by an emotionless mask. On her lap was the new script. She hadn't said so, but her actions said she wasn't going to let this one out of her sight.

"I had a few minutes to talk to Detective West," I said, putting an end to the hush. "He was tied up with interviews, but he wanted me to tell you that he was sorry to have to interrupt your meeting."

"He's just doing his job," Catherine said. "The meeting was important but not crucial. Shooting is still weeks away."

"He also wanted me to tell you that he searched your home again, this time looking for listening devices. He brought an expert with him."

"Did he find anything?" She looked at me.

"No."

"I don't understand," she said. "The mystery script had our words down almost identically."

"That's one of the things that bothers me," I admitted. "If someone was listening in and recording our conversation, then why are there subtle differences between what we said and what was later written?"

"Maybe whoever did this didn't record it. Maybe they just listened in and later wrote it down. I'm not sure I could recite what we said word for word."

"That's natural enough," I said. "Memory is fragile." I waited for a moment, then added what I had been putting off. "There's something else—something Mr. Rockwood said."

"What?"

"He asked where the additional pages appeared. We told him. Then he mentioned the same thing you did about three acts and plot points. He said he wondered if there would be a second act."

"That's frightening."

"I thought so. Could it be a coincidence the pages were placed there and not somewhere else in the script?"

"I suppose," she said.

"You don't sound convinced."

"I'm not convinced about anything."

"How competitive is the movie business?" I asked. "Could someone be doing this to you to throw off the production?"

"It's very competitive. Sometimes it's cutthroat. What about fingerprints? Wasn't he going to check for fingerprints?"

"Yes. He found ours, of course, but he also found several others. That's one reason he is asking for prints from the others. He told me he ran the prints he had through the computer databases and there were no hits."

"So there were no listening devices in my home, and the fingerprints have been a dead end. We're nowhere."

"West is just starting the investigation. Give him some time."

"I hope I have time to give."

"What do you mean by that?" I asked. She returned her gaze to the slow-moving traffic.

"Nothing," she said. "Just forget it."

chapter 10

I dropped Catherine off at the theater at four. That gave me enough time to run by the office and check my messages. Tess was walking out as I was walking in.

"Hey, Tess," I said. "Did you get my message?"

"About the stop sign and the child in the hospital? I got it. We're not dealing with a practical joker anymore." Her tone was dark. "We have two people in the hospital, both in grave condition. One of them just a child. We have serious problems."

"I assume you let Fred know." I started toward my office. Tess stayed at my side. More meetings are conducted in hallways than offices.

"I did. He's anticipating what legal actions we may face and doing the preliminary work to protect the city. You know, some would try to get the family to sign a hold-harmless agreement or try to buy the family off by promising to cover all medical expenses."

"We're not doing anything underhanded," I said. "Everything must be aboveboard."

"I know and I agree. Let me say aloud what we've both been thinking. The city stands to lose a great deal of money."

"We're insured." We crossed the threshold into the outer office and said "hi" to Floyd who was putting files away.

"I know we're insured. Let's just hope we can get insurance this time next year."

I motioned for her to take a seat and glanced at my desk. Very few calls. That was good.

"We'll cross that bridge when we come to it." I took a seat in my office chair.

"That's easy for you to say, Mayor. Next year you may be in Washington, D.C. I and the rest of the council will be left with the problem."

She had a point. "What do you think we should do?"

"We're not in the driver's seat. At this point, all we can do is try and find the perpetrators and prosecute them. We should also work out contingency plans."

"Maybe we should go public," I said. "Ask the public for help."

"I'd clear that with Chief Webb first. He has a man working on the problem. If we get ahead of them and make things more difficult, then he's going to be impossible to live with."

"He's already impossible to live with."

"It can be worse." Tess stood. "I wish I had better news."

"I appreciate what you're doing, Tess."

She left and Floyd flowed in a moment later. "How'd it go?" he asked.

"It went. Anything I need to know about?"

"No. Just the same ol' same ol'. You going to the play tonight?"

"Yes. Catherine arranged for me, a date, and my parents to attend opening night. She got balcony seats."

"Oh." He looked disappointed.

"Jerry is going to meet me there, but I've got a problem."

"Problem?"

"My parents are out of town. That means I have two extra tickets. Got any ideas who might like to go to a dinner theater tonight?"

His eyes widened. "Yes. Me!"

"And . . ."

"And? Oh, and Celeste."

I shook my head in disbelief. "Give her a call. This is your chance to make things up to her. It's short notice, but she might like an impromptu date."

"I'll call right away." He turned to leave.

"Oh, Floyd?"

"Yes."

"If you spend the evening telling Celeste how wonderful Catherine is, I will throw you off the balcony. Understood?"

He smiled, embarrassed. "Understood."

I have never been much for the theater. Most of my entertainment comes over CNN. It's sad, I know, but it is what I've become. Sitting in a balcony room of the Curtain Call dinner theater was changing that. The theater was divided into three seating areas. Long rows of tables filled the floor area closest to the stage. People in padded chairs lined the sides and talked freely as they ate. Farther from the stage, but still at floor level, were two banks of booths. Those seats cost more but provided a slightly better view of the stage and more elbow room.

The balcony rooms were a level above the first floor and were comprised of three walls and a wood rail. Two tables were in each room, situated near the rail overlooking the floor below and the stage. Dark green wallpaper, reminiscent of turn-of-the-century fine homes, covered the walls. A pale beige carpet blanketed the floor. The lighting was dimmed to a warm romantic glow, and the conversations of patrons below wafted up in a murmur.

Rather than sit at separate tables, Jerry and I pushed the tables together. Jerry sat to my right, Floyd to my left, and Celeste anchored the end opposite Jerry. Although still young, Celeste was showing signs that she was crossing the threshold from youth to womanhood. Her cheeks were a little rounder than last year, and her conversation a little more fluid and less encumbered with teenage baggage. Her blond hair was shorter, hovering two inches above her shoulder. She smiled easily, engaged in the conversation, but I caught her casting odd glances at Floyd. Apparently, the stress between them was still there.

We enjoyed light conversation and told a few jokes. A waiter brought an assortment of bread, butter, salads, and finally the main course. On my plate was a nice slice of medium-well beef with a blue cheese sauce, mixed vegetables, and wild rice. I made short work of it.

After the meal, the waiter bussed four empty plates, refilled our drinks, and took dessert orders, which would be fulfilled during intermission. As we chatted, I studied the program that had been given to us when we arrived. Normally a detail person, I felt a little embarrassed that I didn't even know the title of the play. *Too many thoughts and too few brain cells*. I made up for my oversight. The first thing I noticed surprised me.

```
TAKE MY HEART
A Comedic Murder Mystery
Written and Directed by Harold Young
```

Harold Young, the high school drama teacher I had met when I came to the Curtain Call to meet Catherine. *Teacher, writer, actor, director.* He's a busy man.

The program included pictures of the actors and a brief biography of each. Leading the list was Catherine Anderson. Her picture was a professional headshot and her smile gave color to the black-and-white photo.

"She is lovely," Celeste said.

I took a quick look at Floyd. His mouth opened, then closed again. *Good boy.*

"The joke in my family is that all the genes for good looks migrated to her," I said.

"You're very beautiful, Maddy," Celeste said. "Don't sell yourself short."

"That's what I've been saying," Jerry added.

"All right you two," I quipped, "I'll give you thirty minutes to stop that kind of talk."

"Just thirty minutes?" Jerry said.

"I don't want to be too dictatorial."

"Maybe I should be an actor," Floyd said with a whiplash change of subjects.

I bit back a smile. Floyd was a chameleon, always wanting "to be" whatever was in front of him. Now in a theater, he was considering a life upon the boards.

"How come you never want to be a doctor, Floyd?" Jerry asked.

"You have to do yucky stuff," he replied with simple innocence.

"It's true. I look at lots of yucky stuff. In fact, just the other day, Maddy was cooking dinner—"

"Careful, Dr. Thomas. Your future is flashing before my eyes."

"An actor?" Celeste said. "Floyd, you get nervous talking to new people. What would you do with a roomful of them every night?"

"I might get used to it." He was becoming defensive.

Celeste pressed a little more. "Why do you keep changing your mind about things? One day, you want to be a preacher like your father, the next day you want to be a teacher, the next a businessman. Why do you do that?"

"I don't want to miss my calling. I'm just trying to be open to possibilities." There was a bite in his words.

"You're afraid of making a mistake," Celeste said.

"That's right, I am. I don't want to waste my life."

The conversation was headed down a slippery hill. I was about to shift the topic when the lights dimmed and a statuesque woman with red hair, high cheekbones, and a clear voice stepped onstage. She wore a gray pantsuit; subdued, but quietly elegant. A string of pearls hung from her neck and were matched with earrings.

"Good evening," she said. The theater's acoustics and electronics augmented her voice. People around the tables turned to face her, and she waited while they repositioned their chairs, her smile as permanent and inflexible as the stage she stood upon.

The mumbling quieted, parents reined children in, glasses and coffee cups were set down. All eyes were upon her.

"My name is Neena Lasko, and I want to welcome you to my theater and the premiere production of *Take My Heart*, an original work by Santa Rita's own Harold Young. The cast and crew have been working very hard to make this play memorable and enjoyable. To make certain that we all enjoy the play to its fullest, please mute or turn off your cell phones and pagers. The play will begin in a few moments. Our servers will be around to fill coffee cups and other drink orders. No drinks will be served during the play, but don't fear. They'll be around again during intermission. Again, allow me to thank you for your patronage. And now, for the first time anywhere, *Take My Heart*, starring Catherine Anderson."

Polite applause rose, servers scurried, and then the lights dimmed.

Catherine walked onstage and delivered the first line, and for the next forty-five minutes, I forgot about dead men in pools, reporters in hospitals, missing stop signs, and a congressional campaign.

I am proud of every member of my family, from my parents to the last uncle and cousin, but had never felt such a swelling of pride as when Catherine walked offstage at the end of act two. She moved in an effortless fashion as if gravity had no sway with her; her voice clarion; her expressions believable. She and the remaining cast had seized us by the lapels and dragged us into the pretend world of the play. I was sad when the first half of the play was finished and comforted myself with the knowledge that there was more to come.

The curtains closed and the lights came up. Several hundred patrons began to talk at once. They were as impressed as I had been.

"I owe you an apology, Floyd," Celeste said. "She is more beautiful than you described." She reached across the table and took his hand. Floyd gave it a squeeze. The evening was turning out all right after all.

Our waiter returned, served coffee and ice cream. I was just two bites into the vanilla bean when the door opened and the woman I had seen on the stage entered. She introduced herself to us. Jerry stood, and so did Floyd—five seconds later.

"Sit, sit," Neena Lasko said. "Catherine told me you were up here. It's not every day that I have both the mayor and a candidate for congress in my place."

"I'm just one person," I said. I introduced the others.

"I know, but it sounds better my way." She laughed, then asked, "Is this your first time here?"

"It is, but it won't be my last. I'm having a wonderful time and the meal was great." She looked older in person than onstage. I guessed that she had left the fifty-five mark behind.

"We have an excellent chef and a superb support staff. I don't think you can find a better meal."

"And a great play," Jerry said.

"Yes," Neena agreed. "Harold has been working on this script for over a decade. I've seen more plays than I can count and this is one of the strongest performances. I wouldn't be surprised if we see it on Broadway in a few years. All Harold needs is the right break."

"Can that really happen?" I asked.

"Sure. Why not? Producers don't care where good ideas come from, only that they make money. It's one reason he wanted Catherine to play the part. He knew she could pull off the part and get the needed attention."

"It's like he wrote the play just for her," Jerry said.

"He did. He told me that he had been working on the play for a few years when she walked into his high school theater class. It wasn't long before he realized that she exemplified the kind of actress needed to make the play work. He began tweaking the script to suit her. Of course, by the time he finished, she had already graduated and gone off to New York. He's been trying to get her to do the play for the last two years."

"I'm glad he succeeded," Floyd said. He was holding hands with Celeste again.

"Me too," Neena said. "I've got a feeling we're going to get great box office out of this. I just wish we could keep her for the full run. That movie deal is good for Catherine but bad for us." She shrugged. "Such is life. I'll take her for as long as I can get her."

"What do the actors do during intermission?" Floyd asked.

"Floyd is wondering about life in the theater," I added.

"Ah," Neena said. "Right now, they're taking a break while the stage crew sets up for the next scene. Some actors review the script; some walk in circles and mumble their lines; others play video games."

"Video games? Really?" Floyd said.

"Sure. Only a few actors are onstage at any one time. They've been over this play so many times that they can recite lines in their sleep and probably do. When not onstage they pass the time any way they can."

"Cool," Floyd said.

"Everything about the theater is cool," Neena said. "It's one rea-son I do what I do—"

The door to the room sprang open so suddenly that I jumped, my knee hitting the table, spilling small waves of coffee.

Harold Young stepped in, looked around, and then closed the door behind him. Even in the subdued light I could tell he was shaken. His skin was pale and small beads of sweat dotted his brow. Aside from the terror on his face, he looked every bit the part of the director: turtle-neck sweater, sport coat, slacks, and tennis shoes.

"What's wrong?" Neena said.

Harold looked at her, then directly at me. He started to speak but managed only to stammer. I rose.

"Is something wrong with Catherine?"

More sweat. His breathing was ragged. For a moment I expected him to keel over from a heart attack.

"Have a seat," Jerry said, springing to his feet. Apparently he was worried about the same thing.

"I don't want to sit down," he snapped. He lowered his voice. "Thank you, but I can't sit down."

I don't know why I didn't see it at first, but Harold was hiding something with his left hand.

"Pull yourself together," Neena said. "What is the problem?"

Slowly, Harold raised his left hand. In it was a script. A script printed on yellow paper.

"That's the script Catherine brought with her today," I said.

"No, it's not," Harold said. "I have that script. She gave it to me for safekeeping. This is a different script. It arrived after the play started. Someone dropped it off during the first act and one of the employees took it to the cast room. After we went to intermission, Catherine saw it and read a few pages. She excused herself. No one

has seen her since. I looked everywhere for her. I even sent someone into the ladies' restroom. She's gone. Catherine is gone, and
we're supposed to raise the curtain in ten minutes."

"We can't go on without her," Neena said. "If we don't find her
I'll have to explain to the crowd why we're suddenly using the
understudy."

"May I see the script?" I asked.

"What?" Harold seemed close to a nervous breakdown.

"The script. May I see it?"

He handed it to me. I know it was my imagination but it seemed
three times heavier than it should be.

chapter 20

O kay," Neena said, "let's keep focused." She looked at her watch. "Harold, do a quick search of the theater."

"I already have."

"Do it again. Take a couple of servers with you. I'm going to search the grounds. Let's meet in my office in five minutes."

"I should alert Jane."

"Jane?" I asked.

"Jane Ash," Harold said. "She's the understudy."

"Let's just hope she went out for some fresh air." Neena started for the door, then stopped. "Wait. Have you talked to . . . I can't think of his name—her publicist."

I said, "Franco Zambonelli? He's here?"

"He was earlier. Catherine asked that I make room for him. This showing is sold out and squeezing one more in a few minutes before showtime was tough. Fortunately, we had a cancellation in one of the booths. I put him there."

She exited with Harold in tow.

"This doesn't sound good," Jerry said.

"No, it doesn't," I agreed. There was a burning in my stomach as I returned to the table and pushed away the dessert dishes. Jerry and Celeste helped reposition the coffee cups to give me room to do the one thing I didn't want to do. I set the script down. I knew where the offensive pages had been in the script now in police possession. I flipped through the early pages until I came to the spot where I expected to find the text of my conversation with Catherine in her home. It wasn't there. That should have been a relief for Catherine, not something to send her wherever she went.

My gut tightened as I faced the dark question floating just below my imagination. *Were there new pages?* It would take some time to read through the whole script. Then it hit me. I began to fan the pages.

"What are you doing?" Jerry asked.

"Looking for pages that don't belong."

"How are you going to know if they don't belong?"

"Pages were inserted into a script delivered to Catherine," I explained. I gave a quick summary of the offensive additions for Celeste's benefit. "The only thing that made those pages different from the real script was the lack of page numbers."

Flipping through the pages I scanned the upper right corner. Numbers fluttered by until I found one that was blank.

I stopped flipping.

I stopped breathing.

Someone had inserted several pages. Like before, these looked like every other page in the screenplay with the exception of the missing numbers. I read.

```
EXT. LACY'S HOME—NIGHT
     The moon rides high in the sky casting ivory light
     on the distant ocean. Lacy arrives home. In the
     distance, a dog barks. She enters her home through
     the front door. It is clear that she is upset. She
     still wears her costume.
```

INT. FOYER OF LACY'S HOME
The house is dark. Lacy turns on a light and walks
into the living room. A noise outside catches her
attention. She approaches the back door. She
reaches for the curtains to pull them back, but
stops with her fingers just an inch from the
drapes. A soft noise pushes through the door. Lacy
takes a deep breath and slowly pulls the drape
back.

                    LACY
                  (Screams)
        No! Stay away. Stay away!

                  INTRUDER
                  (Darkly)
        You know what I want.

                    LACY
        I came just like you wanted. I'm here.
        You promised that you'd let him go.

                  INTRUDER
        Promises can be broken. You should know
        that. You've broken enough.

                    LACY
        Please, just let him go.

                  INTRUDER
        It's too late and it's your fault. It's
        all your fault.

                    LACY
        No. Please no. I'm sorry.

                  INTRUDER
        Sorry doesn't cut it. Never has. Never
        will.

(Laughs)

The Body Count is now two. Ready for three?

The rest of the page was blank.

"Who's Lacy?" Floyd asked.

"That's Catherine's character in the movie," I explained.

"That's terrifying," Celeste said.

"Jerry," I said, rising. "We're leaving."

"I thought you might say that. Don't you think we should call—"

"We can do that on the way." I snatched up the script.

"I'll go with you," Floyd said.

"No, you won't." I was out the door and moved down the stairs as fast as I could. I could hear Jerry behind me. He caught up and put a protective, guiding hand on my elbow.

"Slow down," he said.

"Too much time has already passed." I started to pull away.

He tightened his grip and his words. "I said, slow down. We're going to go to her house, but not in a panic. God gave us brains for a reason. Let's use them."

Hearing Jerry use the word "God" put a hitch in my step. He was spiritually sensitive but not a spiritual man. The odd mixture often bothered me. He had never ridiculed my adult conversion, but he was quick to change the topic when spiritual matters came up. It saddened me. It also slowed our relationship.

"I am thinking." I inhaled deeply, then let it out. "That's why we need to hurry."

He led the way to his Ford Excursion, hit the unlock button on his keychain, and moved to the driver's seat. Seconds later we were on our way to Catherine's home. Jerry drove. I called Detective West.

The moon did hang high in the sky, just like the altered screenplay had said. I prayed that was the only thing it was right about.

Catherine's large home had been lovely to see on my first visit, but in the gloom of night and the darkness of fear, it loomed like a haunted house. As we pulled up her drive, I could see a dim yellow light pouring through the foyer windows. No other lights glowed.

Jerry slowed as we approached the house. He released his right hand from the steering wheel and set it on my left arm. "You're staying in the car."

"No, I'm not."

"For once, Maddy, just once, listen to me. We don't know the situation. The police will be here in moments. If you get out and start running around, you'll make their job more difficult."

"Catherine could be hurt." Or worse.

"I'll get out and take a look around. When the police arrive, you can tell them I'm on the property. I don't want to give your Detective West a reason to shoot me."

"Jerry. I can't just sit and wait—"

A motion from the side yard to my right stopped me. Out of the darkness made dim by the moon, a figure staggered into our headlights. It was Catherine. I was out the door a heartbeat later. Jerry called after me. He said something else but I couldn't hear it.

"Catherine!"

"Maddy? Maddy!" She ran to me.

I started for her. She was still wearing the gown she had been wearing in the last scene before intermission. In the glow of the headlights I could see that things were different. Her hair was ruffled and her gown was askew. It was also streaked with blood.

"Catherine. Are you hurt?"

"No, no, no. I'm ... he's ..." She looked over her shoulder.

He? I thought of the script and the character called INTRUDER and his words about "body count."

Jerry slipped to our side. He looked Catherine over. "Where are you hurt?"

"I ... I'm not ... he's ... he's ..."

"Get in the car," Jerry ordered.

"But—" Catherine began.

"Now." Jerry was done talking. He seized Catherine by the arm and forced her toward his SUV. I followed. He opened the rear passenger door. "Get in. You too, Maddy."

"Do you think—"

"Shut up and get in."

Shut up? I did as I was told and climbed into the back. Jerry trotted around the car and took his seat behind the wheel. He started the engine and dropped it into reverse.

"He's hurt," Catherine said. "Andy. Andy Buchanan. He's in the backyard. He's not moving."

Jerry looked back at the house. *Doctor* Jerry was thinking of a helpless, wounded man. *Friend* Jerry was thinking about two women who might be in danger. He had just pressed the accelerator and started the SUV back down the driveway when the air filled with red and blue lights. I turned and saw a patrol car pull through the gate followed by an unmarked car. Another squad car trailed in.

Jerry hit the brake and slammed the gear selector into park. He popped his door and exited. "In the back," he called.

The lead car stopped and a uniformed officer emerged. In the mix of moonlight, police car headlights, and emergency lights, I could see he had drawn his weapon. "On the ground! Facedown!"

"You don't understand."

"On the GROUND!"

Jerry disappeared from sight as he lowered himself to the driveway. The officer approached. A movement to my right made me jump. An officer with his gun pointed at the car was moving closer.

"Don't move," I told Catherine.

"Why are they doing this?"

"Because they don't know who we are yet. We'll be fine in a moment. Just do as the officers say."

The glare of a flashlight hit me in the eyes and I winced. The light moved around the interior of the SUV in a jerky motion. Another light came through the back window. My mouth went dry.

"Step out of the car, hands above your head." The officer's voice was muffled by the closed window. I reached for the door latch and slowly opened the door. Putting my hands before me, I slipped from the seat. "Step away from the vehicle. Hands over your head. Turn around."

I once watched West help make one of these stops. He called it a felony stop in which everyone was assumed to be armed and dangerous. In less than twenty minutes I had gone from nibbling vanilla bean ice cream in the comfort of a balcony room in the Curtain Call theater to being ordered around like a felon.

"Take two steps back—"

"Hold it." I recognized the voice. It sounded wonderful. West.

"Mayor?"

"Yes."

West stepped forward, looked at me, and looked inside the car. "You can lower your hands."

"That's Jerry you have on the ground," I said.

He smiled at that. "They're clear. Let him up," West said.

His smile eroded when I said, "Catherine said there's someone injured in the backyard. She said it's Andy."

"Andy Buchanan?"

"Yes."

Jerry rounded the car. West eyed him sternly. "Get them out of here, Doc."

"That's what I was trying to do."

"Well, try again." He looked at the other officers. "There may be a man down. The perp may still be on the grounds. Watch each other. Let's go." West moved forward and to the side of the house.

"Come on," Jerry said. "We'll have to walk. The police have me boxed in." Again he took our arms and started walking us down the drive. I glanced over my shoulder and saw West and two officers make their way into the shadows, guns drawn and at the ready.

chapter 21

Andy Buchanan was dead.

The twenty-seven-year-old son of Catherine's producer Charles Buchanan lay in repose upon a deck chair on the upper terrace overlooking the pool, his arms and legs akimbo. His brown hair was askew and his blue eyes gazed over the distant ocean as if counting the moonlight jewels left on the undulating surface. Earrings still hung from their holes. He wore black jeans, black sneakers, and a black T-shirt.

He seemed at peace and the illusion would have been more convincing if not for the ugly round hole in his forehead. The other chairs were scattered about, and leaning against the terrace wall were the landscaper's tools I had seen before.

I walked from the terrace, up the stone steps to the patio where Catherine waited with Jerry and one of the officers. West escorted me.

"You okay?" His voice was soft and kind.

"No. I feel sick."

"If you're going to toss your cookies, I'd prefer that you not do it on my crime scene."

"I don't mean that kind of sick. I feel . . . stunned. Two murders at Catherine's home. I don't think I've ever heard of anything like this."

"It's not normal, that's for sure. Speaking of things not being normal . . ." He stopped while we were still out of earshot of those on the patio. "How well do you know your cousin?"

"That's an odd way to back into a question. What do you mean 'speaking of things not being normal'?"

"It was a poor way to begin. I'm sorry."

"Are you saying that Catherine isn't normal?" The question irritated me.

"I'm just asking how well you know her."

"Fairly well. I'm older than she so we didn't pal around as kids. The family would get together at holidays and birthdays. Why?"

"There's a reason I wanted you to see the body," West said. He looked back at the lifeless Andy.

"You said you wanted me to see things so I could confirm your identification. To be honest, I thought that was an odd statement. You don't need my confirmation. You talked to him earlier today."

"It was all I could come up with," he admitted. "You've spent a fair amount of time with Catherine these last two or three days, right?"

I agreed.

"Has she been acting weird?"

"Weird. Is that a police term? What do you mean weird?" I felt defensive.

"Mayor, I know all this has been rough on you, but it hasn't been a picnic for me either. I'd appreciate a little support here. Now, has she been acting strange?"

"Not that I've noticed. She's been a little reserved, but I'd expect that from someone who finds a dead body in her pool. Her schedule is full, and I'm getting the idea that she's under a lot of pressure."

"But nothing else you'd categorize as being unexpected or out of the norm?"

"Not really. What are you getting at?"

"You saw the blood on her dress?" He started to look at her but caught himself.

"Of course. It's hard to miss."

He blinked a few times as if waiting for me to see the obvious. When it was clear I wasn't putting two and two together, he asked, "Where did it come from?"

"Andy's body, I suppose—" I looked back at the corpse in the chair. There had been very little blood. As with the first victim, there had been an entrance wound but no exit wound. A small streak of crimson ran from the young man's forehead to his nose, but that was all. The rivulet of red didn't look smeared. "I don't know. You'll have to ask her."

"I plan to," West said. "I plan to ask her several things."

"You don't think she had anything to do with this, do you? That's ridiculous."

"Is it? My job is to keep an open mind about everything I see and everyone I meet. Right now I have a young woman who lives alone in a gigantic house and has had two people—both of whom were closely associated with her—murdered on her property. A script goes missing and the replacement copy contains an accurate rendering of your private conversation with her. I've been over the house with a surveillance expert and we could find no listening devices. That means that someone was in the house with you listening to your words, or—"

"Or one of us wrote it down."

"Exactly. And both of you told me that Catherine searched the house for Ed Lowe."

"I doubt she checked the closets," I protested.

"Do you think that someone hidden in a closet could have heard your conversation in the living room?"

"Maybe. It's possible."

"But not likely." He gazed into my eyes and I saw a sadness tucked behind a steely determination. "Did you see her first movie?"

"No. My parents did. They were very proud. The movie came out at a bad time for me. I kept meaning to go see it."

"The director's cut just came out on DVD."

"Director's cut?"

"The version the director intended. Movies are often edited after the director is done, usually to shorten the running time or to remove something that might be offensive."

"Since when is Hollywood concerned about being offensive?"

"You've got a point there, but my understanding is that some scenes may get cut to avoid a possible lawsuit, avoid copyright infringement, or simply because the producers don't like it. The point is, a director's cut will have all the scenes the director thinks belong." He paused. "I got my hands on one of the DVDs and watched it last night—or early this morning, I should say."

"And?"

"The movie is a mystery/suspense, a woman-in-peril kind of thing. There's a scene in it in which the bad guy is seen loading a .38 revolver. He's loading it with Glaser blue-tips. These DVDs often have extras to entice consumers to buy a movie they've already seen at the theater. Some, like this one, have a director's commentary. The movie plays and the director does a voice-over explaining interesting facts about the scene, funny stories, problems, and the like."

"And the director mentions the scene was cut," I said, anticipating where West was headed.

"Exactly. The producers nixed the scene because they thought it slowed the story down. Here's my point. In the theater release of the movie, no mention is made of Glaser blue-tip bullets. The writer intended it to be a key factor, but all references to the bullet type were edited out. Unless you're an avid shooter, a cop, or a gun nut, you've probably never heard of that particular ammunition."

"I had never heard of it until you mentioned it," I said. "So you see a connection?"

"I see a *possible* connection. There's something else," West said, lowering his voice. "You sat through the script meeting today, right?"

"Much of it. I was with you in Rockwood's office. They continued while we met."

"Did you get the gist of the plot?"

I felt stupid. "Yes. It's about a young woman who slowly loses her mind. But you can't be saying that Catherine is living out the script. I don't recall people being shot in the head."

"They are in the first movie," West said. "In the new movie, a model is stalked by a killer who murders to get her attention. She may be pulling from both movies."

"How can you know so much about the new movie? You were interviewing people and not in the reading—You read the script you took for fingerprints."

He nodded. "I had the fingerprint people make a copy of it for me, which, by the way, was no easy task. Do you know how difficult it is to make a photocopy of yellow paper? Anyway, I read the whole thing. I also got a fresh copy from Buchanan before I left Hollywood. I made a comparison. They were identical with the exception of the added pages in Catherine's copy."

"What are you going to do?" I knew I wasn't going to like the answer.

"I have a hundred questions, and I'm afraid some of the answers lay with your cousin." He gave me a sorrowful stare. "I'm stretching investigative protocol here, Mayor, but I'm going to give you a heads-up. I'm going to take Ms. Anderson in for some questioning."

"You're not serious. She's a victim—"

He raised a finger, cutting me off. "Maddy, don't make me regret giving you advance warning. I'm doing so because she's related to you. I'm using kid gloves here. Anyone else would have a tougher go of things."

"But you can't arrest her. She's been through too much."

"I didn't say I was going to arrest her. I'm going to detain her for questioning. She won't be under arrest, but she does have a right to an attorney. I want you to help me."

That angered me. "Help you do what?"

"Advise her to cooperate."

I felt sick before; now I felt completely drained of strength. None of what West was suggesting seemed right, but there was logic to it. "I'm going in with her."

"That's not advisable."

"You want my help or not?"

His face hardened. West didn't enjoy being manipulated any more than I did. "You make certain you don't interfere—Madam Mayor."

A voice drew my attention to the patio. A new figure stood with Catherine and Jerry. "Oh, brother," I said. "You're life just got more complicated." Franco Zambonelli had arrived with the finesse of an army tank.

I followed West up the stone steps and approached the small gathering on the patio. Jerry and West exchanged hard, rigid glances. They shared a mutual dislike of each other and expressed it in the coldest professional manner.

"Doc?" West said.

"I can't do an exam out here, but she insists she is unhurt."

Catherine stood, appearing more child than adult, her hands folded in front of her. Her lace gown was soiled with blood, the hem brown from where it had scraped the still incomplete landscaped yards. Her shoes were dirty.

"Of course, she's okay," Franco said loudly. "She's a trooper. Nothing gets her down." He put his arm around her, and Catherine appeared to shrink before my eyes. Maybe it was the moonlight, but she looked wan, thin, and flimsy.

"I know this has been hard on you, Ms. Anderson, but I'm going to need to ask you some questions."

"Can't you see that she's been traumatized, Officer?" Franco said. "She's not answering any questions tonight." He started to steer her away. "Come on, baby. I'll take you away from all of this."

"Mr. Zambonelli, no one is leaving until I say so."

"That a fact?" Franco blurted.

"Yes, it is a fact," West said. I saw his jaw clench. I expected a grimace but saw a small smile.

Franco spun around. "I don't like being pushed around, buddy."

"I'm going to have to ask you to stand over there," West said. He motioned to the corner of the patio.

"I don't have to stand anywhere I don't want."

West took a step closer, and I took two back. So did Jerry.

"You need to listen to the detective," Catherine said. "Don't be stupid."

"All my life, his kind has pushed me around. I know my rights. No Andy of Mayberry cop is going to treat me like a criminal. I'm just here to protect your rights, baby."

West maintained his humorless smile. "Please stand over there until I call for you, Mr. Zambonelli."

"I'm staying put, pal." He poked West in the chest with an index finger. I cringed.

In movement that was almost too fast for my eyes to register, West had snatched the offending hand and twisted it until

Zambonelli was bent over. West jerked the man's right arm behind him and twisted his hand in a painful-looking direction. Zambonelli cried out. "What are you doing? Ow. Stop. Stop."

The uniformed cops must have heard his cries. Four of them arrived en masse. "Hey, Tom," West said to one of the officers. "This guy just assaulted me. How about cuffing him and putting him in the back of your car while I decide whether to press charges."

"I didn't assault you."

"I think you did." West handed Franco off to the other officer.

"Was that necessary?" Catherine asked.

"Yes, it was. There are a few other things that are necessary. I need you to come down to the station with me."

"Can't you ask your questions here?" Her pale skin had gone white.

"It would be better if we were down at the station. Scientific investigation and the medical examiner have work to do. We'll just be in their way."

Catherine looked at me, pleading for help.

"You should go," I said. "I'll go with you."

West cut me a look of disapproval but said nothing.

"Do I have to ride in the back of a police car?"

"I'm certain Detective West would let us drive you down," I said. "Isn't that right, Detective?" *You asked for my help. This is my brand of helping.*

"As long as you go straight to the station." He directed his words at me.

A clanking caught my attention. Two men with a gurney had been led through the house to the patio. The medical examiner and crew had arrived. With them was a thin, African-American officer. She walked straight to West.

"You requested a female officer, Detective."

He didn't answer her directly. Instead, he spoke to Catherine. "This is Officer Sharon Brock. She's going to accompany you while you change into some more comfortable clothing. I'm afraid that dress is evidence."

"The dress!" Catherine sputtered. "I ran out on the play. I ran off with the dress!"

I tried to calm her. "Harold said the understudy would cover for you."

"She can't. This is the only dress for that scene. I've ruined the play." She began to weep. The mounting waters had topped the emotional dam. It was giving way. The dress was the last straw.

"I'll take care of this," I told West. "Come on. Let's get you changed."

"Mayor," West said. "Officer Brock must go with you. It's a chain of evidence thing."

"Fine, fine. Let's go." I walked Catherine toward her home.

chapter 22

I stood in the viewing area adjacent to the interrogation room of police headquarters. The Santa Rita police department was housed in a mission-style building separated from city hall by a parking lot. Most of the rooms were austere, including the one in which I now waited. Only the foyer, the only room most of the law-abiding public saw, had any flair. Its interior was contemporary, which stood in stark contrast with the California mission exterior.

It felt odd to stand in the narrow room, looking through a see-through mirror at Catherine, now dressed in slacks, tennis shoes, and a gray, unmarked sweatshirt. I had seen such rooms on television but to actually be in one made me feel out of place. Jerry stood beside me. West allowed us to watch as a concession, one he gave begrudgingly. One day, I would no longer be mayor and my ability to stretch privilege would be at an end. I wondered if I could leverage the same kind of favoritism if I won the congressional election. I doubted it.

The door to our dark room opened, then closed. Bill Webb walked in, bringing a goose bump–raising chill with him. He eyed me in a way that made it clear I had once again gotten under his skin.

His face bore the same look of pain that it always did. I tried to remember the last time I saw him smile.

Bill Webb wore the title chief of police, and he wore it proudly. Santa Rita was fortunate to have him. He ran a tight ship, played by the book, and was as dedicated a man as I have ever met. I held his abilities and his position in high regard. The man, however, was a different matter. He was honest, forthright, determined, and possessed a hundred other commendable qualities, but he irritated me beyond endurance. My only comfort was that I had the same effect on him. Over the years, we had butted heads over finances. He wanted more, and I wouldn't give it to him. The money just wasn't there, and he blamed me for it. Every year he'd ask for more money in the budget to hire personnel and to improve equipment; each year I gave him less than he wanted. He was never glad to see me, and I had only been glad to see him once—when he saved my life.

I thought that formative event would change our relationship. It didn't.

A second after Webb entered the viewing area, Judson West entered the interrogation room. I saw Catherine stiffen and my heart melted.

"Detective West said you'd be here," Webb said, his voice low. "He said you've been helpful."

"I want to be here for Catherine," I said, matching his tone. "She's been through a lot for someone her age."

"It wouldn't be any easier if she were older."

"You're probably right," I said. "You know Dr. Jerry Thomas, don't you, Chief?"

"We've met." He gave Jerry a nod.

Voices, picked up by a microphone in the room, played over a speaker mounted in the ceiling.

"I'm sorry to keep you waiting, Ms. Anderson. I needed to report to the chief. May I get you a drink? Water? Coffee? Soda?"

"No, thank you." Catherine's voice cracked and so did my heart.

"First, let me say you are *not* under arrest. You are free to leave at any time. Do you understand that?"

"Yes. Maddy said my being here might help you."

"We hope so. We want to catch the murderer as soon as possible." He cleared his throat. "I also need to inform you that you have a right to have an attorney present during questioning. Previously, you declined an opportunity to call a lawyer. Would you like to do so now?"

"No."

"One last thing before we begin. I wish to inform you I am recording this meeting. Do you understand that?"

"I do." She put her hands on the table, wringing them as if trying to wipe away a stain.

"Earlier this evening you were performing in a play at the Curtain Call dinner theater but left to go to your home. Can you tell me what prompted that?"

"You already know."

"Yes, I do, but I'm trying to create a time continuity. I want to know things in order."

"Okay. I understand, I think." She swallowed. "We were at intermission. I was in a room backstage where the actors meet. One of the theater's employees brought me the movie script, the second one you have now. It scared me."

"Why did it frighten you?" West asked.

"Because I had already picked up a new script, and I wasn't expecting another. And . . . and I was afraid there would be pages like the other pages."

"Like the ones in the script brought to you by Andy Buchanan?"

At the mention of Andy's name, Catherine began to tear up. She dabbed at her eyes with a finger. "Poor Andy. What will his father say? Poor Chuck. Has anyone told him? He should know. Someone should tell him."

"It was another reason I was late," West said. "I called him."

"Thank you," she whispered. "I don't think I could have done it."

"Ms. Anderson, do you know the employee who brought you the script?"

She shook her head. "Tonight was the first time I had seen her."

"How do you know she's an employee?" West pressed.

"She had a name tag. One of those plastic tags with the name of the theater on it. She wasn't a waitress. I think she worked the gift shop."

"What did you do after she handed you the script?"

"I got scared. I made myself look for the pages that someone put in the script Andy brought. You know, the one I needed to replace the one gone missing. Those pages weren't there, but there were others. I was afraid someone was in trouble, so I raced home."

"Why didn't you call the police?"

"I don't know."

"Ms. Anderson," West asked softly. "How did you get from the theater to your home? Mayor Glenn dropped you off, and to my knowledge you don't have another chauffeur, and you didn't have a car available."

That was a good question. I wondered the same thing.

"I took a cab."

"A cab? A taxi." West cocked his head to the side. "You called for a cab?"

"No. There was one waiting in the parking lot. Why are you looking at me that way?"

"Well, Ms. Anderson, I understand that you grew up in Santa Rita, then moved to New York. You should know that while we certainly have taxis in the city, you don't find them on every street corner. If you want a cab in this town you have to call for one."

"I didn't call for one," Catherine said. She was becoming defensive again. "I ran out to the parking lot and saw a cab. I took it."

"How did you pay for it? I mean, you were still in your costume, right?"

"I grabbed my purse before I left. It's instinctive with women." She leaned back, putting another foot of distance between her and West.

Chief Webb leaned my direction. "You can bet Detective West will double-check that."

I chose not to comment. My mind was racing. West had been right. Unlike megacities, cabs in Santa Rita didn't wait at key locations for a fare. They'd starve. Southern Californians were fiercely loyal to their cars. Only those who couldn't drive or needed a ride to the train station or airport called for a taxi.

"So the cab dropped you off at your home. Then what?"

"I ran up the drive and into the house."

"Was there anyone in the house?"

Catherine replied, "No, but the patio light was on. I pulled back the curtains, just like the new pages in the script said, but there was no intruder. I opened the rear door and—"

"Was it locked?"

Catherine thought for a second. "I don't remember unlocking it, but I may have. It's all a little blurry. Anyway, I went out on the porch. I didn't see anyone ... not at first. Then I saw ... I saw Andy in the chair."

"Did you realize something was wrong?"

"No. Not at first. He was on the terrace near the pool. I was still on the patio. The patio is higher up the slope than the terrace. I guess you know that. You were there."

"That's all right. So you saw Andy Buchanan in the chair. Did you recognize him at that time?"

She wrung her hands again. "No. Well, sort of. He has that curly brown hair. Very distinctive. It looked like it could be Andy. I went to see."

"Weren't you frightened?"

"Terrified, but the script had me ... that is, Lacy ... pleading for someone's life. I had to make sure it wasn't Andy and that he was all right."

"So alone and at night, after reading pages of a script that frightened you, you descended the stone stairs to approach someone who might be Andy."

"That's right. I know it wasn't wise, but I wasn't thinking clearly." Her lower lip began to quiver. "I saw ... I saw it was Andy and there was a ... there was ..."

"That's all right, Ms. Anderson. I know what you saw. Tell me what you did next."

I stole a look at Jerry who looked pained at hearing this.

"I heard a car out front. I ran to the drive to get help."

"You didn't touch the body?"

"No. Of course not."

West said nothing, but waited, giving Catherine more time. She added nothing. "Ms. Anderson. The dress you were wearing, the one I asked you to change out of and give to the woman officer, was streaked with blood. How did blood come to be on the dress?"

At first, Catherine looked confused, then she said, "Oh. It's not blood. Well, it's not real blood. It's stage blood."

My mind ran back to the first time I saw Catherine in the Curtain Call. Blood was oozing from her dress. It had been part of the rehearsal.

"It looked like blood to me," West said.

"That's the idea, Detective. It's supposed to look real. In the third act, I'm supposed to be wounded."

"So, when we test the dress we'll find nothing but food coloring?" West pressed.

"You won't even find that. Food coloring stains the costume. Stage blood is designed to clean up quickly."

"So you had just been preparing for the next scene?"

"Yes. I carry a capsule of stage blood in the next scene. I get shot, and I'm supposed to squeeze the packet. The packet must have had a leak, and I wiped my hands on my dress. As I said, I was pretty shaken by the script." She paused, then asked, "What's happened to Franco?"

"He's fine. He's being detained for assault."

"He didn't really assault you. He just touched you."

"Mr. Zambonelli was interfering with my investigation," West said. "But don't worry. I'll cut him loose soon."

"I would appreciate it," Catherine said.

West ignored the comment. "Were you expecting Andy Buchanan to be at your home?"

"Not at all."

"Any idea why he might have been there? Did he say anything to you at the reading today?"

"We barely spoke," Catherine said. "I don't know why he was there."

The questioning went on for another half hour but nothing new came of it. I listened to every word but felt more befuddled than when it all began. I only knew one thing:

Something wasn't right.

chapter 23

"What now?" Jerry asked.

"Back to the theater," I said, slipping into the passenger seat of Jerry's car. I browbeat Chief Webb and Detective West into making promises to keep me posted and to let me know as soon as Catherine was free to go. They drew the line at letting me talk to her before I left, claiming that they wanted to avoid any "appearance of evil."

Jerry started the car. "What a night. I can't believe West took you down to see the victim. What was up with that?"

"He wanted to separate me from Catherine. He had questions." I buckled my seat belt.

"What kind of questions?" He backed out of the stall and moved us through the parking lot and on to the street.

"He wanted to know if Catherine has been acting strangely. If he thinks Catherine is part of murder, then he's on the wrong track."

"Why? Women can't kill?"

"Does Catherine look like a killer to you?"

"I'm not sure appearance is proof of innocence or guilt. Did you tell him about her problem?"

I looked at Jerry. Streetlights cast puddles of light on the road, puddles that oozed into the car as we drove beneath their light fall. "What problem?"

"Oh, surely you noticed, Maddy. You've spent time with her. I noticed it last night."

"What? When we were having pie?"

"Exactly. How much pie did she eat?"

Why is everyone turning against her? "I don't know. A piece."

"Try a half of a slice of pie. And when she ate it she did so in a very specific way. Her teeth never touched the fork."

"So? I don't know where you're going with this."

Jerry steered toward the freeway and pressed the accelerator. "Let me ask you something. How much have you seen her eat?"

"Jerry. This is ridiculous."

"Stop being obstinate. How much have you seen her eat?"

The question came out of nowhere, and I had to give it some thought. "The first evening at my place I came downstairs and she was sitting at the table eating apples and cheese. She had prepared it herself."

"Anything unusual?"

"I don't know how unusual it is, but she had all the cheese and apple slices lined up. Come to think of it, she stopped eating when I appeared. She drank her tea, however."

"Was that her dinner for the night?"

"No, Nat brought grinders over and—"

"Wait. Nat brought grinders, and you didn't invite me?"

"It was one of those spontaneous things. It was Nat's idea. Floyd had come over with some information from the office, and we sat around eating the sandwiches. Don't worry, I won't tell you how delicious they were."

"Thanks. I'm not going to let the fact Floyd was included and I wasn't bother me."

"Weren't you stuck at the hospital? You couldn't have come anyway."

He snorted. "It's the principle of the thing. What did Catherine do with the sandwich?"

"She ate . . ." That wasn't right. "She picked at it. Come to think of it, she didn't eat at the rehearsal party at the theater." I pondered each time I had been with Catherine when food was present and in each case she did little more than nibble. "Do you think she has an eating disorder—but that can't be right. I was with her when she changed out of the costume into the clothing she's wearing now. She's thin but not painfully so."

"I'm not suggesting she's afflicted with anorexia nervosa. In fact, I suspect it's something else."

He had me now. "Like what?"

"I shouldn't be guessing. There are several possibilities and only a proper medical workup including a psych eval could tell."

"Guess anyway."

"Most of the time she's very much in control," he said. "Does that seem true?"

"Yes."

"I wonder if she has a variation of OCD."

"Obsessive-compulsive disorder? You mean like constant hand washing, overorganizing, that sort of thing?"

"That sort of thing, but I'm overgeneralizing. All I've got to base this on is what you've told me and what little I've seen. It might be as simple as not wanting to eat in the presence of others. I had an aunt who felt that every time she ate, people were staring at her, silently making fun of her. It was all in her imagination, but that didn't matter—it was real to her."

"What would cause that?" I asked, suddenly wearied by yet another problem to think about.

"I can't say without some evidence to go on. I wouldn't doubt her sudden rise to fame might have something to do with it."

"Her star did rise fast. A successful start in New York, a starring role on Broadway, and a hit movie. She would have to grow up fast."

"And where was her family?" Jerry asked as he brought the car to freeway speeds and melded into seventy-mile-an-hour traffic.

"Her family—my family—are very tight."

"Where are her parents?"

"Well, they moved to Boise."

"And she was in New York and Hollywood. Very different cultures and the anchors of her life were hundreds of miles away. How social was she in school?"

"As I remember, not very social at all. She's always been a private person. What does this have to do with two murders?"

"Detective West asked you about odd behavior. He needs to know about this."

"I can't imagine that they are in any way related," I protested.

"Again, I'm not saying it is, but West needs as much information as he can get. This doesn't mean that Catherine is a double murderer, but someone is. Any information that may lead to an arrest may be information that saves a life—maybe Catherine's life."

I pulled my cell phone from my purse and placed a call to Judson West.

Jerry pulled into the near-empty parking lot of the Curtain Call. A half-dozen cars were parked at the lot's distant end. Employees still on shift, I assumed. Jerry pulled close to the entrance door, not bothering to line his car between the white lines of the parking stall. I stepped to the pavement and closed the door behind me. A chill ran through me as the breeze whispered past my face. I couldn't decide if the chill was outside trying to get in, or inside me trying to get out. Either way, I was starting to feel miserable.

Jerry, ever the gentleman, rounded the car and put his arm around my shoulders, guiding me to the door. I was capable of finding the door without aid or fear of tripping, but I made no complaints. A strong arm nearby was a blessing.

Since the theater was closed, I expected the glass entrance doors to be locked. They weren't. Jerry opened the door, and we stepped into the warmth of the foyer. The aroma of dinner and coffee still wafted in the air. When we first stepped into the theater earlier that evening, the place was abuzz with a hundred conversations as servers dashed about, each dressed in a tuxedo. Now the place was filled with the clatter of chairs being moved, dishes being stacked, and the loud voices of employees shouting words across the dining area.

We moved from the foyer to the theater. The white tablecloths that had draped the tables with elegance were gone, leaving bare folding tables that had borne too many meals, been kicked and elbowed by too many patrons. The lights were bright, revealing a carpet that bore stains of previous shows. The stage curtains were pulled back, leaving the stage open for critical scrutiny. In the bright lights the backdrops and props seemed common and unbelievable. The mystery I had felt a short time ago when the play ran at full speed had melted through the cracks in the floor.

"I'm sorry, we're closed." The voice came from my left. I turned to see Neena Lasko approaching. "Oh, Mayor Glenn, Dr. Thomas. I didn't realize it was you."

"I should have called," I said.

"No, no. Of course not. Don't be silly. Can I get you anything? I think the coffeepot is still full."

The thought of coffee in my acid-roiling stomach had no appeal. I declined and so did Jerry. "I thought I'd bring you and Harold up-to-date and maybe ask a question or two."

"Certainly." She looked around. "My crew is cleaning up. Would you be comfortable if we talk onstage? That will keep us out of the way."

"Sure. That'd be fine."

Neena motioned for one of her young employees, a college-age man with shirttail hanging out, to come over, then asked him to set up four chairs center stage. He didn't question the request. We followed Neena to the side steps and mounted the treads until we stood on the boards the actors had trod earlier. Promising to return, she slipped backstage.

"I've always wanted to be center stage," Jerry said. "Maybe I should change careers."

"I've heard you sing; stay with medicine."

"Ouch. Must you always be truthful?" He winked.

The employee had just set the last chair in place when Neena reappeared with Harold Young in tow. He looked worn, drained of energy. We sat.

"How's Catherine?" Harold leaned forward, resting his hands on his knees. He looked pale in the harsh lights.

"Physically, she's fine," I said. "At the moment she's at the police station—helping Detective West with a few questions."

"Police station?" Unlike Harold, Neena sat erect as if she had just graduated from charm school. "I don't understand."

"There's been another murder at Catherine's house." It was a bombshell, and I let it explode in their minds before going on. I wished there had been a kinder way to announce the black news, but I couldn't think of one.

"I can't believe this," Harold said. "I can't believe it. It's not possible."

I wanted to tell him that I had stared at the lifeless face with a neat, round hole in the forehead, but I restrained myself. Harold looked brittle.

"Do you know who the victim is . . . was?" Neena asked.

"His name is Andy Buchanan. His father is Charles Buchanan, the director of Catherine's new movie."

"Do I want to know how he died?" Harold asked.

"Gunshot to the head," I said.

"What's this world coming to?" Harold said. "It seems that every year humanity moves one step closer to complete insanity."

I couldn't argue. "I'm trying to gain a better understanding of what happened tonight."

"I can't tell you much," Neena said. "I was in the office helping with receipts during most of the play. I was with you when Harold told me about Catherine running off."

"That was miserable." Harold pushed back and sucked in air as if he had been holding his breath for the last five minutes. "She ran off in costume. We had to scramble to come up with something for the understudy to wear. Jane did a wonderful job, considering the short notice. The crowd knew something was up when I announced the change in cast. They were kind."

"At least none of them asked for their money back," Neena said.

"Will Catherine be available for tomorrow's performance?"

I thought of West's intimation that Catherine might somehow be involved in the murders. The thought made me angry. "I don't know. She's been through a lot." That was vague enough.

"Of course, of course," Harold said. "I just thought it might help get her mind off things—well, it would be good for the production too, of course. I just mean . . . I don't know what I mean." He rubbed his face. "I suppose I should get the gown back. Jane is going to need it tomorrow."

"That may be a problem," I said. "The police have taken it as evidence."

"Evidence?" Harold snapped. "Evidence of what?"

"It had streaks of what looked like blood," I said.

"Nonsense." He swore. "Idiot police. It's stage blood. One of the cast was messing around backstage and broke one of the packets on a table. He was sitting next to Catherine. That was right before that, that script arrived and ruined everything."

"Do you know who delivered the script backstage?" I asked.

Harold gazed at the floor. He fell silent.

"I do," Neena said. "Her name is Bobbi Millard. She works the small gift shop just off the lobby. She's been with me for better than ten years."

"Is she still here?" I hadn't seen a light from the little shop and was worried that she had left.

"I think so. She usually helps the kitchen crew clean up. We let her take home a couple of plates of food. She's looking out for elderly parents and she doesn't earn enough to keep body and soul together. Do you want me to get her?"

"That would be nice."

Neena excused herself and I focused on Harold. I felt sorry for him. He had spent months pulling this play together and years writing it, and opening night fell apart like Tinkertoys in a hurricane. "Are you okay?"

He looked at me. "No, I'm not okay. This night has been horrible. We pulled it off, but there's a good chance that tomorrow night will be an abysmal failure, especially if Catherine isn't here. There are going to be reporters, right? There are always reporters when there's been a murder. Think of the feeding frenzy that will surround this. I can see the headline now: Famous Actress Flees Theater to Murder Scene."

"Maybe it won't be that bad," Jerry said. "Maybe the news will draw bigger crowds."

The scorn on Harold's face was frightening. "It's not about money, Doc. It's about the play, the art. I poured my life into this project. I almost had to beg Neena to let me produce the play here. The news may put more money in her coffers, but my play will always be associated with murder—no, correction—two murders."

"Certainly you're not blaming Catherine." I struggled to keep my words even. "She's more of a victim than you."

"What? Blame Catherine? Why would I . . . ? Of course not. Catherine is my only claim to fame. I couldn't, I wouldn't blame her for anything. I just wish she had waited until after the play to run off."

"She was frightened out of her wits, Harold. She may be an adult, but only barely so. I wish she hadn't run off either, but she did. We're left with that."

"Here she is," Neena said. "This is Bobbi Millard."

Jerry stood and offered his seat. He then scampered down the stairs and brought up another chair.

"What is this all about?" Bobbi looked nervous and I could guess why. She had been pulled from whatever she was doing in the back and summoned to center stage to be asked questions. Her eyes moved from person to person as if one of us might be holding a weapon. Bobbi Millard was tall, thin, and well into her fifties. Black hair that looked like it might be a wig sat atop her head. Her face bore the deep lines of a lifelong smoker. Her sandpaper voice furthered the assumption.

"Hi, Ms. Millard," I said. "May I call you Bobbi?"

"Um, sure. Why not?"

"Thanks. I'm Maddy Glenn."

I watched as she lowered herself into the chair that moments before had been occupied by Jerry. "Maddy Glenn. Like Madison Glenn, the mayor?"

I smiled. "You'd be surprised how few people know the name of their mayor. You've made my day, Bobbi." She relaxed a little. "Not only am I the mayor, but I'm also Catherine Anderson's cousin. I was here watching the play tonight."

"She's an odd one, she is," Bobbi said. I detected a touch of British accent long worn down by American English.

"I understand you delivered a script to her."

"I don't know if 'delivered' is the right word. I walked it from the lobby backstage and gave it to her. Someone else brought it to the theater. All the color from her face ran to her toes when she saw that thing. I thought I had done something wrong. I figured I was in for a chewing out, her being famous and all."

"Do you know the person who brought it?" I asked.

"Never seen him before. I thought it a tad late for deliveries but I guess some of these services deliver until well after dinner. I've had them come to my door as late as eight o'clock, but that was close to Christmastime so I guess—"

"Which delivery service was it?" I asked before she could regale us about last year's Christmas deliveries.

"UPS, I guess."

"You're not certain?"

"He wasn't wearing the usual brown uniform. I suppose it could have been DHL, but they wear yellow, don't they?"

"I think so," I said. "The person who delivered the screenplay wasn't wearing a uniform?"

"No. Just jeans and a pullover shirt."

Jerry asked, "So the script was in a package. Did you unwrap it before taking it back to Catherine?"

"Of course not. That'd be like opening someone else's mail. I have better manners than that, thank you very much."

"I'm sure you do," I said. "Just one last thing: could you describe the delivery person?"

"I don't see why not." She looked up as if his picture were somewhere among the lights. "He was young with thick curly brown hair and had several earrings. I don't think men should wear earrings. It don't look right."

The room chilled like a freezer. "Do you remember what he was wearing?"

"Sure. He was dressed all in black. Even his tennis shoes were black." She studied me. "You don't look so well, Mayor."

I didn't feel so well. Bobbi Millard had just described the corpse I had seen—Andy Buchanan.

Once back in the car I placed another call to West. I had two reasons for the call. First to tell him I had just learned it was Andy Buchanan who delivered the script, and, second, to see if I could pick up Catherine and take her home.

On the first point, West chewed me out for meddling. I expected that, but I had done nothing more than ask questions about Catherine. I knew that West would interview everyone at the theater. He was that thorough.

On the second point, I was surprised to learn that Catherine was already gone, dropped off at my house.

"So you're ruling out her involvement in the murders," I said.

"I'm not ruling anything out. For now, she's not a likely suspect but I'll keep her on my radar. We tested the dress and discovered that the blood was, well, not blood. Nor could we find any gunpowder residue on her hands or on the dress."

"Who took her to my home?" I asked.

"I did. She said she had a key."

"She doesn't." My words were a breath above a whisper.

"What?"

"I said, she doesn't have a key. I never gave her one."

"Why would she lie about that?"

"I have no idea. You didn't watch her go into the house?"

"No. She said her key was for the back door. She went around back."

I rubbed my forehead. "The only back door I have is a sliding patio door. It unlocks from the inside and doesn't use a key. How long ago was this?"

"Fifteen minutes. I just got back in the office."

My heart was having trouble finding its rhythm. "Jerry and I are headed that way now, but you need to get someone over there and make certain she got in." *Make certain she's still there*, I thought.

West hung up without a word.

"What's up?" Jerry asked.

"We need to get to my house as fast as possible. Catherine is up to something. She lied about having a key to my house. She let West drop her off, knowing that she had no way in."

"That doesn't make sense."

"It does if you don't plan on going in the house."

"Maybe she just wanted out of the police station. I can't imagine a girl her age finding the interrogation room an attractive place."

"No one would find it attractive. I'm worried that she's going to do something stupid."

"Like what?" Jerry said as he pressed the accelerator down.

"Like run away."

 chapter 24

When we arrived on my street, I saw a police car out front. A uniformed officer came from the side yard and marched to his car. Jerry pulled in the driveway and we exited. The officer eyed us suspiciously, then recognized me as I stepped into the penumbra of a streetlight.

"Hello, Mayor," the officer said. His nameplate read David Blake.

"Did you find anything, Officer?"

"No, ma'am. I got here a couple of minutes ago and rang the bell. No answer. No lights. I searched around back but didn't see anyone. The call said to look for a woman outside the house, is that right?"

"Yes. My cousin."

"White female, early twenties—"

Another car drove up. I recognized West's sedan. He parked behind the patrol car. "Anything?"

"Nothing, Detective. I was just telling the mayor that I searched around back."

"Thanks, David. I'll take it from here. You can go 10–8."

"Yes, sir."

Officer Blake entered his car. Before he could start the engine, West was moving to the front door. "Let's check inside."

Jerry and I followed behind him. I started to insert my key when he stopped me. He bent forward and studied the doorknob, then shook his head. "Nothing. Go ahead."

I did and swung open the door. I stepped in and flipped the foyer light switch, then moved to the alarm. It was still set with no indication of open doors or windows.

"Does she know the security code?" West asked.

"No. If she came in, the alarm would be sounding and the alarm company would have dispatched one of your men."

West groaned. "Why would she tell me she had a key when she didn't?"

"To get away from you," Jerry said. *Uh-oh.*

"What's that supposed to mean?" West turned to face Jerry.

"Don't read anything into it, Detective. It's just that you asked some pretty invasive questions. After something like that, I imagine that even your dog would want to get away."

"I was doing my job, Doc. Nothing more."

"I wasn't insinuating anything more."

It was time to step in. "What about her house? Could she have used her cell phone to call a cab and return there?"

"I just talked to the head scientific investigator. They and a few officers are still checking the grounds and house for evidence. I'm due back over there in a few minutes. They checked. She hasn't shown up."

"Maybe she will," Jerry said.

"Perhaps," I said.

"I should have seen her to the door and all the way inside," West said. "I just didn't anticipate this kind of deceit."

We moved into the living room. I waited for Jerry to jump on West's admitted oversight. To my relief, he said nothing.

I crossed the living room, turning on all the lights. I did the same in the dining room and kitchen. I also switched on the rear deck lights.

"What are you doing?" Jerry asked.

"If I was dropped off at a house I couldn't get into, I'd wait for the owner to return. I'd also take a walk along the beach to think things through." I opened the sliding glass door and stepped out onto the deck. The salt air swirled around me and the gentle symphony of two-foot waves stroking the sandy beach played along the shore. Jerry and West joined me.

"So the lights are your version of a beacon calling her home," Jerry said. "You never cease to amaze me."

I strained my eyes against the darkness, hoping to see Catherine's thin form walking along the sands. I was disappointed. Then I gazed out to sea and tried to force out the image of her swimming out to meet death, propelled by guilt or fear. The cold of the thought made my bones ache. I shivered.

"Come inside," Jerry said. "I'll make some tea. We'll wait together." He turned me around and led me into my own house. West closed the door.

"I'll make the tea," I said. "It'll give me something to do. Besides, your tea always tastes like coffee."

"That's because it is coffee."

Jerry and West sat at the table. I started fussing in the kitchen. The open floor plan allowed easy conversation.

"Let me ask you something, Doc," West began. "This stuff that Maddy was saying about Catherine and OCD, could that have anything to do with the murders?"

"To make sure we're clear on this, Detective, I'm not saying Catherine suffers from OCD. I'm just saying that she might have some version of it. I've not spoken with her about it. I've not had more than a few minutes of opportunity to observe her. Besides all of that, I'm not an expert in the field."

"But you've seen it before."

"Many times. Obsessive-compulsive disorder afflicts children too. Usually when I see it, I refer the family to a child psychiatrist where they can receive specialized treatment."

"Children come down with this?" West asked.

I set the teapot on the flames and joined them at the table.

"Most cases begin in adolescence or early adulthood. It affects about 2 percent of the population. It can be so severe that it requires hospitalization or light enough to be little more than a nuisance."

"Then it is a mental illness?" I said.

"Absolutely. It is called obsessive-compulsive because the patient obsesses over something. It can be anything from locks, to germs, to sex, to the fear of hurting someone. Patients feel compelled to repeatedly react to the obsession. For example, if my obsession is cleanliness, then I might sink into a cleaning ritual where I wash my hands twenty or thirty times a day—until my skin is raw and bleeding—but never feel clean. If I have an obsession about locks, then I might spend hours locking and unlocking doors trying to convince myself that they really are secure."

"But Catherine hasn't shown any signs of that," I said. "At least not that I've seen."

"Again, I'm not saying she is OCD, and if she is, it might be mild. In her case, it appears she doesn't like to eat in front of people. Her obsession might be a fear of ridicule and her compulsive response is to avoid eating in public."

"How does someone come down with a disease like this?" West wondered.

"It's not like catching a cold, Detective. The disorder seems to be a combination of psychological and biological influences. Researchers have done brain scans on people with OCD and have observed unusual activities in the orbital cortex, cingulated cortex, and the caudate nucleus—"

"You're losing me, Doc," West said.

"Sorry. There's clinical evidence that part of the problem is rooted in certain brain activity, but there's also a link to some psychological causation. Something bad happens to a child because a door wasn't locked; something especially obnoxious gets spilled on a child and now he never feels clean."

"I hate to think what might trigger an eating condition," West said.

"It may not be that she ate something horrible. Maybe as a child she got sick at school and threw up on herself in class. The kids all laugh and tease her and she anchors that embarrassment to eating in public."

"Is there a treatment available?" I asked. The teapot began to boil but I held my seat. I wanted to hear the answer.

"Some. Every case is different. Sometimes psychotherapy and psychoactive drugs work. Some doctors use what's called 'exposure and response prevention.' That treatment requires that the patient be exposed to the obsession but prevented from engaging in the compulsive ritual."

It took me a second to translate that. "If I have an obsession about germs, the therapist might . . . what? Dirty my hands and then deprive me of a sink in which to wash?"

"Exactly," Jerry replied.

"What about medications?" I asked.

"There has been success with certain serotonin reuptake inhibitors like Prozac or Luvox and a tricyclic antidepressant, like Anafranil. About 80 percent show improvement with medication and therapy, but relapse if they stop taking their prescriptions. Exposure and response prevention works about 60 percent of the time."

"And I thought I was depressed before." I rose and returned to the kitchen. Jerry had been very careful not to say that Catherine was struggling with OCD, but I could see why it crossed his mind.

"Doc, I appreciate all these answers, but what I need to know is this: is she a danger to herself or others?"

"I don't know. I wish I did, but since I don't know what the problem is, I can't be predictive."

"That's not a very helpful answer, Doc," West said.

"No, but it is a very honest one." Jerry looked at me. "I will say this. There have been those who link OCD with certain crimes as well as BPD, borderline personality disorder." He paused. "One psychiatrist said Jeffrey Dahmer showed symptoms of OCD. I wish I could be more help. Perhaps you should talk to a criminal psychologist instead of a pediatrician."

"I might do that, Doc. I just might do that."

I carried the teapot to the table. Jerry jumped up and grabbed cups. "Didn't you tell me that you couldn't find gunpowder residue on Catherine or her dress? Why are you still acting like she's a suspect?"

"I don't think she pulled the trigger that killed Andy Buchanan," West said.

"That's good. It doesn't make sense to think she did."

"Maybe not to you."

chapter 25

When the sun rose, it found me awake and staring at the ceiling. Last night ended quickly. West drank a cup of tea more out of courtesy than desire. It was clear that his mind was elsewhere. He apologized again for not seeing Catherine to the door. The fault was not his. He had been lied to. Nonetheless, he shouldered the blame.

Jerry sat with me for another hour, and we did our best to make small talk but we failed miserably. The ability to focus is one of my strengths, but the utter shock of the last two days had pirated away my ability to marshal productive thought. Mostly I stared at the table and worried about Catherine. The sounding of Jerry's cell phone hauled my weary mind back to the present. I watched as his face drew long and dour.

"I have to go to the hospital," he said and rose.

I read his face. "The boy?"

"Yeah. He's taken a turn for the worse."

I saw him to the door, locked it behind him, and started to reset the alarm. The sight of it made me stop. I decided to leave it off. Instead of sleeping in my bed, I chose to leave the lights on for Catherine and to sleep on the sofa so I'd be sure to hear her if she knocked.

At best, I dozed off and on. The lights bothered me. Every sound outside made my heart lurch. And my mind would not stop fabricating tragedies with Catherine at their center. At 4:00 a.m. I knew she wasn't coming, but I waited anyway. At five I rose, took a quick shower, and dressed for work. At six, I made breakfast. At seven I left. Everything in between was a blur.

I arrived at the office uncertain what the day held. I spent the night fluctuating between worry, confusion, and prayer. I prayed for the phone to ring and I prayed it wouldn't, fearful of the bad news that might be waiting on the other end. It was a late-night phone call that had informed me of my husband's murder. That was years ago, but such scarring doesn't disappear over time. Then I prayed that Catherine would ring my doorbell. She didn't. In the wee hours my prayers dissolved into wordless utterances and those were the sweetest of all.

I took the long way to the office, stopping for a latte at a new coffeehouse. With coffee and a cranberry scone in tow, I returned to my car and to the road. The coffee was wonderful, but I never got around to the scone. Hunger was missing in action.

The clock read seven thirty when I strolled into the lobby and drifted like a powerless ship to the office wing that normally made my blood move faster. The cubicles were empty. By eight, however, aides, secretaries, and employees from various departments would be zipping through corridors and firing up computers. I set a course for my office, entered, and plopped down in the desk chair.

On the desk were messages from yesterday, today's calendar, and two newspapers. I set the coffee down, started the computer on the credenza behind my desk, pushed the message slips aside, and opened the paper. I was beginning my daily routine. It seemed an odd, even selfish thing to do, but I wanted it—needed it.

I set aside the *LA Times* and opened the *Register*. Two articles immediately caught my attention, both below the fold. "Register Reporter In Coma" the title above one article read. The byline read "Vincent Branch, Editor." The article was short, rehashing the auto accident and the missing guardrail, and giving a brief vita of Doug Turner's work with the *Register*. I pushed a tear from my eye and reminded myself that at least the article was on the front page and not the obits. There was no mention of the boy injured by the driver who drove through an intersection where once a stop sign had been. They had not made the connection. For that I was thankful.

The second article was very short and clearly had been added at the last moment. No doubt tomorrow's paper would have a thousand words beginning above the fold. The headline proclaimed, "Second Murder at Starlet's Home." Short as it was, it had the six friends of every journalist: who, what, when, where, why, and how. The words were simple but the reading was hard.

I leaned back in my chair and closed my eyes. I so wanted to sleep, not just because I was weary, but because I wanted to escape. I have prided myself on my fortitude, my strength under pressure, my ability to focus no matter how loud and intense the distraction, but this morning my thoughts were controlling me. They bounced like Ping-Pong balls. Where was Catherine? Who was killing people at her home? Was she mentally ill? Was she involved in the murders? Does she know the killer? Is she the third victim? Those should have been enough questions for any mortal, but I couldn't help asking who was stealing guardrails and stop signs and making our streets unsafe? Would Doug live? Would a child whose only crime was walking to school ever be the same? Could his family be repaired? And what of the poor woman who hit him?

"Napping already?" The words followed a gentle knock on the open door.

My eyes snapped open and I jolted in the chair. Tess stood in the doorway. Someone was with her, standing just behind and to her left. "I wish," I said. "Just lost in thought. You're here early."

"I thought I'd grab a few minutes of your time before the hordes arrived."

"Come in and have a seat."

Tess plunged into the room, a man close behind. He was no taller than Tess, had olive skin, and wore a brown sport jacket around a barrel chest. He gave a polite nod as he entered and took the other seat in front of my desk.

"This is Detective Adrian Scott," Tess announced. "He's been assigned to investigate our little problem."

"Little problem?" The phrase irritated me. Of course, I was so edgy that the beating of a hummingbird's wings would annoy me. "There are two people in the hospital because of the 'little problem.' Dr. Thomas was called to the hospital last night because the boy has taken a turn for the worse."

"It's good to meet you too, Mayor," Detective Scott said.

Already, I disliked the man. We sat in silence for a moment. Scott fidgeted, Tess bore a hole in me with her icy stare, and I was wondering if I had lost my mind.

"I'm sorry," I said, ending the standoff. "It's been a rough couple of days."

"I heard about the murder," Scott said. "Two at the same home." He shook his head.

"Murder?" Tess said.

"Last night," I explained. "A man was killed at Catherine Anderson's home. Detective West is looking into it." I didn't see any need to go into detail.

"West is a good man," Scott said. "I suppose we should enjoy him while we have him."

I nodded. "Yes. You're right . . . What do you mean while we have him?"

"The Denver PD has made him an offer. I know I couldn't turn it down." Scott gave a little laugh.

"He's considering going to Denver?" The news rocked me like an earthquake.

"They've offered him a lead detective position. Much more prestige, much bigger bucks."

"He's lead detective here," I countered.

Scott picked up on my attitude and did a verbal backpedal. "Yes, ma'am. He is."

His mouth was silent on the issue but I could read the unspoken phrases. He's the lead homicide detective in a homicide division of one person—himself.

I beat my emotions back and leaned over the desk. "I'd hate to see him go. He's been an important addition to the force."

"Yes, ma'am," Scott said. "He's taught me many things."

"Well, I don't suppose you're here before office hours to talk about Detective West."

"No, we're not." Tess clipped her words. I had done it again. "I've asked Detective Scott to brief you on the situation as it stands. He came on shift early to do so."

"I appreciate that," I said. "What have you learned?"

"Deputy Mayor Lawrence has been turning up the pressure on us to discover who's behind what we first thought were pranks. Of course, with the two serious injuries, it is no longer a matter of pranks. If either victim dies, we'll be looking at far more serious charges. At Deputy Mayor Lawrence's insistence, I conducted a deeper survey of the extent of the crimes. Working with public works, I've revised her list. As of last night, twenty-two stop signs, six yield, two dip, and two slow curve signs have gone missing. The problem began a month ago."

"If memory serves that's two more stop signs. Is that right?"

"Yes, ma'am," Scott said. "Two more were reported last evening. Still on the list are four fire hydrant caps, one manhole cover, and three segments of guardrail. Everything has been replaced."

"So the problem continues."

"Yes," Tess said. "Chief Webb has put as many officers on the street each shift as he can. We believe the thefts are happening late at night or in the early hours of the morning. I have talked to the principals of every school in the district and asked the superintendents of neighboring districts to do the same. There are a couple of other things you should know."

"Oh?"

"We believe that the perpetrators are local. No other police agency in the region is having the same problem. Also, whoever is doing this is tool savvy."

"What do you mean?" I pressed.

"In some cases signs and even guardrails can be removed with simple hand tools. But the public works department has been retrofitting signs with bolts that require special wrenches to remove. In about a third of the cases, a saw had to be used to remove the sign. In several cases, they sawed right through the pole. I'm assuming it's faster that way."

"What kind of saw would they need?"

"A cordless reciprocating saw would do the trick," Scott said. "With the right blade, that is."

"I'm not familiar with a reciprocating saw," I said, although I remembered someone using the term earlier.

"You've probably seen one. They come in twelve-, fourteen-, and eighteen-volt versions and are battery powered. A single, changeable blade sticks out front. They're used in the construction trade to cut through wood, drywall, and even metal."

"So these kids are unbolting what they can and cutting what they can't?"

"Exactly." Scott was becoming more animated. "But I wouldn't call them kids. They have to be old enough to get their hands on such a tool and know how to use it. I've contacted the high schools and colleges that have shop classes. None report stolen tools."

"They might be using a saw belonging to their parents, or perhaps even have bought their own," Tess suggested.

"But why?" I asked, not expecting an answer. "Surely they know the danger they're creating."

Tess turned to Scott, and he to her as if silently arguing about who got to speak next.

"Detective Scott found something yesterday."

"Oh?" I looked at him.

He took a deep breath. "This is going to be hard to believe, Mayor, but it's as true as me sitting here. While investigating one of the scenes, I found a video setup. They're recording the events or at least some of them."

"What? Why would they do that?"

Scott pressed his lips together. "I can't be sure, but I'll bet this month's salary that they're compiling video footage and plan to sell it."

"Sell it to whom?"

"To the same kind of sick minds that can conceive of this kind of thing," Tess said. "Do you remember a few years ago a pair of young men paid homeless men to fight each other and do other nauseating acts? They preyed on the desperation of the homeless. They video-taped everything and sold it over the Internet."

Scott interjected, "They were arrested and faced several felony and misdemeanor charges."

"People actually bought that kind of footage?" I asked.

"They made a lot of money," Scott said. "I think we may have something similar here, but a little more sophisticated."

"How is it more sophisticated? It sounds like the same barbaric behavior."

"Not more sophisticated in content, but in execution. In the street-fighting case, someone stood around with a camera. It's hard to prove you're not involved when your buddy is filming you paying the men to fight. What I found were inexpensive cameras hooked to a power supply and a small transmitter. I don't have the recorder. I assume it's hidden somewhere where it can be easily retrieved."

"I'm . . . shocked." It was all I could think of to say.

"In a way, this is good news," Scott said.

"I don't see how," I admitted.

"That's why you're mayor and I'm a cop." Scott surrendered a friendly grin. "The good news is that we'll be able to charge the perp with a higher crime if we find the recordings in his possession. By placing a camera at the scene it shows that the nutcase was looking for an accident to occur and therefore contributed to its cause. It's going to be much more difficult to plead, 'It was just a prank. I didn't mean for anyone to get hurt.'"

"So, whoever is doing this knows how to use tools and is familiar with electronics."

"That's right, Mayor," Scott said.

I studied Tess for a moment. She had something rattling around in her brain. "What's on your mind, Tess?"

"It's time to go public. You need to hold a press conference."

"A press conference?"

"Yes," Tess said. "We can't watch every stop sign or supervise every guardrail. Someone is setting up accidents for their own profit. We need to let the public know so they can not only be alert to the problem but also keep an eye out for suspicious behavior. Ask the citizens to help. I was hesitant at first, but it's time."

Scott shook his head. "I've already told Deputy Mayor Lawrence that I'm opposed to the idea. I want to catch this guy. It's going to be much harder to do if he knows the whole city is looking for him."

"It's not unusual for the police to ask for public help or to issue a warning," I said.

"With all due respect, Mayor, it's not unusual for them not to involve the public. The police should decide such matters. In this case, Chief Webb should make the call."

"I see your point," I said. I saw a deep frown pinch Tess's face.

Scott seemed pleased. "That's good, Mayor. I'll tell the Chief that you see it our way."

"No, you won't." I rose. Tess and Detective Scott followed suit. "Your argument is logical but not convincing. My priority is the safety and well-being of our citizens. I want this guy behind bars as soon as possible, but I'm not willing to see another child hit by a car or another citizen roll his or her car down some ravine."

"But, Mayor—"

"Tess, will you set up the press conference?"

"I will." The frown was gone.

"I want you there. I want the public to know who their champion has been."

Scott tried again. "But, Mayor, if you'll only listen."

"Thank you for filling me in, Detective Scott. You have my complete support in your investigation—although you probably don't believe that at the moment."

"No, ma'am. I don't."

chapter 20

I was on the phone with Nat when Chief Webb plowed into my office like a runaway ship crashing into a pier. His face was a dark red, his shoulders pulled back, and his jaw so tightly clamped that I expected to hear teeth shattering any moment.

He arrived with such force my heart seemed to bounce around in my chest as I pushed back from the desk. "Um, I'll have to call you back, Nat," I said and hung up. Webb was breathing in gulps, sucking air through his teeth. I stood and looked at Floyd who had followed him in. It was his job to show guests in, an impossible task in this case. "Close the door behind you, Floyd." He got the idea.

"Won't you sit down, Chief?" I noticed that he had an envelope in his hand.

"No, Madam Mayor, I will not. This will only take a moment." He tossed the envelope on my desk.

"What's this?"

"It's my resignation," he announced, his voice just a few decibels below a shout.

I opened the letter. It was short and neatly typed on police letter-head. I read it aloud. "'Whereas I no longer feel able to lead the fine men and women who make up the Santa Rita police; and whereas my authority is continually undermined by city hall; and whereas my opinion and leadership is routinely ignored, I hereby tender my resignation effective at close of business this date. Signed, Chief William "Bill" Webb.'"

"Well?"

"That's a lot of 'whereas,' Chief."

"So you can't even take my resignation seriously."

"I take it very seriously. Please sit down."

"I prefer to stand."

I sighed and sat, folding my hands on my desk. I said nothing. The thing with Bill Webb is that he's gruff, opinionated, impossible to intimidate, and quick tempered. He's also a man of old values and a believer in authority, even if that authority requires he do something he doesn't wish to do. His mayor was seated and he was not; it was ungentlemanly to hover. Finally, he eased into one of the desk chairs.

"I take it Detective Scott complained to you about our decision to have a press conference."

"He did."

I waited for more but nothing came. "You think the press conference is a bad idea."

"I think when one of my detectives tells you a press conference will interfere with his investigation, you should listen."

"I did listen and I weighed the pros and cons before making a decision."

"He's of another mind."

"Chief," I said. "I know you want to catch this guy. I want you to catch him too, but I also have to be concerned about the legal exposure of the city, the safety of its citizens, and—"

"Please don't lecture me about law and safety, Mayor. I've logged over twenty-five years with a badge."

"Exceptional years, I might add," I said. "Look, we've never gotten along, but I have never once considered you anything less than the finest police chief in the country."

"My resignation stands. I'm tired of your meddling in my department. I'm tired of being told no on budget and hiring issues. It's time you got a new patsy. There are people out there who would kowtow to your every whim."

I glared at him for several moments, holding back what I wanted to say in deference to what I should say.

"Let's go." I shot to my feet and retrieved my purse from the drawer where it rests while I'm in my office.

His angry countenance morphed into confusion. He stood. "Go where?"

"You're going with me. Do you want to drive, or shall I?"

"Are you daft? I just resigned."

"I'm tired, I'm confused, I'm worried sick about one of my relatives, I'm stressed from a campaign I haven't been able to participate in for over a week, I'm sleep deprived and many other things, but I am not now, nor have I ever been, daft." I rounded the desk and opened the door.

"But—" he began.

"Two things, Chief. One, your letter says your resignation is effective at close of business today. My watch says that it's only eight thirty in the morning, so you're still mine. Second, I haven't accepted that letter yet. Let's go."

I marched from my office, glancing at a very pale, stunned-looking Floyd. He had heard it all. Behind me I could hear angry grumbling. At least he was following me.

Webb consented to drive, more to express control than anything chivalrous. We made the drive in arctic silence but we arrived at our destination. I led the way, Webb saying nothing but giving off vibes that threatened to wilt flowers. I kept my head up and my expression neutral. That was proving to be a more difficult job than I anticipated.

As we walked through the automatic glass doors and the lobby, Webb struggled to keep his tongue. I could see it on his face and his ever-deepening scowl. As we strolled through the lobby, we were greeted by the same elderly ladies I had met last time I entered the hospital.

"Excuse me," one said. "You need name tags—"

Webb pulled back his dark suit coat, showing his badge. We walked down the hall, leaving the two volunteers to their bewilderment. Outside the ICU doors, I pressed the call button on the intercom and announced my presence.

"I'm sorry," the unseen nurse said. "These are not visiting hours. The hours are posted on the placard below the intercom." The wall speaker went silent.

"Excuse me," Webb said. He pushed the button. The same voice answered. "This is Chief of Police Bill Webb. Send your supervisor out or let us in. I don't care which you do."

There was silence for a moment, then the double doors swung open. We entered but stopped the moment we saw a wide and determined nurse. Her hands were planted on her hips.

"I had better see a badge pretty quick or there's going to be trouble."

She was frightening. Webb removed his badge from his belt and held it out. "Will this do?"

"I suppose," she said. "How can I help you?"

I thought it wise if I took over. "I'm Mayor Madison Glenn, and you've just met Chief Webb. Two of your patients were involved in accidents being investigated by the police."

"You're talking about Mr. Turner and little Byron Slater."

Byron Slater. I was awash in shame. I had never asked the boy's name. He was just Jerry's patient or "that six-year-old boy."

"That's right," I said.

"Neither is in a position to talk to you. I'm afraid you've wasted your time."

"We're not here to talk to them," I said. "We won't bother them; we just need a few minutes."

She gave us the once-over. Webb could intimidate paint off walls, but he seemed to have no sway with this woman. "Be certain you don't disturb them." She turned and returned to her place behind the nurse's counter.

I led Webb to the cubicle that held Doug Turner. Doug looked the same as when I last saw him: frail, swollen, bruised, bandaged, and almost unrecognizable. "He's a pain at times," I said, "but he always dealt squarely with me."

Webb said nothing. He studied Doug for a few minutes but seemed unmoved. Over twenty-five years of police work, I knew he had seen more than I could imagine.

"Last word I had was that he was still in rough shape," I added. I couldn't say anything more. "Come with me." I led Webb to little Byron Slater's cubicle. Like Doug, he was attached to tubes, heavily bandaged, and his face was swollen. Both eyes carried black bruises beneath them. It seemed wrong for someone so young to be so battered and broken.

This time, Webb wasn't so stoic. He stared at the lad and the harsh, granitelike scowl softened. "I hate seeing kids busted up. I can't get used to it."

"I don't think we're supposed to get used to it." I felt flush.

"You probably don't know this," Webb said, "but I almost ruined my career when I was a patrol officer."

"I didn't know that."

"I was called to a disturbance at a grocery store. It must have been twenty, no, twenty-three years ago. Some man was yelling at his wife and son. Right there in the canned vegetable aisle. I had just rounded the corner when I saw him backhand the kid. The boy couldn't have been more than four or five."

"That's horrible."

"I approached, and as I did, I felt something snap in my brain. I pride myself on my control but I lost it that day."

"You pride yourself on your *control*?"

"Have you ever known me to do more than bluster?"

"No, I guess not, but you've got that blustering thing down pretty good."

His eyes didn't move from Byron. "Anyway, I told him to back away from his family. He refused. I continued forward. He took a swing. Caught me on the right jaw."

"Couldn't get out of the way?" I guessed.

"Didn't want to. I wanted the blow to land."

What? "Why would you want to do that?"

"Assault on a police officer is a serious offense. The punch hurt in the most wonderful way. I had my excuse."

"What did you do?"

"I arrested him. I arrested him real hard." He shrugged. "Some thought I might have been a little rough. No charges were brought. I got a nonpunitive reprimand in my employment file. It didn't affect my career, but I still can't look at a boy his age without hearing that backhand."

There was a pause. "I have a grandson his age." He nodded at the comatose Byron. "That boy is nothing but a sack of energy. He's wearing his parents ragged, but he lights up a room when he enters."

"This is why I have to do the press conference, Chief. I don't think I could live with myself if another little boy ends up in this place. I know it might interfere with the investigation. I know that it might drive the criminal into hiding so we never find him, but it might also help. Even if it doesn't, and another Doug Turner or little Byron Slater ends up in a hospital bed, I'll be able to say, I tried everything I knew to try."

I paused and stared at the child. "I'm not trying to meddle, Chief. From time to time our authorities cross paths. I must do what I think is best, just as you must, but it is never personal. I don't think you know how much I admire you."

"Admire? Me? I've given you more grief than you deserve."

I grinned. "I think I probably deserved more than I got."

Webb's eyes moistened. "You never get used to this, Mayor. I've seen children killed in auto accidents, suicides, even murdered. It never gets any easier."

"Let's pray that it never does."

"Come on, I'll take you back to the office," Webb said. "I seemed to have left some trash on your desk."

I reached out and gave his arm a squeeze. It was the closest thing to a hug that Webb would allow.

We thanked the nurse who seemed to have softened in the few minutes we were in her domain, but also seemed relieved to have us go. We passed through the double doors and into the hall. Just across the corridor was the waiting room. Something familiar caught my eye. A second later, I realized the something was a some-one. Jerry was in the waiting room. I poked my head in to say hi, then realized that he wasn't alone.

"Maddy? What are you doing here?"

"I was visiting in the ICU."

"But it's not visiting . . . never mind." Jerry stood. "This is Ron and Kay Slater. Their son is—"

"Byron Slater. Chief Webb and I were just looking in on him."

"Really?" Mr. Slater seemed suspicious. "Are you a doctor?"

"No." I entered the room. "I'm the mayor of Santa Rita."

Jerry made introductions. He seemed uneasy. I had walked into a sensitive moment and was trying to think of a gracious exit. "I didn't realize Dr. Thomas was with someone. I saw him through the door. I'll leave you alone."

"Figures," Ron Slater said. He was bristling.

"Ron, don't," Kay said. His wife took his arm.

I looked at the father and then at Jerry. "I'm sorry. I truly didn't mean to intrude."

"It's not the intrusion, it's the apathy."

I could almost feel the heat. A movement at the door reminded me that Webb was still in earshot. He moved closer. I raised a hand and stopped him in his tracks. I stepped into the waiting room and took a seat facing the couple. "I'm afraid I don't understand." I had an uneasy feeling I was about to find out.

"This may not be the best time." Jerry had the look of a nervous bomb disposal officer.

"I see." I started to rise.

"Will there ever be a good time?" Ron asked. "I don't think so. The doc here tells me that my son isn't gonna make it. He says the head trauma may be too great and the brain continues to swell."

"Is there no hope?" I asked Jerry.

"There's always hope, but things look pretty grim."

"And it's the city's fault," Ron said.

"Please, Ron, don't," Kay said. Tears were rolling down her cheeks.

"Why not, Kay? Why not? What should I do, just sit here until Byron is dead and cold?" That started a flood of tears. "I'm sorry, baby. I'm sorry." He took her in his arms. "I shouldn't have said that. It's just that . . . it's just that . . ."

"Jerry?" I said.

"The Slater's have no health insurance. They may lose their son and everything else. I'm doing what I can to get social help, but—"

"We'll never dig out from under. Not that that matters. Very little matters without Byron. And all because the city can't keep the streets safe for our children. A missing stop sign. I can't believe it. We should sue."

"Yes, you should," I said.

"What?" Kay said.

"I don't know how much you know," I said, leaning forward, "but the city didn't take down that sign. There's been a rash of vandalism. Someone is stealing traffic signs and other things. The police are investigating."

"Vigorously," Webb said behind me. He moved into the doorway.

"A detective has been assigned to the case, all field officers have been alerted, and this afternoon I will be holding a press conference to ask the help of Santa Rita residents. The Chief's office and my office are doing everything we can. If you feel you should sue the city, then I encourage you to do so. It's your right."

"I can't believe the mayor of the city is saying this," Ron said.

"Well, I'm having a little trouble believing it myself. There are legal reasons why I shouldn't even be talking to you, but I believe that people matter more than law."

Ron buried his face in his hands and began to sob. I tried to fight back my own tears but I was too tired, too frustrated to try for very long. I let them flow.

"I feel so guilty about not being there when he needed me, about not having insurance. I'm self-employed. I drive a truck. I can barely pay the bills and buy gas for my rig. Kay, she ain't been all that healthy herself. She won't go to the doctor because we can't afford it."

"You're not alone, Mr. Slater," I said. "As Dr. Thomas can tell you, there's a health care crisis in the country. Forty-four million people in our country have no health insurance; another thirty-eight million Americans have inadequate insurance. That means that one in three people are in a similar situation."

"What do we do?"

"Hang on to each other," I said. "Hang on to friends and family. Follow Dr. Thomas's advice and don't give up hope. I'm praying for your son, and I will continue to do so." I opened my purse and removed a business card. "Call me anytime. Even if it's just to talk. I know what it is to lose someone you love. I can't make it easier, but at least you can talk to someone who understands."

Kay took the card. "Thank you, Mayor."

I excused myself and walked with Webb to his car. Once inside, he said, "Sometimes you amaze me, Mayor. Not many people could have handled that as well as you did."

I burst into tears.

chapter 27

ebb drove around the city until I had pulled myself together. To his credit, he didn't try to comfort me. He let the relief valve that had been holding my emotions in check flow freely without comment, complaint, or intrusion. It felt like I had wept for an hour but it had been less than five minutes, followed by another five minutes of the obligatory sniffing and nose blowing.

"I'm sorry," I said, feeling like a high school girl.

"Don't be," Webb said. "Honest emotion is a good thing."

I chuckled. "Isn't this where you tell me that even big strong men like you cry from time to time?"

"Not likely," he said. A moment later he asked, "Back to the office?"

"Yes. I'm better now. I haven't lost it like that in a long time." More sniffing. "I don't know what brought that on."

"Sure you do, Madam Mayor. It's part of your affliction."

"My affliction? What affliction?"

He shifted his gaze to me for a moment, then back to the road. "You have a terminal case of caring. It's gotten worse since your conversion, but you had it bad long before that."

"I didn't know caring was an affliction."

"It's probably a good disease to have but it comes with a price. You're the strongest woman I know. You have courage, determination, and a commitment to make wrong things right. You annoy me beyond words, but I do admire those qualities. By the way, if you repeat this in public, I'll deny it."

"I'll keep it a secret." I dabbed at my eyes.

"What I'm getting at is that you not only involve yourself in the problems of others, but you *invest* yourself. Investment is pricey. Take what just happened at the hospital. I walk in your office angrier than a bee in a bottle and slap my resignation on the desk. What do you do? You read it like it was a column in the entertainment section of the newspaper, then drag my fanny down to Pacific Horizon and march me into ICU to see Doug and the Slater boy. Now how am I supposed to feel sorry for myself when I'm looking at them?"

"It wasn't a scheme on my part," I said.

"That's the point. That kind of behavior is second nature to you. I have been a thorn in your side for years. A big thorn. I gave you a golden opportunity to be free of me, and you take steps only to shame me into staying."

"Chief—"

"I'm not finished, Mayor. Then what happens? You end up speaking to the family of a boy who is probably going to die. They threaten to sue the city and what do you do? You encourage them to do so. What kind of mayor does that?" He paused. "I tell you what kind of mayor—a caring mayor. Not a politician. No sir, a politician would try to deflect attention away from themselves. You give the parents your business card. And that's just this one situation. There are two murders at your cousin's home. You're running for congress. That kind of publicity is the last thing you need, but what do you do? You take her in, and dive headfirst into the process of making her life easier, no matter how much more burdensome it makes yours."

"I'm not hearing the downside to this."

"Yeah, I didn't think you would. I'm not sure you can hear the downside. One of the first things we learn as cops is not to invest ourselves in the lives of the victims. Oh sure, we take up offerings around Christmastime or collect food for needy families during Thanksgiving, but we don't stitch our hearts to the people we serve. We can't. If we did, we'd all go crazy by the end of the month. You have forgotten how to weigh the price of involvement. And ..." He took a deep breath and let it slide past his lips. "And I admire you for it."

"Thank you, Chief." In his awkward way, he had made me feel better.

"Yeah, well, you still annoy me."

"That's sweet. And you annoy me too."

The granite-faced Chief Bill Webb smiled.

I looked out the window to see if the sky was falling.

Webb walked me to my office and snatched up his letter of resignation. I offered to shred it for him but he said he might need it in the future. Then he did a favor for me: he called Detective West and got an update on the search for Catherine. There was no news and another piece of me died.

"You know," Webb said, "this makes her look pretty guilty. Fleeing after being interviewed about the second homicide at her home."

"Guilty? Detective West said that no gunpowder residue was found on her hands or clothing. She didn't shoot Andy Buchanan."

"I didn't say she pulled the trigger, but two murders at her home, both people she knew, both connected to her work, is more than a little suspicious. Then she lied about having a key to your place. Why do that?"

"I don't know. I just know she's not a killer."

He looked at me hard. "Terminal caring." He walked away.

No sooner than Webb had left, Floyd appeared at my door. "Do I want to know what all that was about?"

"You don't want to hear it, and I don't want to tell it. Bottom line is that everything is as it was—at least with the chief." I waved him in.

"Has there been . . . I mean, is there any word?"

"About Catherine? No. I wish there was. Sit down, I'll bring you up-to-date." Floyd did, looking like a lost puppy. I shared what I knew about Catherine and her disappearance. He took in every word, looking more worried by the moment.

"Do you think that someone abducted her?" he asked.

"I don't think so. She purposely led Detective West to believe that she had a key to my home, knowing that she didn't. If she couldn't get in and knew it, then she must have had some other plan. I had hoped she intended to wait for me to show up, but I don't think that's what she had in mind."

"But why? Why would she run away?"

"Fear," I suggested.

"What could Catherine be afraid of? Arrest?"

"Perhaps, but I doubt it. I think she may know something we don't. Two people associated with her have died. Maybe she left to protect others, to protect me. The question remains, what does she know that we don't?"

"And who helped her get away? I mean, she didn't just walk from your house."

"Floyd, I want you to do a few things for me. Detective West mentioned a director's cut of Catherine's movie is out on DVD. I'd like to see it."

"That's easy. I bought a copy the night you let me join you and the others for dinner at your home. I have it in my desk. I was hoping that you could get Catherine to autograph it for me. I can set it up so you can watch it on your computer. It has a DVD player, you know—"

"I know that. Just bring me the DVD. I need your computer skills for something else. Search the Internet and see if the script A LONG WAY FROM NOWHERE has been posted. Maybe someone leaked it. Catherine told me that that happens a lot.

"Also," I continued, "run over to the police station and pick up a copy of the script that was dropped off at the theater last night. West said he made a copy of the first one, I'm sure he made a copy of the second. I'll call ahead and pave the way for you. In fact, I'm going to ask for copies of both scripts."

"Do you think he'll give you any trouble about the scripts?"

"Of course he will. I just have to be more insistent and since I'm not asking for actual evidence, just photocopies, he'll relent. He'll complain, but he'll give in." *I hope.*

Floyd wasted no time in retrieving the DVD for me. I set it aside and called West. He relented faster and easier than I expected. Truth was, he sounded preoccupied. I used that to my advantage. City employees seldom hang up on their mayor.

I was eager to start the DVD but decided to wait until Floyd was back. I wanted to give it my full attention and answering the phone would break my concentration. West had said that the first movie had scenes showing the loading of a gun with Glaser blue-tip ammunition but those scenes had later been cut. I doubted I'd see anything important but it was better than sitting in one spot worrying.

A motion at the door caught my attention. I expected to see Floyd, but I saw someone else, someone I never expected to see. He was standing at the threshold watching me. Fritzy stood by his side. She had escorted him from the lobby to my office. I rose from my chair and cleared my throat.

"Mr. Buchanan." The words crawled out, far weaker than I intended. He wore a button-down patterned sweater, a polo shirt, and tan slacks. He looked twenty pounds lighter than when I saw him a short time ago. I knew it was an illusion. He was carrying himself like a man who bore the weight of several planets on his back.

"I hope I'm not disturbing you. I should have called."

I said thank you to Fritzy, dismissing her from the uncomfortable situation. To Buchanan I said, "Nonsense. Come in. Sit down." He did and I started to ask, *How are you doing?* But I caught myself. How would any man be doing whose son had just been murdered? As he sat, I had the sense I was watching a hollow man cored out by violent tragedy.

"I was . . . I was just at the police station. Detective West had some questions. Your aide was over there making copies or something. That made me think of you."

"You drove all the way out here to talk to Detective West?"

"No. I came in late last night. I had to . . . I was asked to . . ."

"Identify the body?"

He lowered his head. "Yes."

"Mr. Buchanan, I wish I could do more than tell you how sorry I am over your loss."

"There's nothing to say that would do any good. It's happened and no matter how many times I tell myself it's not true, I keep seeing him lying on that table looking like my son but with no life in him." His voice choked.

"May I get you something? Water? Coffee?"

He surprised me by chortling. "Have you ever noticed in old movies and television shows, that when someone is upset another character offers them water as if it's an elixir. I don't know how many times I've had to cut a line like that from a script."

"I suppose we do that because we don't know what else to say or do."

"I guess you're right." He took a deep breath and tried to square shoulders that weren't through slumping yet. "I have a favor to ask. I have no right to ask it, but I will."

"Please, go ahead."

"I know there are so many crimes these days that the police get overloaded, and their attention shifts to more recent crimes. I want my son's killer found. Would you ... could you make sure that his death doesn't get stuck on the back burner?"

"Things are a little different here, Mr. Buchanan. Normally, our crime rate is very low and murder is something rare. I can guarantee that Detective West won't put this on the back burner."

"That means a lot to me."

"Mr. Buchanan, may I ask you a question? I don't want to add to your grief but maybe you could help me understand something."

"You can't add to the immeasurable, Mayor. Ask your question." He ran a hand along his shaved head.

"You know about the additions to the first script, the pages that someone added to terrify Catherine. Your son delivered that script and apparently he delivered another one last night. Do you know why he would bring another screenplay to Catherine?"

"Your Detective West wanted to know the same thing. I don't have an answer. I know I didn't send him. And where he got the script, I can't say."

"Was he normally ... impulsive?"

It seemed the question piled another planet on his shoulder. "He was a troubled young man. I thought maybe he had rounded the corner and left his problems behind. Maybe he didn't." He bit his lip.

I waited, mustering all my strength not to ask the question. I didn't need to.

"My wife and I divorced when Andy was ten. I was in the middle of a project and ... well, I was very self-absorbed. When my wife left, she went to Europe and took Andy with her. She's not a good mother, and I'm only a slightly better father. She played the field, living off the massive alimony and child support I agreed to pay. When Andy turned fifteen, he became too much for her to handle. She sent him to me. She left with a good ten-year-old and returned a drug-addicted teenager."

He waved a dismissive hand. "It's not all her fault. I wasn't there for him when he needed me. He had no father image during those formative years. Of course, if I had been there, I wouldn't have been much of an example. I was an alcoholic—I *am* an alcoholic … Been dry for almost twelve years. When Andy arrived on my doorstep, I realized he had a problem. I also realized I had a similar problem. He came by his addictive personality honestly, if *honestly* is the right word. I checked us both into a rehab hospital. We kicked our problems."

"That was a courageous thing to do. You've been off alcohol for over a decade."

"Yeah, I've been able to stick with it. Andy, not so much."

"I'm sorry." I was saying that a lot lately.

"He kept falling back into the old habits. I took him out of school and had him tutored. He did well with that. I also hired him to work with me. He did a little acting; just a line here and there. I also tried to teach him the business. He was interested in directing and writing. He even surprised me with a screenplay one day. It was passable but not great."

"When did he write the screenplay?"

"At college. He had been drug free for a couple of years so I felt comfortable sending him to New York for film school. That's where he met Catherine, in New York. Anyway, he came home with the script. I should have been more encouraging, but screenwriters are a dime a dozen. Only the best make it to the top and those who do make a great deal of money, but the odds are against anyone who tries. I thought he had a better chance at directing. That's where my real contacts are."

Over Buchanan's shoulder, I saw Floyd enter. He had the screen-plays in hand. I asked Floyd to join us and made introductions. Floyd took the other seat but leaned away from Buchanan as if grief were contagious.

"Did Detective West show you the second script? The one that arrived at the theater last night?"

"No. He mentioned it."

What Floyd brought was an unbound set of pages, dark but leg-ible. I turned to the inserted pages, pushed them toward him. "I don't know if you can tell me anything about this."

"I'm sorry about the quality," Floyd said. "I had to make copies of Detective West's copies which were made from the original that was printed on yellow paper."

"It's okay, Floyd. We can read the words and that's what matters."

It took only moments for Buchanan to scan the pages. Clearly he was used to reading screenplays. He handed them back. "I can tell you it's not part of our script. It's a little cheesy but at least the format is right."

"Cheesy?"

"It's a little over the top and a little sloppy."

"What do you mean sloppy?"

He leaned over the desk, looked at the pages again, then pointed. "Right here."

I moved the pages closer and scrutinized them.

LACY

Please, just let him go.

INTRUDER

It's too late and it's your fault. It's all your fault.

LACY

No. Please no. I'm sorry.

```
                    INTRUDER
       Sorry doesn't cut it. Never has. Never
       will.

                    (Laughs)

       The Body Count is now two. Ready for
       three?
```

"What am I supposed to see?"

"See the last line of the insertion? Just below the direction 'Laughs'?"

"The one that reads, 'Ready for three?'"

"Right before that. 'Body Count' is capitalized and it shouldn't be. Sloppy. There's nothing more distracting than a script filled with typos." He rose. "Thank you for your time, Mayor, and your commitment. I need to go make arrangements for my son and . . ."

"And?" I prompted.

New sadness shadowed his face. "I'm going to tell Rockwood to get a new director. I don't think I can continue the project. Thank you again." He started toward the door, then stopped. "You know, that is odd about the typo."

"Odd? How?"

"I told you that Andy surprised me with a script when he came back from college in New York. That was the working title: Body Count."

I returned my gaze to the pages. That was odd. Coincidence? When I looked up Buchanan was gone. A commiserating sorrow filled me. I didn't envy what he would have to face in the days ahead.

Body count. Body Count. A title? I studied the two words, then noticed what followed. I had seen them but they had not registered before.

                    INTRUDER
Sorry doesn't cut it. Never has. Never
will.

                    (Laughs)

The Body Count is now two. Ready for
three?

Who was number three supposed to be?

chapter 20

I had to make the call. The clock was crawling toward noon and still no word from Catherine. A police officer had been assigned to her property, forbidding access to the curious, protecting unfound evidence, and watching for my missing cousin. There had been no sign of her. West had done what police do. He put out an APB, got the necessary legal permissions to monitor her cell phone usage, and asked Detective Brian Duffy to check the home and office of Franco Zambonelli. So far, nothing.

I had to make the call.

My stomach churned as the phone began to ring. It rang five times, and I was prepared to leave a message on an answering machine when I heard a breathless, "Hello."

"Jenny? It's Maddy."

"Oh, hi, Maddy. I almost missed you. I was putting wet laundry in the drier." She sounded unperturbed. "How's my daughter treating you? Is she okay?"

"She called you about the . . . the tragedy at her home?"

"Horrible. The poor thing was shaken to the core. I tried to get her to come home, but she said she was all right and that she was staying with you."

I wanted to move forward gently. "Was that the last time you spoke with her?"

"Yes."

"She didn't call yesterday?" I pushed.

"Maddy, what's wrong? Has something happened to Catherine?"

"There was another murder at her home. Someone she knows from the studio."

"Oh, no, no, no. How can that be? Two murders?"

"Jenny, is Neil there?" Neil was Jenny's husband, Catherine's father.

"No. He's . . . he's golfing. Tell me what happened."

I did, being as brief as possible and leaving out some of the more gruesome details. "I was hoping she had called you."

"I'm coming down there. I'll . . . I'll call Neil on his cell phone and he'll come home. I can throw a few things into a bag and be on an airplane right away—"

"Jenny."

"If I can't get a plane this afternoon, we can drive. If we drive all night—"

"Jenny. Stop." She did. "Listen to me. You need to stay right there."

"I want to be where my baby is!"

"I know. I know. But you need to stay there. Catherine might call. She might even show up on your doorstep before the sun goes down. If she does, the police need to know."

"Why? Is she in trouble? They can't seriously think she's responsible for those horrible things."

"Jenny. Take a breath." I didn't hear anything. "I'm serious. Take a breath." She did and I heard her exhaling over the phone. "Do it again." A few seconds later I said, "Okay, here's what we're going to do next. I'm going to talk. You're going to listen. Got it?" My tone was steady and firm.

"Okay. I'm listening."

"Catherine may be with her publicist. He hasn't shown up at his office or his home, according to the LAPD. She may be trying to distance herself from those she cares about. Two people she knows have been murdered. I think she's trying to protect herself and others. That means she may call you, or she may call some of her old friends. If she calls, I want you to phone Detective Judson West. Can you write down a number?"

"Yes."

I gave her the number as well as my office and cell phone. "All the police want to know is if she's safe. That's all any of us want." I paused. "Are you going to be all right?"

"I think so."

"That's good. Call Neil. He needs to know and you shouldn't be alone. Will you do that?"

"Yes. You'll call the instant you learn something, won't you?"

I promised I would and hung up. It was my turn to take a few deep breaths. I felt like I was on the eleventh mile of a ten-mile race.

I instructed Floyd to hold my calls except for Catherine or West. I closed my door, turned to my computer, and dropped the director's cut DVD in. For the next two hours I watched a movie I should have seen last year. West had described it as a woman-in-peril suspense story. He was right about that. *Night After Night* was dark and moody but well done. The story flowed and the characters were believable. Catherine's acting anchored the whole production. In several scenes it looked as if she might lose her life. Had I been watching in a theater, I would have been less moved, but with two murders and Catherine now missing, the story seemed too real.

I did my best to not lose myself in the movie. I was looking for clues but found none. West had mentioned a scene in which the killer loads a .38 with Glaser blue-tips, just like the one that killed Ed Lowe and presumably the kind that killed Andy Buchanan. That had yet to be demonstrated, but it was a reasonable assumption.

Frustration filled my mind. I had hoped some crime-ending clue would pop off the screen in an *"Aha!"* moment. It didn't happen. The only connections I could make were Catherine was the star, a .38 revolver with Glaser bullets was used, and people died.

I thought about the screenplay being used for the next movie. West was right when he noticed that the story revolved around a model being stalked by a killer who murders to get her attention. Was that what was happening here? Was some soulless, love-crazed killer showing off to get Catherine's attention?

The thought made the strength flow from my body. I had been telling myself that Catherine was safe, hiding of her own accord, but I could be wrong. I could be very wrong.

I paged Floyd. He was in my office five seconds later.

"Did you find anything on the Internet?"

"I did a search for A LONG WAY FROM NOWHERE but came up empty. The only thing I found was a database of movies in production. It's mentioned there, but that's all. Sorry."

"Do another search. This time look for a script called BODY COUNT."

"Okay. How did you like the movie?"

"I don't know. I was looking for something, but I don't know what. Every time Catherine appeared, I felt frightened for her."

"I'm worried," he said.

"Me too."

He started to leave, then he stopped. "Remember, you have that press conference in twenty minutes."

"I remember." I rose and stretched my back. "I'm going over to see Tess now. Give her a call and let her know I'll be there soon."

Leaving the office behind, I stepped into the ladies' room. I stood before the mirror and began to touch up my makeup. I moved slowly, waiting for the surge of excitement and nerves that course through me before every speech. It wasn't there. My emotions were shutting down, having been overworked the last few days.

Where was Catherine? All of my consoling words to her mother were not working on me. I assumed she left to hide, but I was losing confidence in that position. Maybe I was lying to myself.

I finished the touch-up and exchanged the restroom for the office area, moving through the cubicle forest to Tess's office on the other end of the building.

Tess and I walked down the hall to the council chambers exchanging last-minute details which were few. In large cities, a press conference could bring twenty or thirty media representatives. An afternoon conference not laced with scandal in a city the size of Santa Rita would be a small affair.

As we walked into the chamber I saw a small but active crowd. There were two camera crews, Vincent Branch of the *Register*, two from local radio stations, and a stringer from the *Times*. I recognized a reporter from a Ventura newspaper and one from his counterpart in Santa Barbara. All in all, as good a group as I could expect.

As we walked in, Tess and I avoided the large, wide, curving council bench. It had room for each council member and a smaller extension had seats for the city attorney, city manager, and the city clerk. It was familiar territory. Council met in this room most Tuesdays. We avoided the council bench because two women standing behind the elevated bench would have been showy. Instead, Tess had requested maintenance to turn the public lectern, normally used by citizens to address the council during meetings, to face the chamber seats. The dark wood of the room gave the place a somber feel.

I stepped to the podium. "Good afternoon," I began and gave a practiced smile. "Thank you for coming. As some of you may know our city has been experiencing an elevated period of vandalism. Unlike most vandalism, like spray painting buildings or breaking school windows, these crimes have taken a dangerous turn. In the last few days, two individuals—one a child—have been injured and hospitalized. Both are in grave condition. We at the city take public safety seriously and have been actively seeking to end these offenses and bring the perpetrators to justice."

The room was silent. The two cameras were rolling, the radio reporters held out tape recorders, and others took notes.

I continued. "Deputy Mayor Tess Lawrence has taken the lead in the matter and will now brief you about the nature and extent of the problem and what is being done." I stepped to the side and Tess took my place.

She was smooth. From the moment she stepped behind the podium she was in charge. Her tone was pleasant but seasoned with just the right amount of indignation at what was happening. Over the next five minutes she gave a detailed account of the missing signs, the police investigation, and the promise that she and the city would not quit until those responsible were arrested. My admiration for her grew. I regretted the years of animosity between us. That being acknowledged, I knew her feelings about me had not changed. We had reached a workable relationship but little more.

"We are asking for the help of the citizens of Santa Rita. First, we ask that you be aware of the problem. If a sign that was there earlier is now missing, please report it as soon as possible. Also, please be alert to the activities in your own neighborhood. If you see any suspicious person or group, call the police immediately. By working together, we can solve this problem in short order." She looked over the crowd, then said, "The mayor and I will take a few questions."

"What are the police doing about the matter?" one of the radio reporters asked.

Tess fielded the question. "A detective has been assigned and is hard at work on the matter, patrols have been increased, on-duty and off-duty officers have been instructed to look for and report any missing signs, guardrails, or anything else that has gone missing."

"Any ideas who is doing this?" the Ventura reporter asked.

"It looks like something done by high school or early college age people."

"Building on that," a television reporter asked, "*why* would anyone do this?"

Tess hesitated before answering. The police had found a camera and transmitter, but they had asked us not to mention the find. It was best to keep some things secret for a time. "We won't truly know why until those responsible are caught."

"Mayor Glenn," the radio reporter began, "there's been two murders at Catherine Anderson's home in the Oak Crest Knolls area. You were at the home after each murder. Why is that?"

I tried not to frown. "Catherine Anderson is my cousin. I gave her a ride home. But let's remember, this press conference is about the dangerous vandalism in our city."

"Do you think these murders will affect your campaign?" the television man asked.

"No, I don't. The tragedies have drawn my attention from campaigning, but I see no reason why my campaign would be adversely affected."

"Is that why the deputy mayor is in charge of this investigation?" someone asked. It was Vincent Branch and his words were bitter.

Tess elbowed in front of me. "Let me answer that, Mr. Branch. The mayor is fully apprised of all elements of the problem and investigation. She has been instrumental in putting an end to the crime."

I had a sudden urge to buy Tess lunch. My first impression was that she was playing the party line well, showing a unified front before the media, but something in her voice rang with sincerity. She looked at Branch and I expected one of her patented withering stares, but her expression was soft. "We are aware, Mr. Branch, that Doug Turner is one of the victims and that he is one of your prized employees."

"He's a friend, not just an employee." Branch looked in pain. "When the responsible people are found, what charges will be brought against them?"

I took that one. "That will be up to the district attorney. I plan to ask for a very aggressive prosecution."

"Injured parties also will be able to bring suit of injury and damages," Tess added.

More questions were asked, but soon petered out. We fielded each one, then thanked them all. As the gathering began to break up, I called out to Vincent Branch and motioned him over. He frowned, lowered his head, and started in our direction.

"What are you doing?" Tess asked.

"Stay with me," I said, avoiding her question.

Branch approached and gave a polite nod. "You wanted to see me, Mayor?"

I studied him for a moment. He looked drawn and worn and near empty. "Are we okay?"

"What do you mean?"

"Is there a problem between us?"

He lowered his eyes for a moment. "Look, Mayor. I probably could have asked that question a little better, I know that. I just think it's odd that someone else seems in charge of the problem."

"The police are in charge," I said. "What's the real problem?"

He worked his lips before speaking. "I spoke to the doctors this morning. Doug has no family to speak of. His mother died earlier this year."

"I remember. She was up in Oregon, right?"

"Yes. Doug was married for a while but that didn't last. I don't know why. He seemed to enjoy the lone life. Because no family is available the doctors have been a little more forthcoming with me."

"I visited yesterday," I said. "There was no change."

"No change today either," Branch said. "It doesn't look good." He seemed to shrink before my eyes.

"You two are close?"

"Yeah, we've been buds since college. He was my chief competition for editor at the *Register*. He pulled out of the running. When I asked him why, he said he'd rather write stories than assign them. I think he gave it up for me."

"That sounds like Doug," I said. "We knocked heads more times than I can number. I'm sure I aged him more than time itself."

Branch looked at me. "He would never tell you this. It goes against a reporter's instinct. If he were here, he'd beat me to keep from saying it, but he is one of your biggest supporters. When you chose to run for congress, he was thrilled. His words were, 'It's about time.' He was right."

"Thank you," I said. "What can I do to help?"

"Catch these guys. Catch them soon and parade them in front of city hall. Hang them by their thumbs if the law will allow it."

I smiled. "It won't, but you do have my promise—our promise, that we will do everything we can to put an end to it."

"I can't ask for more," he stated, then added, "I'm sorry if I came off too brusque."

"I can overlook it."

chapter 29

I had just returned to the office when Judson West walked in. "Need some air?" he asked.

I said I did and we walked from the building, making use of the front doors instead of the private entry at the back. Anyone approaching city hall would walk by a long rectangular fountain and reflecting pool. The burbling fountain, a warm October sun, clear blue sky, and a fresh breeze made me glad to be out of the building.

"You've had a rough week." He reached in his suit coat pocket and removed a small plastic bag. Cashews. He ripped open the top and offered me one. It would have been rude to have declined.

"I've had rough weeks before."

"And that makes it easier?"

I chuckled. "Not even close. Just because I've had a migraine before doesn't mean the next one will hurt any less. It only means that I know that it will end sometime."

"I didn't know you suffered from migraines." He poured a couple of cashews in his palm.

"I don't. It was an illustration. However, I have worked with a few migraines."

"Haven't we all? I don't suppose you've heard from Catherine."

"No. I called her mother in case she phoned."

"That had to be difficult. I hate calls like that."

"There are more enjoyable things." He handed me the bag. I took it and fished out another cashew.

"I promised to keep you posted. I just left the autopsy of Andy Buchanan. He was killed by a .38 Glaser blue-tip just as we suspected. He also had defensive wounds on his arms. It looks like he took a couple of blows to the belly and jaw."

"He was in a fight?"

"It looks that way. I went back to the house and reexamined the site. There are several places in the soft dirt that indicate a struggle. Since landscapers had been there several times over the last few weeks, I hadn't made the connection. Some tools they left behind were moved. Crime photos show that they were neatly stacked before."

"Who would he be fighting? Not Catherine. You can't be serious."

"No, not Catherine. Whoever he fought with had a good punch. Besides, when I examined her hands and tested for gunpowder residue, I didn't see any bruising. I would expect to see some evidence. Her dress didn't look like it had been through a struggle—despite the fake blood."

"So you're taking her off your suspect list," I said. "She never should have been on it."

"She may still be involved somehow. She has skipped town." He reached for the cashews. I pulled them out of his reach.

"You call my cousin a criminal, then want my cashews?"

"Your cashews? I brought those and shared them out of the goodness of my heart. You're stealing food from a cop."

"I'm not stealing. It's ... eminent domain," I said. "Seriously, she's the victim, not the criminal."

"I will agree that she didn't pull the trigger, but there are other ways to be involved. Both murders are closely tied to her. I take nothing for granted and dismiss nothing."

"Whatever happened to a person being innocent until proven guilty?"

"That's court thinking. In my world, everyone's guilty until I know they're innocent." He snatched the bag out of my hands. "Eminent domain. Clever, but possession is nine-tenths of the law."

"Now that you know the bullets are the same, what do you conclude?"

"There's still ballistic tests to do. The DRUGFIRE search came up negative on the first bullet. What I really need is the gun. The bullets are only half the equation."

There was another matter on my mind, and I weighed the wisdom of bringing it up. There was already so much to occupy my mind, so many things demanding West's attention, I didn't want to add to the burden. It was best to let it go. I didn't.

"I hear you've been offered a position in Denver," I said without preamble.

"Really. I didn't know it was public information. You have spies following me?"

"Not this week." The comment was light, the opposite of how I felt. "A little birdie told me."

"Did the little birdie have a badge?"

"Maybe. I don't want to get anyone on your bad side." I looked at the concrete beneath my feet. There was nothing to see, but it was easier than looking at West.

"I don't have a bad side. I'm patient and pure through and through. Did Chief Webb tell you?"

"The chief doesn't tell me much of anything. He didn't let your secret slip."

"Then it must have been Detective Scott. He's the only other cop you've dealt with lately."

"I see why they made you a detective. It was Scott. When were you going to tell me?"

"There's nothing to tell. A friend from San Diego moved to the Denver PD. He learned they were looking to recruit a detective or two who could also train the young guys. It's a pretty good deal."

"Sounds like you're considering it. I think I have a right to know." I sounded more testy than I intended. I was feeling more hurt than I expected.

"You do?" West smiled. "Did we get married recently and I missed it? I think I would remember something like that."

"You know what I mean," I countered.

"I don't have a clue what you mean. I've made no decision. Truth is, I've barely had time to think about it. I talked it over with Chief Webb and a couple of other detectives. Wisdom can be found in the opinions of others. I read that in a fortune cookie."

"I meant I have a right to know because we're friends."

"Okay, Maddy, what's the problem? You're put out because someone has shown interest in me, and I didn't immediately send you an email?"

What am I put out over? It was a fair question but that didn't mean I had to like it.

"I just would hate to see you leave."

"There are many detectives who can do what I do. Or did you mean something else? I was under the impression that our relationship would never be more than professional and friendly."

I had no idea where to go from there. West had tried to ratchet up our relationship several times, but it never felt right. "I'm meddling and I shouldn't be. Denver is a long way away."

"How far is Washington, D.C.? If I remember my geography right, it's a lot farther to the East Coast than to Colorado."

He had me. I watched people move in and out of the building. City hall always had something going on. It was then that I saw a familiar form burst from the front doors. He stopped and searched the grounds. Floyd saw me and scampered my way. Adrenaline began to flow.

I stood, waiting for Floyd to close the distance. He stopped a foot away and looked as if he had run a mile instead of fifty feet. "What's wrong?"

"It's ... it's ..." He fell silent and looked at West, then me.

"Start talking, Floyd," I said.

"It's ... Catherine."

"What about her? Did she call?"

West stood.

"No, no," Floyd said. "She's in your office. Right now. In your office. I've been looking all over for you. I called your cell phone and everything."

My cell phone was in my purse, which was still in a drawer in my office.

I started moving.

I walked at a deliberate pace. Seeing the mayor and a police detective running through city hall might cause concern among some of the employees, so I moved at a quick but steady pace. West was to my right, Floyd to my left. On the way, Floyd filled us in.

"I was sitting at my desk when the phone rang. It was Catherine. She was calling on her cell phone. She said she and Mr. Zambonelli were in the parking lot and wanted to talk to you. You were gone. I wasn't sure what to do, so I told them how to come in the back way and unlocked the door for them. I put them in your office and went looking for you."

"You done good, kid," West said. "You handled it perfectly. Let's just hope they're still there."

"Why wouldn't they be?" I snapped.

West gave me a disappointed look but didn't answer. We walked into the small lobby that leads to the executive area of city hall. Fritzy was at her place. She pressed the button that opened the small wood gate in the pony wall that separated the public area from the office area where city council members, their staff, and support personnel work.

"I see Floyd found you," Fritzy said, as we passed through the gate. "While you're here, Mayor, I have a question for you."

"Not now, Fritzy." We pressed on and entered Floyd's office. "Close the door, Floyd." He did. I went to my own door, which was shut as it should be. I turned the doorknob and stepped in. West was so close I could feel his breath on my cheek.

Sitting in front of my desk were Catherine and Franco. Franco wore the same clothing he wore on the night of the play. Catherine had changed. The clothing looked new. My guess was that she bought new threads.

Catherine stood. So did Franco.

"Hi, Maddy," Catherine whispered.

"Hi? HI? You run off without a word and all you have to say is, 'Hi'?"

"I know you're angry—"

"You don't know the half of it. Do you know the worry you've put us through? You're mother is beside herself."

"She knows?" Catherine's eyes widened.

"Of course she knows. I called her to see if you had made contact."

"Um, Mayor," West said.

"How could you just take off like that?"

"I know, I shouldn't have. I was just scared."

"So you thought you'd spread that fear around a little." My anger surprised me.

"Mayor, if I could—" West started.

I stepped toward Catherine until we were eye-to-eye. My jaw was tight, my stomach felt full of magma, and my hands clenched into fists. I took a breath. Then another. Catherine said nothing, and I could no longer speak. A second later I took her in my arms and held her tight. I felt her arms rise and encircle me.

The anger that boiled in me cooled and drained away. In its place rose the joy of knowing that Catherine was safe. "Thank you, God," I whispered. "Thank you, thank you, thank you."

"If you two are done with whatever it is you're doing," West said, "I'd like to ask a question or two."

I pulled away but before stepping back I raised my hands and placed them on the sides of her head. I pulled her forward and kissed her on the forehead. Then I took a step back and moved to my place behind the desk. I felt as limp as a used washrag. Catherine sat, looking frail. Franco slipped back into his chair.

"I'm sorry about the outburst," I said. "I shouldn't have snapped at you."

"I had it coming," Catherine said. "I didn't mean to cause so much trouble."

West sat on the edge of my desk, normally something I would never allow, but there was no other place for him to sit. "Okay, who's going to start?"

"Me," Catherine said. "It's my fault. I was afraid and humiliated. I just wanted to get away. When I was at the police station I saw that you had let Franco go. He didn't deserve to be arrested, you know."

"I had a point to make." West looked at Franco but the publicist didn't react. "Go on."

Catherine rubbed her thumbs together. "When you offered to take me to Maddy's I said yes, even though I didn't have a key."

"You said you did," West said. "When you saw the house was dark, you told me you had a key."

"I know. It was a lie and I feel bad about it. But all I could think of was that someone killed Ed and someone killed Andy, and that line in the script came to mind."

"Which line?" West prompted.

I knew. "'The Body Count is now two. Ready for three?'"

"I thought that I might be number three. Worse, I thought Maddy might be next. I couldn't live with myself if ... Anyway, after you dropped me off, I went around back to the deck and called Franco. He picked me up."

"You thought that was a good idea, Mr. Zambonelli?" West asked.

"No, I thought it was a lousy idea," Franco shot back.

"He tried to talk me out of it, but I threatened to take a cab someplace."

"What was I to do?" Franco said. "She was leaving one way or the other, so I figured better with me than alone. Am I right or am I right? I took her to a place north of Santa Barbara. I got us a couple of rooms." He turned to Catherine. "Everything I do, I do for you, baby. Everything."

"It took awhile, but this morning, Franco talked me into coming here." Catherine rubbed her thumbs together harder. I was afraid I was going to see bone soon. "Do I have to go to jail?"

She asked the last question with her head down. She couldn't look at me or West. Seeing her so innocent, vulnerable, and frightened tore my heart in half.

"After what you put us through, Ms. Anderson, I should lock you up—except I don't have any real reason to do so. You broke no laws."

"What about Franco?" Catherine said.

"You said you went of your own free will?" West asked.

"Yes. Like I said. He was against the whole thing."

"Then I have no reason to hold him—yet."

Catherine looked at me. "I should call my mother. Then I should talk to Harold and Neena. Will you go with Franco and me?"

"Of course." I stood. "Catherine needs to make a call. Let's give her some privacy. Go on, get out of my office."

The room emptied. I stepped to Catherine and reached for her hand. "I was out of line earlier. Forgive me?"

"If you'll forgive me," she said. "Besides, I'm well aware of the family temper."

"Call your mom. Take as much time as you need." I left my office and closed the door behind me, but not before I saw her take her cell phone in hand.

Floyd was at his desk looking as if he had just witnessed open heart surgery. I felt a little drained myself. I just hoped I wasn't showing it as much as he. I glanced around, wondering why only Floyd and I were still around.

Floyd saw my confusion. "Detective West said he was going back to work. Mr. Zambonelli asked where the bathrooms were. I told him."

"What a day," I said and pinched the bridge of my nose.

"I found this for you," Floyd said. He pushed a stack of paper my way.

"What is it?"

"It's the BODY COUNT script you asked for. Andy Buchanan had his own Web page; one of those sites where a person posts their résumé, work history, and interests. It looked like he was trying to get someone interested in the screenplay. He uploaded the whole thing as well as his contact information. I downloaded it as a Zip file, extracted it, and printed it for you."

"You're the best, Floyd." I picked up the stack of paper and thumbed through it. I was not an expert but it looked like a complete script. My mind was humming. I felt like I was holding something important but didn't yet know why. "Floyd, I want you to print another one of these and deliver it to Detective West. I want you to deliver it personally. Tell him that I asked you to do some research and that I thought you found something important. Make sure he sees Andy Buchanan's name."

"What are you going to do?"

"I'm going to drive Catherine to the theater and wait for her. I think she wants to mend a few fences." I held up the screenplay. "I'm also going to do a little reading."

"Is there anything else I can do?"

"There is. I have another research project for you. I'm certain that the police are already doing this, but I think your youth might give you an edge on them."

"More Internet searching?"

"Exactly. You know the problem with the missing signs and guardrails. The police are keeping this part secret so you are to keep this to yourself. Understood?"

"Got it."

"The police have found a simple video camera and transmitter at one of the scenes. I want to know how someone would do that and if they are selling the footage on the Internet."

"You're kidding."

"I wish I was."

I heard my office door open. "I'm ready now."

Catherine oozed out of the office. Her eyes were red and puffy and her nose pink. It must have been a difficult phone call to make.

chapter 30

After waiting for Franco, the three of us hopped in my car and I plowed onto the freeway. The conversation was minimal, each of us lost in our own thoughts. I was certain Catherine needed time to recover from her telephone conversation with her mother and plan what she was to say to Harold and Neena.

It was just before two thirty and traffic was lighter than I expected. Thirty minutes from now it would be a different matter. I didn't push the speed. We had no appointment time. We would get there when we got there.

"I just had a thought," I said. "Do you know if Neena and Harold will be there?"

"No," Catherine said, "but I'm sure they will be. Neena works from about one until the theater closes in the evening. Harold showed up at two yesterday to check things over. He will be there."

We fell back into silence.

Fifteen minutes later, I pulled into the lot of the Curtain Call dinner theater and parked close to the front door. A half-dozen other cars were there. Early employees, I assumed.

Once out of the car, Catherine and Franco started toward the door. I left the script in the car and followed. We stepped into the empty lobby.

"I would like to talk to them alone," Catherine said.

"I understand." I started to say something else when a young man in a clean white smock walked by. I assumed he worked in the kitchen, arriving early to set up for the evening's meal. He saw us and stopped.

"May I help you?" He looked at me, then at Catherine. "Oh." I waited for more but nothing came.

"We're here to see Ms. Lasko and Mr. Young," I said.

"Um, sure. Have a seat in the theater, and I'll let them know you're here."

Catherine was slow to move so I took the lead, walking through the lobby and past the curtained doors. Inside, the lights burned brightly as a worker covered the tables with white cloths and another set out silverware and glasses. The theater was gearing up for another evening of great art. We stood by the first row of booths and waited. It didn't take long for Neena to appear.

"Catherine, dear." Neena moved straight to Catherine and gave her a hug. "Are you all right? We've been so worried."

"Catherine!" The voice was familiar. Harold Young bounded down the stage and jogged to us, taking Catherine in his arms.

At least they're not throwing things at her.

"I, um, I thought we should talk." She reminded me of a child waiting for a scolding. It was heartrending.

Harold said, "You know, you left us in a bind."

"I know. That's what I want to talk about."

It was time to make an exit. "We'll wait over there." I motioned toward the tables nearest the stage. "Come on, Franco, you can regale me with stories of New Jersey."

We retreated. Before I sat down I looked back at the trio. They had settled into the booth and Catherine was talking. I took a seat; Franco sat across the table.

Franco eyed me. "You don't like me much, do you?" Straight to the point.

"I don't know you well enough to have an opinion."

He smirked. "Don't give me none of that political smooth talk. I make my living by sizing up people and making other people look good. I know a snow job when I see one."

"Okay, Franco, I'll admit you've irritated me on several occasions."

"I've been nuthin' but a gentleman," he said.

This time I smirked. "Within five minutes of arriving at my house, you insulted my city and our police force and forced yourself into this situation. Of course, what really sticks in my craw is that you let me, the police, and everyone who cares about Catherine worry all night and most of the day."

"I told you it wasn't my idea, it was hers. Everything I do, I do for her. I did talk her into coming to talk to you. You heard her say that herself."

I had heard that.

"Look, Mayor. I know I can rub people the wrong way. Maybe it's the East Coast accent; maybe it's because I can be a little blunt; maybe I don't think before I speak, but you gotta believe I ain't got nuthin' but the best in mind for Catherine. She's my best client. Whatever happens to her happens to me."

"Franco, I don't know what to think of you. You're a stranger to me, one Catherine seems to trust, but after two murders at her home, I'm not inclined to trust anyone but my closest friends."

"Then why did you let me come along?"

"Because Catherine sees something in you. It is obvious that you've won her trust."

"But I haven't won yours?"

"No. You haven't. Have I won your trust?"

He laughed. "You're the mayor. You're Catherine's cousin. She thinks you hung the moon. Yeah, I trust you."

I hadn't expected that. "Let me ask you something. Why would Andy Buchanan be at Catherine's home?"

He sighed. "I don't know, Mayor. I really don't. I've been asking that myself. I even asked Catherine while driving to the hotel. She said he had a crush on her at college—you know, when they was in New York. But she said that was over several years ago."

"Do you read her scripts?" I asked.

"Nah. I'm sure her agent does, but I learn what I need from her. After the movie is shot and they're ready to start to promote it, I get a DVD copy to review. The whole crew does too. That way I know what the movie is all about."

"So you don't know who would be doing this to Catherine?"

"Mayor, if I knew for sure, it wouldn't be a problem no more. You know what I mean?"

I was pretty sure I did.

"How did you get to be a publicist?" I asked. "If I'm not prying."

"Hustle, Mayor. Pure and simple, hustle. I grew up on the edge of the projects. It was a rough neighborhood. Future didn't look good for me. I was pretty good in school but good grades was just an invitation to get beat up. I watched my friends die from drug overdoses, get locked up for selling things they shouldn't, or get shot while standing on the street corner. I knew that wasn't for me. I used to spend as much time out of the area as I could. Usually, I sat in movie houses taking in the latest flicks. I fell in love with the business. In school, they took some of us up to Broadway to catch a play. It was an old play. A revival of *42nd Street*. Not much to the story line but seeing all those actors, hearing the music—it got in me."

"So you wanted to be an actor?"

"No, no way. I'm no actor. I know that. I can't write worth a dime, either. I don't have what it takes to be a director of a play or a movie, but I do know how to hustle. I can sell anything to anyone, or anyone to any group. Yes sir, that I can do. During my last year of school, I talked my way into working for a local publicist. I worked for free and learned a few things. After school, I did the same thing in New York. A few years later I started my own firm."

"How did you meet Catherine?"

"I was representing one of the actors in her Broadway play. He made a recommendation, and she hired me on. When she came to Hollywood, I thought it would be a good time to open another office."

Catherine approached. "Thank you for bringing me," she said.

"Did you say what needed to be said? Are they okay with everything?" I asked.

"Yes. They were very disappointed in me, but they said they understood. They want me to perform again."

"That's great, baby," Franco said. "But maybe you should take this whole play thing off. You need some rest."

"They want me to act tonight."

"Tonight?" That surprised me. "What did you tell them?"

"I owe them. I told them yes."

I offered to drive Catherine to my home so she could rest before the play, but she declined. She wanted to help Harold any way she could, refresh her lines, and "get in character," something she felt she could do better by being in the theater. She also admitted she wanted to talk to the other actors. "They deserve some explanation," she said. I admired her humility.

That left Franco. He made a couple of attempts to talk his client out of doing the play, but Catherine carried many of the same genes for stubbornness I do. Franco was wasting his breath. He offered to stay with her but she said no. She needed things to be as close to normal as possible, and she insisted that he leave. He looked crest-fallen. I was expecting a protruding lower lip, but Catherine made everything right with a little, platonic kiss on the cheek. He melted.

The polite thing to do was offer to drive Franco back to his car in the parking lot of city hall, but he declined. I had the feeling he'd had all of me that he wanted. He said he'd call a cab to take him to his car but promised to be back for the play. Catherine said she'd like that.

Franco's fierce independence freed me to escape the office. I placed a call to Nat and asked if she was up for company. She was and I was on my way.

Part of my reason for visiting with Nat was more than to spare me a drive back to the office. I also wanted to spend some time with my friend and campaign manager. I had only been back from Sacra-mento for a few days—very long days—days of great distraction as far as the campaign was concerned. If there had been any luck in this horrible week it was that Nat and I planned a light schedule, know-ing my desk would be full of work when I returned. Next week I was back to having two jobs: mayor and congressional candidate.

I said a few good-byes, made Catherine promise not to run off again, and drove to Nat's Santa Barbara home. I parked out front and walked up the concrete path to her porch. I waved at the small camera I knew was tucked away in a soffit above the door.

I didn't bother knocking. She knew I was there. Since her acci-dent, Nat had become a self-educated expert in electronic gizmos, at least those that could make her life easier. There were times when a woman in a wheelchair didn't want to answer the door. She could see her porch, front and rear yards, and the street in front of her house. She was a wired woman.

A speaker above my head sounded, "Come in, Maddy."

I did and found the living room and the adjoining dining room empty.

"I assume you're hidden away in your office," I said loudly.

"Brilliant as usual." The voice rolled down the hallway that led to Nat's bedroom and the room she had converted into an office. "There are diet sodas in the fridge. Grab a couple."

I set my purse on the dining room table, walked into the kitchen, scooped up two Diet Cokes, and headed down the hall. Nat was sitting at her computer. A large monitor was positioned to her right, revealing what her unblinking cameras saw. Several video recorders were stacked on one side. Whenever Nat left her home, she activated these recorders and then played the images back at high speed. She liked to know who'd been by while she was gone. I was surprised to see she was on the phone. A headset pressed her blond hair to her scalp.

Popping the soda, I set it on a coaster near her right hand. She mouthed the word, "Thanks." I took the only seat in the office, a chrome and leather chair that had once been stylish but would now be called classic modern.

"And you said you searched some of the blogs," she said into the mouthpiece while typing commands into her computer with one hand. "And that led you where?"

Blogs?

I opened my can of soda and took a sip. Watching Nat work was amazing. Confined to the chair and having full motion of only one hand, she could still do more than most people I know.

The soda tasted sweet and the bubbles felt soothing. I've learned to rest in forced downtime. This was a good time to take a deep breath and sort my thoughts. The first thing on my agenda was prayer. Catherine was back and safe. Two murders remained to be solved, the theft of signs and other safety items remained a major problem, Doug and the Slater boy were still in the hospital, and the election was less than a month away and aside from a speech I gave at the chamber of commerce, I had done nothing to solicit more votes. The problems piled before me like tons of mounded snow ready to give way in a town-eating avalanche. But Catherine was home and safe. God was good, and with soda in hand and eyes closed, I told him so.

When I opened my eyes I saw a short video playing on Nat's computer screen. The quality was poor, the image grainy, and the motion a little jerky. At first I assumed that Nat was talking to one of her clients. I could see a car moving forward. The video was shot from an elevated position. Occasionally something blurred the edge of the frame. Something happened I didn't quite catch but Nat pulled back and groaned.

"Hang on," she said to the caller. "I'm running it again."

There was something familiar about this. I rose and stepped behind Nat.

She turned her head my direction. "Brace yourself."

"For what?"

The video started again. I could see that although the overall image was poor, it was in color. The car appeared from the left of the frame and approached the intersection. It was a Ford minivan. Time seemed to stretch as a half second later I realized what I was watching.

The minivan moved forward. A young boy stepped from the curb. Nausea filled my belly and burned my throat. I had no words. I had just seen a child hit by a car. The sweet taste of the soda turned rancid in my mouth.

"Is that . . . ?"

"The boy in the hospital you told me about? I think so. The police can confirm it . . . what's that? Hang on." The last comment was directed to the caller.

"Who are you talking to?" I asked.

"Floyd, Maddy is here, I'm going to put you on speakerphone." Nat punched a button on the phone and removed her headset. "Can you hear me?"

"Yes. I hear you fine. Are you there, Mayor?"

"I am, Floyd, but I just got here. Someone needs to fill me in."

"That would be you, Floyd," Nat said. "You're the genius who found this."

"I'm no genius. I just got lucky. Really anyone familiar with—"

"Floyd," I interrupted. "Talk about the video." I looked at Nat who made no attempt to conceal the smile.

"Oh, sorry. You asked me to do some research for you and I did. First, I searched for a way to videotape an accident and sell it on the Internet. I found small video cameras are easy to buy over the Internet. Some people use them as nannycams—you know, a way to make sure their babysitters aren't stealing the silverware or beating the kids. Others set up surveillance of their homes so that they can check things while they're at work or on a business trip."

"That's what the police found in the tree?" I asked.

"I guess so. I asked Detective Scott if I could see it, but he said no. He also said a couple of other things you probably don't want to hear. Anyway, I started searching the Internet and learned that there's a whole industry that sells covert video cameras and other spy stuff to the public. They have all kinds of neat stuff. Some of it's kinda scary."

"Tell me about the cameras," I said. Nat took a sip of her soda and looked very proud.

"They come in various sizes, but most are small. The quality varies depending on how much you want to spend. Most are little black plastic boxes. Some come with transmitters and receivers. For example, you can buy a spy camera and set it up in the cafeteria and sit in your office and see who is stealing granola bars."

"You can do all this wirelessly?"

"Yes. Some systems are good for a thousand feet or so. The good ones are expensive. It would be easy to spend over a thousand dollars for one system. Cheaper ones are available."

"That seems out of the range for high school kids," I said.

Nat jumped in. "Are you kidding? Between iPods, laptops, tricked-out cell phones, and other gadgets, kids own a lot more technology than a grand can buy. And that's assuming they bought it. The devices could be stolen."

"I knew you were busy with Catherine so I called Nat. She knows more about this stuff than I do. She's been a big help."

"Nonsense, this is all Floyd's doing. All I did was guess the level of sophistication of the camera. Like Floyd, I hadn't seen it, but based on the image quality I would guess that it's a higher-end camera but the signal is being stretched to the limits. In other words, the receiver is a little too far from the transmitter. They still got footage but the quality isn't as good as it could be. I'm kind of thankful for that."

So was I. "But where did you get the video?"

"You said that they might want to sell this stuff on the Internet. That's easy enough, but it isn't something you want to advertise. This isn't the kind of thing you put on a billboard. So I did some basic searches but came up with nothing. Then I thought, what would I do? Blogs was the answer."

"Blogs?"

Nat answered. "It's short for 'Web log.' Take the 'b' from Web and add it to 'log' and you get 'blog.' Think of them as online journals. In some cases, others can post to your blog. People with common interests exchange information through blogs and bulletin boards."

"Exactly. I found a posting about a gross video of an auto accident. The guy was bragging. I followed the link and found the video. It was uploaded to a personal website but the only way to view it is to have the exact URL."

"I'm not following," I admitted.

"Let me explain it this way," Nat said. "A client hires me to do some research. I do my job and I want to post pictures, text, video, and the like on my website but I don't want others to see it. I upload the information to my site as a separate page and give it an address like www.natsanders.com/client101 or similar. Then I call or email my client and give her that address. Only people who know the address can access the site. Sometimes I add a password."

"So that's what happened here?"

"Yes, except there's no password. That's kind of stupid."

"Even considering this is kind of stupid," I said. "Someone buys or steals the camera and recorder, sets up the scene, records until there is an accident, then uploads it to his or her website."

"Not his or her website. They were smart enough not to do that. They uploaded it to someone else's site."

"Can you do that?"

Nat nodded. "If you have the transfer protocols you can."

My mind was chugging like an old percolator. "Whose site?"

"Santa Rita High School."

Our suspicions had been right. "This isn't good."

"Actually, it is." There was a pause. Floyd never contradicted me. Having just done so must have shocked him. "You see, the police might be able to find out who knew the transfer protocols and who had access to the computers at the time the video was uploaded. Or if it was uploaded from someplace else, where that was. I don't know if they need search warrants or anything."

"We can leave that up to them—"

"There's more," Nat said. "Go on, Floyd."

"Well, there's a limited range on the spy camera's transmitter. Nat thinks it's a thousand feet or so. That fits with the specs I found. That means that the receiver must be close. Unless the guy is sitting in a car recording this stuff, then the recorder is most likely in one of the houses. The police should be able to find out if any students live within a thousand feet of the camera location, and see if that student has access to the high school website. At the very least, it's a start."

"And," Nat said, "your brilliant aide had another idea. He searched the business license records to see if there was a local electronics shop that specialized in spy equipment. Want to guess what he found?"

"That there is?"

"Yes. It's called Eye-Spy."

Energy fired through me. We were making some assumptions but they were reasonable and based on solid evidence. It was time to act. "I'll be right back." I stepped out of the office and returned with my cell phone. I called the police station and asked for Detective Adrian Scott. He was on the line a moment later.

"Good afternoon, Mayor. Did you know your assistant was over here a little while ago nosing around in my investigation?"

"Nosing around?"

"That's right. He wanted to see the camera we retrieved. We're trying to keep that information from the public so as not to alert the perp."

I sighed for effect. "Okay, Detective, here's what I need you to do. I need you to get up, walk across the parking lot to city hall, and go to my office. My nosy aide is going to show you the video that was taken from the camera you wouldn't let him see, then he's going to tell you where it is on the Internet and how it probably got there.

Then he's going to give you some more information that will send you to the high school to talk to a few people."

"He found the video on the Net?"

"That he did. You may choose to apologize to him, anytime you wish. I'll leave that up to you." I hung up. "Floyd, if Detective Scott isn't there in the next ten minutes, call me back. Also, I want you to share everything you've found with Tess. Is she in the building?"

"I think so."

"Good. Oh, and Floyd. You're the best. The absolute best."

"Um, thanks. Just doing my job."

Nat said, "Hey, Floyd, if you ever get tired of hanging around city hall, I'll give you a job."

"Knock it off, Nat," I said before Floyd could speak. "He's mine. You try and steal him again, and I'll tell everyone you dye your hair."

"I don't dye my hair."

I smiled. "They won't know that." I laid a hand on her shoulder. "Thanks, Nat. You and Floyd may have saved lives."

chapter 01

I spent the rest of the afternoon and early evening meeting with Nat. We discussed the campaign and just about everything else. It was the everything else that got to me. An hour after I arrived, and a second can of soda later I let slip that Judson West had been offered a position in Denver.

"That doesn't surprise me," Nat said. We were seated around her dining room table, nibbling crackers.

"It certainly surprised me," I admitted.

"Of course it did."

I eyed her. "What does that mean?"

"You don't want to ask that."

"I just did," I insisted.

She raised her soda. "We've talked about your personal life a few times, haven't we?"

"Yes."

"You know that West is still in love with you, and if not in love, then infatuated."

"I know that he still has interest, but I've done nothing to encourage it. Jerry and I are officially seeing each other."

Nat chortled. "I didn't know that could be done officially." She paused, then looked me straight in the eye. "Sometimes you amaze me, Maddy. There you sit, smart, beautiful, driven, living life with purpose and intensity, yet you can be as dumb as a brick."

"I beg your pardon?"

"I just watched you assimilate a ton of information about spy cameras, broadcast distances and more, then ring up a police detective, read him the riot act, and then shift gears into discussions of the campaign, but for the life of you, you can't see what you're doing to those two men."

"What I'm doing to *them*? Exactly what am I *doing* to them?"

"Stringing them along. You're going out with Jerry, giving him hope for a future with you, but you won't move out of the present. West is still in your orbit, hoping Jerry will tire of waiting. It sounds like he's the one giving up on waiting."

"You think he's considering taking the Denver job to get my attention, is that it?"

"No, I think that he's considering it so he can get away from you."

I blinked. "That's a little harsh."

"No, you're being a little sensitive. Your love life is your business, but right now you have two men who desire you and you're willing to let them hang out there until you make up your mind."

"I didn't know relationship counseling was part of a campaign manager's job." I was being defensive. Her words pinched a nerve.

"Hey, I told you that you didn't want to go down this path."

She had warned me. "All right, what do you suggest?"

"Get off the dime, lady. Make a decision and stop stringing these poor guys along."

"Some decisions shouldn't be rushed." I leaned back and crossed my arms. More defensiveness.

"Rushed?" She laughed. "At this rate, Maddy, you'll be in a convalescent home gumming applesauce before you get around to choosing Jerry. And you know what? Jerry will be at the home with you, showering you with admiration and love."

"How do you know that Jerry is the right one for me?"

"Oh, come on, Maddy, the man's heart pumps gold for you. He'd eat glass if it would make you happy. Let me ask you something: can you picture yourself married to Judson West?"

There were moments when I had tried, but it never felt right. "No."

"Good, a straight answer. What about Jerry? Can you see yourself married to him?"

I had imagined that many times as well, often against my will. "Yes, I can."

"So you don't want West to leave because you need a safety net. Let him go, Maddy."

That hurt. "I don't view him as a safety net."

"So what then? You're angry he didn't tell you about Denver because you fear the loss of a good cop?"

"Now you're being unfair."

Nat raised the can of Diet Coke to her lips and said nothing. Her eyes, however, said enough.

She set the drink down. "Has Jerry been supportive of your run for congress?"

"Very supportive."

"Don't you realize how special that is? If you win the seat, you're going to be spending a lot of time in D.C. He's willing to let you go so that you can be happy; so that you can fulfill your dream—your heart's desire. Listen, Maddy, there aren't many men like that."

"It's not that simple."

"Isn't it?"

"No, it's not," I snapped. I cooled my tone. "No, it isn't. He doesn't share my faith. I've become a believer and he's not."

"Uh-huh. He's hostile to Christianity?"

"No, I didn't say that."

"What does he believe?" Nat's words had taken on an edge.

"I know he has doubts and questions."

"Don't you?"

There was a time when I could have dropped a couple of quick lies and moved on, but not now, not here, not with Nat who saw deeper into my being than anyone else. I was still so new in the faith, less than a year and a half, and every day I learned how ignorant I was. "I admit I don't have all the answers."

"So having questions doesn't disqualify you as a believer."

"No."

The cracker nibbling had stopped and the soul rending had begun. "Maddy, I have seen you change. This faith of yours has altered you. When we first met, I thought, 'Now here is a woman I can respect: sharp, strong, edgy.' Then you gave your life to Christ or whatever you call it and I thought, 'Well, there goes the edge; there goes all those qualities that make her wonderful.' I was wrong. Some things in your life have softened, but only those things that needed it. I've watched you over the months, as a friend, as your campaign manager, and I have seen intriguing things. You are better for having faith."

Tears were edging up to my eyelids. I felt as if all my internal organs were made of wax and were melting and draining into my feet.

"Did you come to your spiritual decision all by yourself?"

I shook my head. "I read some passages from the Bible they found with my husband after he was killed. Paul Shedd had given it to him. I went to Paul with questions. He led me to Christ."

"I'm certainly no expert," Nat said, "but isn't that what Christians do? Don't they share what they found?"

I dragged a dry finger beneath my eyes and pulled it away wet. "Yes."

"Talk to Jerry, Maddy. I think you may find he's more open than you think. He's never ridiculed your faith, has he?"

"No, never."

"Talk to him. Share what you know."

"I don't know where to begin."

She smiled. "Begin with the heart. That's where you two communicate the best. Always start with the heart."

I looked down at the table. Everything Nat had said was right. I didn't like it. I wasn't enjoying the conversation, and a huge part of me wished I had gone back to the office. Just the other day I had tried to express my faith to Catherine, but I felt I had failed. Maybe I was too vague, too inexperienced. Maybe I gave up too soon.

The conversation was forcing a sharper focus. I did love Jerry. West was attractive and I was drawn to him, but I was connected to Jerry. We had been through so much, and he was always there, always supportive, and always patient. Patience was a requirement for those who hung around me.

"You're right. Thank you for being so honest. I just wish I knew how to begin." I raised my eyes from the table and saw something I had never seen before: tears brimming in Nat's eyes.

"You can start with me," she whispered.

chapter 82

I left Nat's emotionally drained. At least I was drained for a more joyful reason. I did my best to explain a person's need for Christ and for the forgiveness of sins. I was clumsy but I persisted, explaining what I knew, what I had learned from the Bible, and most of all, how it changed me. I confessed that I was not the ideal Christian, that I was a person in the act of becoming, and that becoming would take a lifetime. With Catherine I spoke in generalities but with Nat I just opened my heart like it was a steamer trunk and let her peek inside. When I was done, she asked questions. Some I had answers for, others I promised to get answers to. I made no pretense at being an expert, made no claims of being a theologian. I presented myself as I was, a new Christian who knew she had been changed and who knew that there were more changes on the way.

When all the talking was done, I waited for flashes of lightning, a heavenly beam to shine down from the sky, pierce the house, and fall upon Nat. It didn't.

"I need to think," Nat said, but there was something different in her tone and in the glow of her eyes. I understood. We were carved from the same granite slab. I wouldn't press because I hated being pressed. It was taking time to learn, but I was realizing that sometimes the best thing to do is get out of God's way. I did as I was led. The rest was out of my hands.

At the front door we hugged, and I walked to the car. Before starting the engine, I made two calls: One to Neena Lasko at the Curtain Call dinner theater and one to Jerry. In each phone call, I asked for a favor.

Neena had to do some rearranging, but she made it happen. Jerry and I would have the same balcony room we had last night. This time, however, it would be just the two of us. Although the room was designed to hold four or more, we would be alone. I offered to pay for the tickets that would normally have been purchased for the other table, but she declined and I let her.

Traffic back to the theater was lighter than I expected so I arrived early. I visited with Neena for a moment, checked in on Catherine, telling her in old theater tradition to "break a leg," then went to the balcony room. I took the BODY COUNT screenplay that I had been carting around all afternoon with me. Jerry wouldn't arrive for an hour, giving me time to glance through the script.

One of the servers, dressed in street clothes, brought me a cup of coffee compliments of Neena. I imagined he would don his tux when the theater opened for dinner. I slipped my feet out of the pumps I had been wearing all day, granting a short furlough to my toes. I set the screenplay in front of me.

```
                    BODY COUNT
              An Original Screenplay by
                   Andy Buchanan
```

Unlike the other scripts I had seen this week, this one had no revision dates in the bottom right corner. It had never reached the stage where revisions were required. I started reading. Screenplays are different than books. Each page has more white space than text, so the reading was fast.

I had turned the last page when Jerry walked through the door. His hair was slightly mussed, his shirt a little wrinkled, and his face drawn with weariness. Boy, he looked good. I rose, kissed him, and wrapped my arms around him. He seemed stunned and stood motionless. Then I felt the tension pour from his body, and he slipped his arms around me.

"This day just got better," he said and rested his chin on the top of my head. "This is good medicine."

"You can say that again." With reluctance, I let go and moved back to the table. "I wasn't expecting you for another half hour."

"My last two appointments canceled. Apparently, kids can get well all on their own. The nerve of the little curtain crawlers. Don't they know I'm trying to make a living?"

"It's a pain when health gets in the way of a good business plan." We both laughed, and his laughter sounded better than any music I've ever heard. It isn't falling in love that is so liberating; it's realizing you've fallen in love.

"What's this?" He pointed at the script.

"It's a screenplay written by the young man killed at Catherine's."

"The second murder."

"That's right. Ed Lowe, the chauffeur, was first, then Andy Buchanan."

"What are you doing with a dead man's script?"

I told him that elements of the murder appeared in two scripts. "In Catherine's first movie, a scene was cut that showed a man loading Glaser blue-tip rounds into a .38 revolver. In the script for her next movie, a stalker kills people associated with a famous model."

"Okay, I can see the connections," Jerry said. "Is this script connected to the murders too?"

"Yes. It's not very subtle. The male protagonist is a rogue movie security guard who falls in love with a leading lady. Want to guess their names?"

"Not Andy and Catherine?"

"You got it. In one scene, a remote listening device is used to eavesdrop on people inside of a house. It's one of those that supposedly picks up the vibration from windows. Everything is recorded, nothing is left behind. Lots of fighting and gunfire. The Catherine character becomes a female Rambo. Can you imagine Catherine running around with a machine gun? No wonder this hasn't been produced."

"Worse movies have been produced," Jerry said.

"Maybe that's what kept Andy going."

"Didn't Catherine see the words 'Body Count' in the added pages?" Jerry asked. "Wouldn't she make the connection?"

"If she did, she didn't say anything. I plan to ask her."

"What are you thinking?"

I weighed my words. "I'm wondering if Andy killed Ed Lowe. I can't be certain about motivation, but the mind that came up with this script might be capable of trying to get her attention by acting out a portion of the play."

"You mean he killed Ed Lowe just to add some kind of reality to the script?"

"No, I don't think he planned to actually kill anyone. No one was supposed to be there. Catherine was at rehearsal. She sent Lowe back to check on the house and to wait for some electricians. We know the electricians came because the power to the remote control shades was working, and Catherine said they weren't when she first arrived."

"So Lowe is at her house and catches sight of Andy Buchanan."

"Maybe. Rockwood says he has met Lowe previously. The same may be true for Andy's father, Chuck, who's directing the movie, but would Andy and Lowe know each other? Probably not. Lowe sees someone lurking around the house. Goes out back to investigate. Maybe he thinks it's one of the workers, only to find out it's some guy with electronic equipment. An argument breaks out. There's a bit of a fight. Andy loses it and shoots Lowe in the head."

"But why would Andy even have a gun?"

"Because he's playing out the part of the male lead in his movie. His father told me his son had a drug problem. He had been hospitalized for his addiction."

"Psychosis has been associated with certain addictions," Jerry said. "How would you prove this?"

"Me? I can't prove anything. Perhaps West can check on past mental problems Andy might have had. The coroner could screen for drugs, I suppose, but that would be up to them."

"I don't know, Maddy. That only solves one murder. If Andy killed Lowe, who killed Andy?"

"I don't have a clue."

I looked over the balcony railing. Early diners were making their way in. The noise level rose.

The door to our room opened, and Neena stepped in again. "Ah, I see that company has arrived." She offered coffee and we accepted. "I have a special treat for you. Harold and I are so relieved to have Catherine back that we'd like to invite you backstage during the intermission. I'm afraid we can't have you back there during the performance because our stage just isn't big enough, but I think you'll enjoy seeing all the activity."

"That would be wonderful," I said.

Neena left us to ourselves.

"I should have asked sooner," I said, reaching for Jerry's hand. "How's the Slater boy?"

"I phoned the nurse's station just before I left. He has stabilized. We're starting to hope again."

"That's good. I've been praying for him." My stomach started doing flips. "I've made arrangements. You and I are going to be the only ones in this room tonight."

An eyebrow rose. "Really?"

"I want to talk to you about something."

"Uh-oh."

I grinned. "Nothing bad, silly. It's just time that I share with you."

"About your faith?"

"How did you know that?"

He gave my hand a squeeze. "I've known you for a very long time. I've loved you for years. I know you better than you might think. I've been watching you change and I like what I see. I'm not sure what to think about all this church stuff, but I'm willing to listen to anything you have to say."

I took him at his word. We talked during the appetizers and the meal that followed. I tried to be as open with him as I had been with Nat.

Five minutes before the play began we prayed.

chapter 33

The play moved forward effortlessly. Catherine took the stage as if last night had not happened. She seemed to float across the boards, and her lines were crisp and clear. The other actors rose to the occasion. I sat in my chair, my shoulder touching Jerry's, my hand on his elbow. My tears of joy had dried, and I was lost in the play. For a few moments, everything seemed perfect in the world. The evil I had seen now seemed far away.

As we finished our meal, the server took our dessert order, and we told him we had been invited backstage for a few minutes and to leave the dessert on the table. We'd eat it during the second portion of the show.

The curtains closed to loud applause. Jerry and I slipped out of the balcony room, and like salmon swimming upstream, worked our way through the lines of people moving to the bathrooms or outside for fresh air. Most of the attendees stayed in the dining area and chatted in good-natured tones, punctuated with laughter.

Room on the floor was slim, the aisle filled with people standing or chairs pushed back so the users could stretch their legs. Nonetheless, we managed to make it to the stage and up the short flight of stairs.

As I hit the top tread a familiar form caught my eye. Franco Zambonelli was seated near the front. He looked lost and concerned. Earlier today we sat and had a heart-to-heart. He was irritating, brash, and not always aware of how others perceived him, but he had brought Catherine back to her senses. I owed him something. I motioned for him to join us.

We passed through the curtains stage left.

"Did you know stage left is to the right of the audience," Jerry said.

"I didn't know that."

As we started backstage he pointed at a black curtain in the wings. It hid the working area from the sight of the audience. "That's called a tormentor curtain."

"Why do they call it that?" I asked.

"I don't know. I only took one theater class in college."

"Decided that acting wasn't for you, eh?"

He looked back at me. "Actually, the professor decided it wasn't for me. 'The theater has wide arms, young Mr. Thomas, but not that wide.' I was crushed."

"I'll bet."

Just beyond the tormentor curtain stood Harold Young. He was all smiles while calling out orders to the stagehands.

"Mayor! You came back to my world."

"Thank you for the invitation." Two men carried a sofa by. "There's a lot of activity back here."

"At times it's bedlam," Harold said. "Follow me; we need to get out of the way." A few steps later we were deeper in the setup area. I could see the place where actors passed their time waiting for their next scenes. Two actors played handheld video games. One of the older thespians was reading a newspaper. It was surreal. I felt like someone had put the world on a coffee break.

Catherine skipped over to us, more animated than I had seen her all week. She threw her arms around my neck, did the same to a very surprised Jerry, and then to Franco. "Are you having fun?"

"Very much. You're wonderful. The whole play is fabulous."

"It is. Harold's a genius, isn't he? This play is going to outlive us all."

"You seem lively," I said.

"She was always that way," Harold said. "A nervous wreck before the curtain goes up, then there's no stopping her."

"Yeah, well, wait until after the play. I'm useless." Catherine took my hand. "Come on, I'll introduce you to the cast. These guys are great."

"It's your fault." The voice was familiar and dark. It came from behind me.

I pivoted and found myself facing Chuck Buchanan. Judging by the reeking smell coming from his clothing, he had been in close contact with booze of some sort. He had told me that he was a recovered alcoholic. His glassy eyes, swagger, and demeanor told me he was no longer recovering. I couldn't blame him. Just this morning he had to identify his dead son; a son with a hole in his forehead.

Without thinking I took a step back. He wore a large leather jacket, and he had both hands plunged deep into its pockets. His face was drawn, his mouth a deep frown.

"Chuck," Catherine said. "I didn't know you were—"

Chuck pulled a gun from his coat and held it in his right hand. Catherine inhaled noisily. I stopped breathing. His hand had a subtle, frightening shake.

"He loved you, Catherine," Buchanan said. "I told him to take his time. To win you bit by bit, but he was impatient. I brought him onboard so you could see him work, see that he had licked his problems, found his center, but you rejected him."

"Chuck," Catherine began. "I'm sorry—"

"It's too late for apologies. You're on stage. Everyone loves you. Andy is lying on a metal slab in a cooler. Naked and locked in a coroner's drawer. It's all because of you."

Jerry inched his way closer to me, standing a foot ahead. He was trying to put his body between me and the gun. "Listen . . . Buchanan is it? Mr. Buchanan. I'm Jerry Thomas. Dr. Jerry Thomas. I think I can help you."

"Can you raise the dead, Doc? Can you? That's the only way you can help me." Tears began to run down his face.

"I think it's the alcohol, Mr. Buchanan. It's a depressant, you know. I think if you give yourself a couple of hours, you'll see what a mistake this is."

"I've lived most my life with booze, Doc. I know what it is. It doesn't matter any more." His voice broke. "I failed my wife, then I failed my son. He followed in my footsteps. He copied me. Read the same books, went to the same college, chose the same career— chose to be an addict. Different drug, same effect."

He returned his pitiful gaze to Catherine. "You have everything, girl. Everything. Looks, fame, money, people who love you. All I had was Andy; all he had was me. He loved you. You could have been good for him. He even wrote a script for you. You wouldn't even read it with him."

"I gave it to my agent," Catherine said. "She said I had to pass."

"He was stalking her," I protested. "Maybe he was lovesick, maybe it was the drugs, but he was stalking her, just like the movie you're making. He spied on her using equipment like that described in his screenplay."

"How do you know what's in his screenplay?"

"I've read it. My aide downloaded it from the Internet."

Jerry took a step forward. "She's right. She showed it to me. We have it up in the balcony room. Come on, I'll show you."

"Take one more step, Doc, and you'll die along with Catherine." He raised the gun and his trembling hand settled. That made me more nervous. "An eye for an eye; a life for a life—a family member for a family member."

The last part confused me. Until he aimed the gun at my forehead. The barrel was directed at the same spot where a nasty bullet took his son's life. "You may not have killed him with your own hands, but you stripped his heart from him. You took someone from my family, now I'm going to return the favor."

"I killed your son," Franco said as if he were ordering a sandwich. "I pulled the trigger, pal. Not only that, he had it comin'."

Buchanan shifted his gaze to Franco.

"That's right, buddy boy. I figured it out." Franco was taunting him and backing toward the stage, redirecting Buchanan's attention from me and the others. "I killed your boy with his own gun."

"Not possible," Buchanan said.

"You're so drunk you don't know what's possible and what's not." He backed up another step. "I was here last night, watching the play. At intermission I had to use the head. When I came out I saw your boy drop the script with the lady in the gift shop. I followed him."

"You're a liar."

"He couldn't deliver the script himself. No guts, I guess. Hiding in the shadows. Sending someone else to deliver it."

"I'm going to kill you where you stand," Buchanan spat.

"Not yet, you're not. You want to know the whole story. You live for story. That's why you're a director." Franco gave a quick look at Jerry. He expected Jerry to do something. I saw Jerry give the subtlest of nods. "As far as I knew, Catherine didn't need another script, so I was curious. I followed him outside and into the parking lot. There was a cabby there. He walked over and gave him something. Money, I guess. Maybe some kinda drug. What'd your boy prefer? Smack? Meth? Crack. I'll bet it was crack. He struck me as a crackhead."

Franco kept ratcheting up the insults, antagonizing Buchanan. At first I thought Franco had lost his mind, but then I saw what he was doing—getting Buchanan to transfer his fury.

"SHUT UP!" Buchanan waved the gun.

Franco backed up until his back was next to the tormentor curtain.

"Yup. I watched your boy give the cabby something. I realized later he was paying the man to sit and wait just in case Catherine came out. You know how Catherine is. Mercurial. Is that the word? Like mercury in a thermometer, up and down. Kinda endearing most of the time, but he knew those extra pages would send her over the edge. He gambled and he won. She came charging out looking for the quickest way home. It was a good thing he paid the cabby."

"He couldn't know she would do that," Buchanan said through clenched teeth.

"Well, you're right there, but so what? He would just try something else stupid, the next night, or the next." He stopped at the curtain. The sound of patrons enjoying conversation, coffee, and dessert drifted backstage. "I watched as your boy went to his car. I decided to follow him. He went straight to Catherine's house. It went downhill from there."

"What did you do? Answer me. What did you do?"

"I parked on the street. He did the same but went further down. I bet his car is still there. After that, there isn't much to tell."

Jerry reached back until his hand touched mine. I gave his arm a squeeze. He pulled away and motioned for me to go backstage.

"No," I whispered.

He motioned more fervently. He slipped an inch closer. Franco couldn't back up anymore without moving beyond the side curtain.

"I watched him walk onto Catherine's property. I followed and confronted him in the backyard. Do you know he killed Catherine's chauffeur? You know Ed Lowe, don't you? Ed caught him in the back. They argued. They fought down by the pool. Andy isn't much of a fighter, so he gave up and promised to leave. Instead he pulled his gun and shot Ed Lowe in the head. Ed was unarmed. Just like me. But your boy shot him anyway, just like you want to shoot me."

Jerry moved before I could speak. But not before Buchanan could turn. He swung with his arm still extended. The gun struck Jerry in the right temple and went off with a deafening crack. Something swept past my ear. Catherine screamed. Jerry fell, his hand cupped to the side of his head. I saw blood trickle from his fingers. I ran to his side as Buchanan, surprised by the recoil and roar of his own gun, paused for a half second.

Franco needed no more. He sprang forward, seized Buchanan by the back of the shirt and yanked hard. The thinner, lighter man lost his footing and tumbled into the side curtain. Franco charged like a bull, burying his head in Buchanan's middle. The two men plunged past the curtain and onto the proscenium.

Someone in the audience screamed. The gun went off. Several more people screamed.

I pulled Jerry's hand away. A straight crease in his scalp poured blood. A quarter inch more to the right and Jerry would be dead.

"I'm okay," Jerry said. "I'm okay. I'm okay." He was trying to convince himself. And me.

"Catherine, take Jerry and get out. Help her, Harold." They approached.

"Maddy, no," Jerry said.

Against my screaming conscience I peeked around the tormentor curtain. Franco had Buchanan pinned to the stage, but Buchanan still had the gun in his hand. It was pointed into the audience. People were scattering, screaming, scrambling. Parents scooped up children. Couples ran together. All jammed at the exit.

Franco was a frightened man trying to subdue a desperate, drunken man. The gun moved in the direction of a mass of bodies trying to flee the theater. Another inch or two and the barrel would point at the heart of the bundle of bodies. I sprinted forward and dropped to my knees, my hands grasping Buchanan's gun hand and pushing it away from the crowd.

It went off.

I jumped and Buchanan's hand came free. The gun came up and plowed into my nose. Tiny lights sparkled in my eyes and something warm dripped down my face. The gun hand was moving again. Franco reached for it at the same time I did. I felt Buchanan's wrist in my hands and I leaned forward with all my weight. His arm moved down as I pressed myself to the stage.

"Maddy!" A voice behind me. Jerry's voice.

I had to hold him. For just another minute or two, I had to hold him. Then the crowd would clear. Then the police would come. Then—

There was a muffled pop.

"MADDY!"

Something hot stabbed my belly. A searing hot.

Warm. Sticky.

"Mad—"

The theater darkened.

Twilight.

Pitch black.

chapter 34

Pitch black.

Twilight.

The room lightened.

"Maddy?"

My eyes were gritty, my mouth dry, and my abdomen hurt like I had just finished a thousand sit-ups.

Something was stuck up my nose. I reached for it.

"Just leave that alone."

I blinked a few times. My vision was blurry, my mind disoriented. A vague shape hovered over me. My eyes cleared and I saw the face of an angel, an angel with a large bandage on the side of his head.

"Jerry. Where . . . What . . ."

"Shush. I'm a doctor. I can tell you that." He leaned forward and kissed me on the forehead. Wonderful. "You're in ICU. It's your third day."

"I don't . . . remember."

"You're not the first surgery patient to say that. Sometimes the medications erase the short-term memory."

Images began to swirl in my mind, all of them unpleasant. "Catherine?"

"She's fine. Still a little shook up, but she's going to be all right. She's staying with Nat right now, but has plans to move back into her home soon."

"Catherine and Nat living together? I'm doomed."

"Yeah, that's pretty much how I see it," Jerry said. "How are you feeling?" He touched my forehead with the back of his hand.

"Five steps beyond lousy and don't you medical types have thermometers to check for fever?"

"I went to an old medical school. Besides, I just like touching you."

"ICU?" I said. "Kind of ironic—" My mind cleared a little more. "Doug. How's Doug doing? Is he still in ICU?"

Jerry shook his head.

Oh no. A torrent of sadness cascaded on me.

"We moved him to the second floor. He was complaining about being so close to you."

"You mean—"

"Yup, he came out of the coma the night we admitted you. His doctor kept him a couple more days. He was transferred to a regular bed just before lunch."

"Thank God."

Jerry smiled. "I did. While I was at it, I thanked him for Byron Slater."

"You've moved the Slater boy to a regular bed?" That was great news.

"No, he's still here in ICU, but his fever has broken, the brain swelling is decreasing, and he's conscious. Not happy, but conscious."

"My nose feels funny," I said and tried to wiggle it. It hurt.

"I don't doubt it. It's broken, and by the way, you have two wonderfully black eyes. I think you should get some more campaign pictures taken."

"Jerry Thomas, you had better be lying to me."

"I wish I were. You look like a long-haired raccoon." He laughed,
said, "Ow," and touched his bandaged head. "Still a little sore."

I reached for his hand, brought it to my lips, and kissed his
knuckle.

"You may have saved a lot of lives, Maddy," Jerry said softly.
"Buchanan kept squeezing the trigger. He was bound to hit someone. You're a hero."

"He did hit someone." I winced as I tried to reposition myself.
"As for being a hero, I'm giving it up. It hurts too much. Besides,
Franco is the real hero."

"He is that, all right. The round that hit you was the last one
fired. Franco was able to free a hand and punched Buchanan. I saw
it. It's a wonder it didn't kill him."

I was getting sleepy again. I fought it off. "What happened to . . .
Franco?"

"I'm afraid he's in jail. West was by to check on you earlier, and
he filled me in. He said Franco admitted killing Andy. He confronted
Andy and they fought. Andy pulled out his gun and they struggled
for it. Franco was able to pull it from Andy's hand but he fell back-
ward. Do you remember any tools by the pool?"

"Some. A shovel, a pickax, and a trowel. West mentioned them
too. I assume they belong to one of the landscapers."

"Andy picked up the shovel and raised it over the fallen Franco.
Franco shot to defend himself."

"He admitted to all of this?"

"West said he kept it quiet because he was concerned what it
would do to Catherine."

"'Everything I do, I do for her,'" I said.

"What?" Jerry looked confused.

"Something Franco said to me while we waited for Catherine at the Curtain Call. He said that everything he does, he does for her."

"West said they also found Andy's car down the street from Catherine's house. They searched it and found a tape recorder with a cassette of your conversation with Catherine when you saw Lowe's body. He had been using the recorder to dictate notes for himself. He was hiding in the house when you two were there. He wasn't expecting you, just Catherine. We'll never know what he planned that day, but your presence messed up his plan."

"The BODY COUNT script mentions one of those eavesdropping devices. I thought maybe he used one of those."

"Nothing that sophisticated. West said they found his fingerprints throughout the house, including Catherine's bedroom. They also found his fingerprints inside the closet. Best guess for now is that he hid the recorder, then hid himself. When Catherine followed you out back, he retrieved the recorder and slipped out the front door."

"It frightens me to think he was so close. If it weren't for Franco, Andy might still be playing games."

"The legal system will decide what happens to Franco now."

"Uh-huh . . ." My eyelids had turned to lead. "When do I get out of ICU?"

"The bullet wound was clean. Lucky for you it wasn't one of the funny bullets you were talking about."

"Glaser . . ."

"Yeah, those. Buchanan used his own gun. Franco buried Andy's gun in the flowerbed. Your bullet went in clean and came out clean. Of course, it messed up some of your innards. If you behave, then you should be in a regular room tomorrow. I'm thinking of asking admitting to put you in the same room as Doug. Just think, he can interview you hour after hour."

"Innards. I love medical talk."

Jerry kept talking but I ceased to hear him. I surrendered to sleep again.

The next day they moved me to a room on the second floor. It was a private room with a television that needed color tuning. I was trying to lose myself in a CNN report when Tess and Floyd walked through the door. Floyd was carrying a box of chocolates, which I took to be a cruel joke, since I wouldn't be allowed such things for a while. Tess carried flowers. At least I didn't want to eat those.

I was glad to see Floyd and surprised to see Tess.

"Aren't you supposed to be minding the shop while I'm out?" I asked her.

She gave one of those rare and stunning smiles. "I have everything under complete control—your office is now where the janitor closet used to be. How are you feeling?"

"Horrible. Nauseated, sore, and I'm tired of lying around in bed."

"Now that sounds like the Maddy Glenn I know." She placed the flowers on the windowsill. "I thought you'd like to know that the police have arrested everyone involved in the sign stealing debacle."

"That's good news," I said. "Sit down, Tess."

She shook her head. "It seems that all I ever do is sit. I'll let Floyd have the chair." He took it. "Thanks to Floyd and his ability to think outside the box, the police were able to track down the hoods who were stealing the signs, barricades, and other things. It was a club. Initiation required the theft of city property. Someone stole a traffic sign and that became the rage. There were six high school students involved. All of them juniors."

"And they videotaped all of these?"

"Oh no. I thought the same thing," Tess said. "When Floyd showed me the video of the vehicle-pedestrian accident, I asked him about the other videos he found. He hadn't found any others. That was the only one. At first, I thought, well, that just means that the other signs and the like were replaced before anything bad happened."

"But that left Mr. Turner's accident," Floyd said. "That would be the kind of thing these guys would post."

"Turns out," Tess said, "only one video was made and posted by a student working alone. He's the president of the computer club at the school. He confessed to making several others but hadn't posted them yet."

"How did they find him?" I asked.

"Floyd did his research, remember. He assumed that the spy camera had a limited range and sure enough, the kid lived within a thousand feet of the camera. Not only that, he bought the device locally, and the police have that bill of sale. I was there when Detective Scott interrogated the student. First Scott showed him the seized camera system, next he showed him the video, then he showed him when and from where it was uploaded. It was enough. The kid started talking, told Detective Scott all about it, and gave names of everyone involved. Detective Scott can be intimidating."

"Floyd, you're a hero," I said. He blushed, a true old-fashioned face reddening. Then to Tess I added, "You too, Tess. I thank God I asked you to be involved in this. You were the best person for the job."

I got another smile.

Epilogue

We had decided to go ahead with the fund-raiser at the Spaghetti Warehouse. Invitations had been sent weeks before, a special announcement had gone out about our special guest, Catherine Anderson, and I couldn't see wasting the effort.

Jerry wheeled me into the restaurant and to the back area where our fund-raiser was to be held. The smell of Italian sauces, garlic, cheese, and bread made my stomach hurt, this time in a good way. Still, I'd have to eat light and little. Pity.

As Jerry pushed me into the expansive room, the gathered crowd rose and applauded. They must have stirred up some dust because my eyes began to water. I waved like a queen on a flowered float as Jerry propelled me to the head table. He stopped the wheelchair by my seat. I rose and took my place in a more standard chair. Next to me was Nat, looking lovelier than I had ever seen her. At the end of the table, near a podium, sat Catherine. She seemed a half decade older but she smiled, waved, and carried on a conversation with one of my campaign staff.

Nat leaned my direction. "You want to race after dinner? My wheelchair against yours. Remember, mine's battery-powered."

"You need to remember that mine is powered by an M.D."

Jerry parked the wheelchair and took a place next to me.

Dinner proceeded like clockwork and noisy conversation filled the room. Spread out among the tables were businessmen, housewives, teachers, grocery clerks, and more. Each had paid four times the amount for their meals than they normally would. The extra was to go to my campaign fund. Also there were my friends and colleagues from city hall. All except Jon Adler. Even Tess had bought a ticket.

We had lively music and every once in a while someone rose to give a toast.

After we had eaten, after dessert had been served, I stood—very slowly—to my feet. The room went quiet.

"I want to thank you for coming tonight and for your great generosity and support—mostly your generosity." That garnered polite laughter. "The doctors say that I can't exert myself yet and even sent Dr. Jerry Thomas along to supervise. Although my wound was to my abdomen, my mouth still works pretty good." More laughter, which grew louder when someone in the audience shouted, "Amen!"

"I'm not going to give a speech this evening. You know where I stand and what I hope to achieve. I do, however, have an announcement to make—a surprising announcement." I looked at Nat, and she returned a worried expression.

I continued. "When someone like me runs for office, we make a lot of promises. We talk a great deal about what we're *going* to do once elected. Tonight, I wish to do more than talk. Recently Santa Rita suffered from a type of vandalism that led to a child being hit by a car. His name is Byron Slater. He's doing better now, but has a very long road ahead of him, including a year or so of therapy."

I paused and looked around. "I'm not going to sing you a sad song. There's a law on the books that prohibits me from singing in public." I took a breath and wished I had spoken to Nat about this first, but I was afraid I would change my mind. "Since choosing to run for congress I have given speeches about our growing health care crisis. Little Byron Slater's family is a victim of the crisis. They have no insurance. Dr. Thomas and I have worked with the hospital and social groups to help them as much as possible, but when the final tally is made they will still be far short of the goal. In a nutshell, this accident will break them financially.

"So here's the big news. The money from this fund-raiser tonight will go not to my campaign but to the Slater family. That means less direct marketing and fewer radio ads. I don't know how it will affect the election. I believe word of mouth is the best way to promote anything. I still need and depend upon your vote. Now, should any of you be bothered by this, please know that your contribution will be refunded to you—less the price of tonight's dinner, of course."

Thankfully, there was another wave of laughter.

I sat down. The loud conversation of ten minutes before settled into a soft murmur, then a man stood. I recognized him as the vice president of one of our local banks. "Excuse me, Madam Mayor. Please correct me if I'm wrong. Since the money given here tonight isn't going to your campaign coffers, then there is no legal limit to what we can give. Is that correct?"

I looked at Nat and she at me. She nodded.

"That's right."

He smiled and pulled his checkbook from his pocket. "That's good to hear."

Suddenly there was applause and that same pesky dust got in my eyes. I turned to Nat. "Hate me?"

"I'm trying to, but you make it so hard." She gave a one-shouldered shrug. "Who knows? You might win anyway."

After dessert and while coffee was being served, Catherine, who had been sitting next to Jerry, stepped to a podium and began to speak. She spoke of the need for character in every walk of life, then told stories about her experiences on Broadway and in Hollywood. It turns out she is very funny.

"I'll bet you're wondering if she ate any dinner tonight?" Jerry said. "She didn't."

"Don't let him pull your leg, Maddy," Nat said. "She has an issue or two to deal with. Mostly, she doesn't like to eat in public. She ate before she came."

"Not OCD?"

Jerry answered. "No. More a social paranoia. I've encouraged her to talk about it. Once she gets settled in, I think she will. Since Buchanan's arrest has put a hold on the movie, she is free to finish the full run of the play. She seems happy about that."

I watched as people visited and wrote checks. Many came by to express concerns for my health and their commitment to vote for me. I thanked each one but was glad to see the party wind down. I was exhausted and ready for my own bed.

Jerry put his arm around me. Catherine leaned forward to look around him. Nat turned my way. Something was up.

"That was a very noble thing for you to do," he said. "I don't know if you'll win or lose next month but I plan to cast my vote for you. But you probably already knew that. What you may not know is that I'm going to ask you to vote for me."

"Vote for you?"

"That's right, Madam Mayor."

"What election are you in?"

"One that requires only one vote to win. In fact, it just so happens that I have a voting booth right here." He reached in his suit coat pocket and pulled out a small black box. He opened it. A diamond ring looked me in the eye. A small, white silk banner was sewn into the top of the box. It read, VOTE FOR JERRY.

I took the ring from the box, slipped it on my left hand, and cast a different kind of vote.

The Incumbent

Madison "Maddy" Glenn is the contro-
versial mayor of the beautiful tourist
town of Santa Rita, California. Lisa
Truccoli, her friend and treasurer of her
last campaign, has been abducted. The
only thing left at the scene of the crime is
a shocking clue—a clue with Maddy's
name on it. And the game begins. She
embarks on a desperate hunt for answers,
finding more shocking clues in a dangerous game the abductor
wants to play—with Maddy.

Softcover: 0-310-24958-9

Before Another Dies

Running the coastal city of Santa Rita.
Campaigning for a congressional seat.
Staying one step ahead of a high-powered
corporate broker's demands. Life couldn't
get more difficult for Mayor Maddy
Glenn—or so she thinks.

For Maddy, the search for answers
about three murders is about to become
personal. Refusing to play it safe, Maddy
is caught in a lethal game in which seconds count. But even her
renowned grit and tenacity—and her emerging faith—may not
be enough to prevent more brutal deaths.

Softcover: 0-310-25935-5

A Ship Possessed

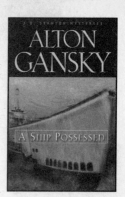

The *USS Triggerfish* has returned, but she has not returned alone. Something is inside her—something unexpected and terrible. To J. D. Stanton, retired Navy captain and historian, falls the task of solving the mystery surrounding a ship possessed. What he is about to encounter will challenge his training, his wits, and his faith.

Softcover: 0-310-21944-2

Vanished

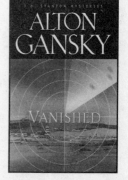

High-level Pentagon orders call J. D. Stanton, retired navy captain, back to active duty to investigate a town gone missing. Food still on dinner plates, gas nozzles still in the fuel ports of cars at the filling station ... Whatever happened took the people of *Roanoke II* completely by surprise. But took them where? Stanton faces a choice that will stretch his Christian faith to the limits. It could supply answers to the mystery of *Roanoke II* ... Or unfathomable and irrevocable horrors.

Softcover: 0-310-22003-3

Out of Time

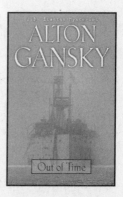

It starts as a trip to help five troubled teens, courtesy of a new Navy youth program. With retired submarine commander J. D. Stanton serving as captain and two young naval officers heading the expedition, the state-of-the-art catamaran leaves port. It's a routine voyage ... until a mysterious storm pulls Stanton and his crew into an eerie world of swirling mist and silence.

Softcover: 0-310-24959-7

We want to hear from you. Please send your comments about this book to us in care of zreview@zondervan.com. Thank you.

GRAND RAPIDS, MICHIGAN 49530 USA

WWW.ZONDERVAN.COM